Me and My Dog

Chicken Soup for the Soul: Me and My Dog
Amy Newmark

Published by Chicken Soup for the Soul, LLC www.chickensoup.com
Copyright ©2024 by Chicken Soup for the Soul, LLC. All Rights Reserved.

The publisher gratefully acknowledges the many publishers and individuals who granted Chicken Soup for the Soul permission to reprint the cited material.

Front cover courtesy of iStockphoto.com (©PK-Photos)
Back cover and interior photo of puppy over man's shoulder courtesy of iStockphoto.com (©Georgiy Datsenko), interior photo of woman with dog courtesy of iStockphoto.com (©PumpizoldA), interior photo of african american woman with dog courtesy of iStockphoto.com (©Halfpoint)
Photo of Amy Newmark courtesy of Susan Morrow at SwickPix

Cover and Interior by Daniel Zaccari

Publisher's Cataloging-In-Publication Data

Names: Newmark, Amy, editor.
Title: Chicken soup for the soul : me and my dog / Amy Newmark.
Description: Cos Cob, CT: Chicken Soup for the Soul, LLC, 2023.
Identifiers: LCCN: 2023943556 | ISBN: 978-1-61159-110-1 (paperback) | 978-1-61159-345-7 (ebook)
Subjects: LCSH Dogs--Anecdotes. | Dogs--Literary collections. | Dog owners--Anecdotes. | Human-animal interactions--Anecdotes. | BISAC PETS / Essays & Narratives | PETS / Dogs / General | HUMOR / Animals
Classification: LCC SF426.2 .C458 2023 | DDC 636.7--dc23

Library of Congress Control Number: 2023943556

Me and My Dog

Amy Newmark

Chicken Soup for the Soul, LLC
Cos Cob, CT

Changing lives one story at a time®
www.chickensoup.com

Table of Contents

❶
~Meant to Be~

❷
~Miracles Happen~

3

~My Very Good, Very Bad Dog~

4

~Who Rescued Whom?~

5

~What I Learned from the Dog~

❻

~Best Friends~

❼

~Natural Therapists~

⑧

~Feline Friends~

⑨

~A Dog's Purpose~

Chapter
1

Meant to Be

Two Pounds of Divine Intervention

Angels deliver Fate to our doorstep —
and anywhere else it is needed.
~Jessi Lane Adams

There was a time I believed in coincidence. But that was prior to meeting my four-legged soul mate. Now, I am sure there is something much bigger at work in the universe. There also was a time when it irritated me to have people equate their pets to humans. Again, that was till it happened to me.

I had just been given a death sentence. At forty-five, a random virus had attacked my heart and left it functioning at a mere thirteen percent. Just like that. Active, working, raising kids one day. Being wheeled out of the hospital and lifted into the car to go home and die quietly a week later. What happened during that week is still a mystery to me.

Unable to take care of even the basics of my everyday living, I spent my days looking at cute puppy faces at various pet adoption sites online. Quite a contrast... someone who should be making her final arrangements, instead, filling every moment viewing and fantasizing about owning one of these yipping, yapping little furry balls full of life. Even I, the eternal optimist, knew this was the most ridiculous idea I had ever entertained. But I wasn't hurting anyone. And it filled my days and gave me hope. It became an obsession when I had nothing left.

The days stretched on. My test results remained grave. There was no improvement. And yet, I was still here. Sort of in limbo. Then, one day I received an odd and unsolicited e-mail from a woman who stated she had just the puppy I was looking for. What? What puppy? I hadn't made any requests for puppies (except in my mind). I was only window-shopping! She said she would be at an address near my home that Saturday and to please stop by.

Against his better judgment, my husband drove me to this mysterious location. I huffed and puffed up the driveway and into the yard where puppies of every size, shape and color ran with wild abandon. People were coming and going quickly and leaving with "puppy care packets" and their new additions. I still was a little mystified about how I even got here or why I came.

Soon all the puppies were off to their respective new homes, the yard was empty and quiet, and the woman turned to me.

"Can I help you?" Our brief conversation revealed that she had no idea about any e-mail regarding a puppy. I felt a little silly and more than depressed as I headed back down the driveway. It was about this time that a matronly woman emerged from the house and into the yard, wearing an old-fashioned floral apron. I offered a weak smile as we passed, and from the corner of my eye noticed a shaggy black and white head and little black nose poking out to see what was going on. I was immediately intrigued. As I got closer, the nosey little rag mop nearly jumped into my arms. If I had died right then, I would have died happy.

But my excitement was soon derailed when the woman said, "Don't take an interest in this one. She has severe heart problems and won't be with us much longer." What? Did she say what I think she said? Heart problems? Jackpot! My new "baby" was already in my arms and covering me with kisses.

After lots of grave warnings and signing of waivers, etc., my new puppy and I made our way to the car to break the news to the next naysayer. But jumping from seat to seat and right on my husband's shoulder, I didn't have much to do with convincing him. He was sold. So home we went. To our home that would never be the same.

And, as they say, the rest is history. And still is. That was ten years ago. Jasmine and I haven't spent a day apart since then. The vet never found a trace of any heart issues with her, and my test results began to show gradual improvement from the day I brought her home, and I am still here a decade later.

So, yes, I'm a believer in fate, divine intervention, or what have you. Coincidence? Not so much.

—JP Jackson—

Puppy Love

I don't like dreams or reality. I like when dreams
become reality because that is my life.
~Jean-Paul Gaultier

My husband Roy was driving. He was the Commodore of the Houston Canoe Club and we were taking flyers for the San Marcos River Clean-Up to Whitewater Experience, a business run by Don Greene. "I had a dream last night," I began hesitantly. "I never had one that seemed so real. I saw every detail."

"Yeah? What was it about?" he replied, getting interested.

"I dreamed that we were getting a little black and tan puppy. In the dream, we got it from a business that was run out of a house."

We had not been married very long and been talking about getting a puppy, but the time never seemed right.

"That's nice. What kind of dog was it?" Roy was almost parked in front of Whitewater Experience.

"I'm not sure," I replied. "But it was small and energetic, and we both just adored it."

"Well, maybe after we get through today, we'll visit the SPCA and see what they have for adoption," Roy responded. "I don't want a frou-frou dog. It's going to have to be a dog that will camp and go canoeing with us."

We parked and got out of the car, and as we approached the building, I couldn't believe my eyes. Whitewater Experience was doing business out of a refurbished old house. *No, it couldn't be*, I thought, yet it looked vaguely familiar. Roy grabbed the flyers, and we walked through the front door. I stared and grabbed Roy's arm.

"This is the place in my dreams, Roy, right down to the Indian blankets on those old Army footlockers."

About this time, Don Greene greeted us and Roy introduced him to me. After exchanging niceties, I couldn't stand it any longer. "I know this is going to sound strange, but you wouldn't happen to have a small black and tan puppy for sale, would you?"

Just as I posed this question, a small Yorkie puppy emerged from under Don's desk. He ran directly to me and gave me puppy kisses.

"It's him, Roy. This is *our* puppy." It *was* the puppy I had seen in my dream the night before.

Don looked confused by our exchange, so we explained my dream to him. He was mesmerized. "Well, I wasn't going to sell this one. I was going to keep him for myself. You see, he shouldn't even be here. I call him Gordo the Magnificent because he was the first puppy born in his litter. He was so big that his head was stuck in the mother's birth canal. I had to hold open the birth canal and drive a stick shift twenty miles to get them to the vet for an emergency operation to save the litter. The vet was successful, and four puppies were born. The rest of the litter has been sold, but Gordo is something special. He has even been with me on several canoe and raft trips.'

Don said that Gordo never approached strangers. But he ran directly to me. He *was* the dog I had seen in my dream, and I was crestfallen when Don said he was going to keep the puppy.

Don saw the sadness in my eyes as I played with Gordo. "Well, I have the mother and the father. There will be more puppies. You folks are good folks and would take him in the outdoors with you. I guess I can let you have this one," Don said.

I was ecstatic. Now the big question… "How much do you want for him?"

"I got $250 for the other puppies," Don said. "Guess I'll ask the same for him."

Now I was saddened for the second time. There was no way we could afford that.

"But for you guys, I would let him go for $225."

Don agreed to a payment plan. We made the first payment and got ready to take the pup home. Then Don said there was one stipulation—that he keep Gordo long enough to teach him how to eddy turn in moving water before we took him home. We agreed, and two weeks later, Gordo was ours.

Most dogs only respond to one person, but from the beginning, Gordo was always *our* dog. He was smart, friendly and not afraid of anything—except thunder. We registered him with the AKC with a name that fit our lives—George Mutt. George because I always wanted a dog named George, and Mutt (Roy's contribution) because this was the first registered dog Roy had ever owned. George went on many adventures with us and was indeed a water dog. He had his own life jacket and understood currents. He loved to "fish" in the shallows, and when he got hot on a summer canoe trip, he would jump into whatever body of water we were paddling.

George Mutt brought us joy for fifteen years. We have owned other dogs since, but none of them was a "dream" dog, and none measured up to George. His pictures are still in our living room and bedroom, and Roy still carries a picture of him in his wallet. He will be with us always—if only in our dreams.

—Janice R. Edwards—

Black Dog

*What seems to us as bitter trials
are often blessings in disguise.*
~Oscar Wilde

As we lowered the skinny body of what had been my big, fluffy, platinum-blond dog, Woofie, into his grave, I erupted in primal sobs. I didn't know a dog could make her way so deeply into the center of my heart and soul. I swore I'd never have another dog again... I didn't think I could live through the heartache of losing another one.

Six months later, I was invited to speak at a conference in New Mexico — state slogan the "Land of Enchantment" — spearheaded by our dear friends George and Sedena Cappannelli. To sweeten the pot of an already sweet opportunity, they offered my husband and me the opportunity to stay in their lovely guesthouse for the weekend. How could we resist?

We drove the long but scenic fourteen hours from Los Angeles to Santa Fe. We arrived the night before I was to speak so we could experience the acclaimed mythologist, author, and storyteller Michael Meade.

He strutted onto the stage with a conga drum. The lights went dim, and a faint spotlight found him. He told us a story in rhythm with his drum. I was transported back in time to a grassy field, starry sky, and open fire. He mesmerized us with this raspy, staccato fable (allow me to paraphrase):

There's an old woman... as old as time... long, gray hair... lives in a cave... with her black dog sitting by her side... all day and night... she rocks in her chair and weaves... the most beautiful weave you've ever seen... blending all the fabric of time and space from the far reaches of this universe... She's been weaving since the beginning of time... and it's now almost finished... and it's beautiful.

Just a few stitches left, and it will be perfect... but she can smell the aroma of her hearty stew that's been brewing in a pot in the back of her cave... All that weaving made her hungry... She lays her weave down on her rocking chair while she hobbles to the back of her cave to feast on her delicious stew.

While she's enjoying her feast, her black dog sniffs around at her weave, and begins playing and pulling on the string with his teeth and paws... it's a toy, a game, it's having a great old time... and by the time the old woman returns to her rocking chair, the entire weave — the one that has taken millions of years to perfect — is completely destroyed.

So, what does the old lady do? She sits back down in her rocking chair, picks up her needle and pieces of string, and resumes her weaving.

He paused dramatically, stopped drumming, and asked the audience point blank:

Who is your black dog?

Who or what in your life gets in the way, just when everything is going perfectly? Just when everything is exactly the way you want it, just when you're at the finish line of an important plan or project, when you're so close you can taste it?

Everyone has a black dog.

Is it a person, an injury, a political leader, a parent, a child, your job that rips it all into shreds?

And you might think it strange, but be grateful for your black dog.

When something is perfect, in Latin, it also means finished. Complete. Done. No more. If the old lady had finished her weave, it would mark the end of time, perhaps the end of the world, and maybe the universe, for that matter.

Thank God for the black dog — that troublemaker, saboteur, nuisance we blame for our problems. But, in fact, if we looked at the situation differently, we'd see that it's the black dog that keeps us in the game, that triggers our passion, keeps us going, engages and challenges us to be more creative and alive than we ever were before.

I was in tears as we drove through the high desert with the sky brightly lit by more stars than I'd ever seen. I thought about the legions of "black dogs" that lined my path. I saw so many of what I deemed horrible interruptions to my life's "perfect" path: almost getting the starring role in a TV series back in my acting days — subverted by a producer who wanted a relationship with me I wasn't willing to have; nearly adopting a child who mysteriously died the day before the adoption would be finalized; and the business deals my husband had been involved in that would have made us a fortune — sabotaged by a person or situation that was a "black dog" in disguise.

We made it "home" to our guesthouse situated amid red rocks and cacti, and our friend/host George yelled out to us, "Welcome home. Hey, don't be scared of the BLACK DOG sitting on your porch. She's a stray. She has been hanging around the guesthouse for the past few weeks. We don't know where she came from, but she's friendly."

Sure enough, a beautiful, shiny Black Lab was sitting on our porch, waiting for us, with her pink tongue out and tail wagging.

George was right. She was friendly. I asked her to sit, and she sat. I asked her to shake, and she lifted her right paw to shake my hand. I asked her to lie down, and she did. After fumbling with the keys, we opened the door, and she walked right in like she owned the place. I had a few bites in a "doggy bag" left from dinner that I fed her. She seemed very happy.

We slept that night with the black dog curled up in a ball on the rug right next to our bed.

Without going through all the details, suffice it to say, Shadow has been our dog now for the past six years. And as adorable and loveable as she is, true to the "black dog" story, she has been a force of destruction in our lives as well. She refuses to be left alone, and we've nearly gone broke paying for "doggy day care" every time we want to go on a date or out of town. She's made the interior of two of our cars look like Freddy Krueger and Edward Scissorhands had a fight inside.

But, on a positive note, she's also managed to rip my heart open in a whole new way. Despite the challenges that come from our black dog, Shadow, I love her with my entire heart and wouldn't trade her for all the perfectly well behaved dogs on the planet.

My dear friend and world-class fusion artist, Rassouli, is famous for saying: "There can be no creation without destruction. Destruction always precedes creation!"

About a month after Shadow entered our lives, my stepdaughter, Meesha, was moving into a new apartment that did not allow dogs. She asked if her dog, Lola (a Chiweenie — half Chihuahua, half Dachshund) could live with us.

Before my heart had been opened by Shadow, I would have never been open to such a proposition. Add to it the fact that my stepdaughter and I had a strained relationship at that point.

But with my now opened heart, I surprised myself by responding, "Why not? Let's take her. She'll be a playmate for Shadow, and it will help Meesha — a win-win all around."

Lola and Shadow, despite being an "odd couple," are the best of friends. In fact, I could not imagine Shadow without Lola, or Lola without Shadow.

Little did I know the ripple effect of embracing our black dog into our lives would be the catalyst for my stepdaughter becoming a wonderful part of my life and a healing balm being released throughout my husband's family. Where there once was anger and resentment, there is friendship and warmth… and it all started with the unexplainable trail of coincidences (synchronicities) that all led back to our black dog.

Every day, I hug her big, fluffy black self, and she reminds me not to cry over the near-perfect plans I weave that get thwarted. Instead I embrace the "black dogs" that life brings me as the source of untold blessings in disguise.

— Kelly Sullivan Walden —

Filling a Need

The purpose of life is a life of purpose.
~Robert Byrne

As I approached my fortieth birthday, I realized that my life was quite meaningless in the larger scheme of things. I had friends and a loving husband and yet something was missing. With no children, I felt that I hadn't done anything that would help mankind or change the world. I would have no legacy to leave.

I was watching TV one day and I saw Billy Graham speaking about prayer. He said that we should ask God for the "desires of our hearts." He explained that this is different than just asking for your wants and wishes. It is not like asking for a new red sports car. He was talking about the deepest and truest desires of your heart.

My desire was to be someone who mattered. I wanted to make a difference in the lives of people and in the lives of animals. After all, dogs had always been a large part of my life, from the time when I was a little girl growing up in central Oklahoma. I thought that my "purpose" would somehow include my love of singing, writing, travel, and of course, working with animals.

Then, something happened that shook my entire core. The "love of my life" dog, my Nicholas, was diagnosed with terminal cancer. He died thirteen months later. I became quite concerned for Bear, our remaining Cockapoo, who was six years old. Bear had been Nicholas's shadow and now that Nick was gone, Bear wouldn't even eat. Our vet suggested that we get another dog to see if that would encourage

Bear to eat.

I found an online ad for a Bichon Frise and when we arrived at the place it was a nightmare, like one of those puppy mills you read about or see on the television news. I decided to delay my search for my "purpose" as I needed to tell the world about the horror I had discovered right in my own backyard.

I had even a bigger fight ahead of me than Nicholas's cancer. This was a fight that would take years. I did research and then I spread the word on the Internet. People began to listen and we formed a small group of Bichon Frise lovers called Small Paws Rescue.

I started out sending the latest news on our rescue efforts to about twenty-five people. Within a few months we had grown to a group of several hundred. Some had Bichons and some had other breeds of dogs.

I felt bad about the delay in finding my "purpose in life," but after all, I was now on a mission.

A few years passed and my rescue stories were being read by more than six thousand people in twenty-eight different countries. National media outlets began asking me to do interviews and to film episodes for Animal Planet.

It took me a while to realize that I had not only found my purpose in life, but each of the desires of my heart had been included as well.

Yes, losing Nicholas was part of this journey. If I hadn't lost Nick, I wouldn't have found myself involved in this magnificent obsession called Small Paws Rescue, along with some of the finest people anywhere. Now my days are filled with helping people and animals. I travel this beautiful country attending Small Paws Rescue functions.

Because of this awesome and wonderful gift to me, in the past thirteen years, Small Paws Rescue has rescued more than 8,000 Bichons and has made a difference in the lives of thousands of people, too.

I've been made whole and complete, and what more could any person ever ask? The sheer joy of doing what I do overflows from every pore of my body, and I can never repay this wonderful gift that has given my life purpose.

You too can find your purpose in life, and the desires of your heart.

And look behind you. You may even be followed by a few thousand small, white, fluffy dogs.

—Robin Pressnall—

A Wanderer in My Dream

Pay attention to your dreams — God's angels often
speak directly to our hearts when we are asleep.
~Eileen Elias Freeman,
The Angels' Little Instruction Book

"How did you sleep?" my husband asked, as he poured me a cup of piping-hot coffee.

"I had a weird dream," I said, blowing soft ripples into the sweet, light-brown liquid. *"I was standing in the yard, and a light-haired dog was running toward me. I stretched my arms wide and called her Lily."*

"Hmm," he said, not looking up from his paper, "wonder what it means."

We didn't have a dog and had not discussed owning one. We also didn't interpret my dream as a sign that we should go out and get one.

A week or so later, I noticed a dog curled up in the corner of our yard. I assumed it belonged to one of our neighbors and thought nothing more of it.

A few nights after that, we came home from a party and saw a dog lying on our porch. It was winter, and we frequently found a cat or two sleeping in the cushions of the wicker furniture. It was comforting to know we were a haven for animals that were out in those cold temperatures. We kept food and water on the porch for those passing through. So, it was no surprise that a dog might take shelter under the cover of our welcoming front porch. We had motion-sensing lights, so I could see how a wanderer might take that as a signal to come up the steps and rest her weary bones.

While my husband parked the car and unlocked the front door, I approached the strange animal slowly. She had chosen our welcome mat for her bed and had her back against the front door. The dog lifted her head and looked at me. She was a beautiful blond husky. Her tail wagged. I reached out to pet her, and she tried to stand. My husband opened the door from inside, and the dog quietly limped down the brick steps and off into the darkness.

"Did she have a collar?" he asked.

"I didn't see one," I said. "She's hurt, though. Should we go look for her?"

"Not at this hour of the night," he said. "Maybe she's going home." I wanted to believe that because I couldn't stand the thought of that sweet dog suffering in pain from an injury.

"I wonder who she belongs to," my husband said, still holding the open door with one hand.

"I don't know," I said, looking out into the darkness, "but I've seen her before."

"Where?"

"In my dream." I looked at him with tears beginning to pool and shivered in the cool night air. "It's Lily."

Days later, she was on the porch again. She let me pet her. I noted that she had hairless spots rubbed down to the bone at her joints. She was covered in fleas, and there were some infected places behind her ears. This poor dog had not been cared for by anyone in a long time.

My husband wrangled her into the truck and took her to a local veterinarian. Unfortunately, her injury had happened some time ago and had already healed. The limp would be permanent. We provided her with everything she needed to recuperate from her other problems — a trip to a groomer, medication, and constant love and attention — and decided to let her stay inside at least until the infections cleared up. We tried to find her owner, but no one claimed her.

She loved baths but was afraid of lightning. She never barked; she talked. She tried to sit in our laps as if she were a small dog. She understood simple commands. She was eager to please. Someone had loved her before; that was easy to see. And having only three good legs did not hinder her ability to run. We found that out the first time we took her for a walk.

Lily decided to keep us.

Even though we hadn't planned on getting a dog, she had sent me a sign in my dream that she was on her way. Call it fate or whatever you want, but Lily would never have to find a place to sleep again. She had found her home, no longer a wanderer in my dream.

— Vickie McEntire —

Shooting Star

For my part, I know nothing with any certainty,
but the sight of the stars makes me dream.
~Vincent van Gogh

I was driving down the highway one night in early spring when I saw the most amazing shooting star fly across almost a third of the sky right in front of me, ending in a brilliant burst of glittering light. It was a spectacular yet fleeting cosmic display. Even though I've been known to set my alarm for the early hours of the morning to watch the Perseids or other predictable meteor showers, I had never seen a meteor so bright and beautiful as that one.

That night, I had a dream where a small lake appeared in front of my house. From the far shore, a puppy swam toward me. His eyes locked on mine, and he made his way to me as if he knew me, with a purposeful stroke and a canine grin of joy.

He leapt into my arms, and the next thing I knew I was holding his squirming, solid body and laughing as he licked me.

Suddenly, in the surreal timeline of dreams, we were snuggling on my couch, and that was when I noticed his short fur was scattered with mocha-colored splotches, including his round puppy belly, which he let me rub while he wiggled into a corner. A feeling of completion expanded within me, like a missing piece was settling into place. This dog was meant to be mine.

The combination of the shooting star and the powerful, vivid dream felt like a portent. Maybe the universe was trying to tell me something. Perhaps there was a dog out there looking for me, and I just had to open my heart to find him.

At the time, I wasn't looking for a dog. I had already rescued two: Jasper, a seventy-four-pound Hound with a touch of Catahoula and maybe Lab, and Lilah, who had Border Collie roots, along with a few other breeds mixed in. I also had rescued two cats — Dawn and Athena — a perfect balance in my interspecies home.

I didn't need another dog. That's what I kept telling myself the next day as I sat in my cubicle at the consulting firm where I worked. But I couldn't shake the feeling that there was a puppy out there who was destined to find me.

So, instead of creating yet another PowerPoint presentation for one of our corporate clients, I went to Petfinder.com, searching for this theoretical dog. I looked at dozens of photos, but none of them seemed like the dog I had dreamt about. Then I remembered another pet-adoption website: Adoptapet.com. I scrolled the pages, reviewing each adorable puppy and sweet dog.

Feeling a bit foolish — and also aware of the pile of work I had to do — I was just about to give up when I saw a face that made my heart skip a beat. I gasped, and my pulse began racing. It was him. I knew it. It *felt* like he was that dog.

He was a scruffy Terrier, and he didn't look exactly like the dog in my dream, but he was staring at me through the picture as if he knew me.

I sent an e-mail inquiry, wanting to know all about him. But the response I received was, "Fill out the application. Then we'll talk." I understood. Rescue groups are run by volunteers who don't have time to answer e-mail from someone who isn't serious about adopting.

Was I serious? Yes, I realized, I was.

So I filled out the application. Coursing through my body and my mind was this feeling of rightness, as if this were a path I needed to follow.

A few e-mails went back and forth between the rescue group and me, and I learned that the puppy was being fostered with — and got along well with — kids, dogs, and cats, which was very important in order for him to fit in with my gang.

I asked if the rescue group had all the information they needed from me so I could meet him. At that point, I thought he was local, but the puppy had been pulled from a kill shelter in South Carolina hundreds of miles away and was being fostered there.

I heard back: "I have no problem if you adopt him." So, while I thought I was arranging a "meet and greet," the rescue group assumed it was a "pick him up and take him home." Things were happening awfully fast. Yet the dream still seemed to be guiding me, so I kept going along with the process.

Several additional e-mails, a set of photos, and a few weeks later, the puppy was on his way to New Jersey.

I couldn't believe I was adopting a dog based on a meteor, a dream, a few pictures and some e-mails. I would never recommend that someone do this, and even today I have no idea why my family went along with the plan.

The woman who set up the adoption didn't want to meet in her home or a park, so we agreed on a Chili's parking lot in a nearby town. I was to bring $250 in cash. It felt like a drug deal, and I told my family that if things seemed weird, we'd get back in the car and drive home without the dog.

But we all fell in love the minute a sweet, wiry-haired puppy greeted each of us individually with a snuggle, kiss, and wag. The woman said, "I love it when they pick their families."

At home, we introduced the dog to Lilah and Jasper. They got along instantly, although it took a little longer with the cats. As a family, we discussed names, and one of my daughters suggested Tucker. Why? "Because he looks like a Tucker." It was true then, and throughout his life he looked like a Tucker.

A few days later, I was rubbing his sweet Terrier belly, and I saw those spots — the ones I had dreamt about.

It was in the stars: Tucker was my dream dog.

He was a ball-obsessed, scruffy Terrier who lived his life to the fullest. He loved to play, and his joy was contagious as he chased balls, squirrels and chipmunks, and barked at deer and the UPS guy. He often slept upside down, with his legs stretched out in multiple directions and his head hanging over the side of his dog bed. He loved to roll around on his back just for the fun of it, serenading us with moans of delight. And even though he was a goofy, silly dog, he was always tuned into the needs of the people around him, offering snuggles, a paw of sympathy, or his signature hugs, leaning into anyone he knew needed comforting. He became good friends with one of my cats, and I often found the two of them hanging out together.

Tucker was only with us for eight years. Like a shooting star, he came streaking into our lives, lit up our home and everyone he touched, and was gone. He was my heart dog, the dog of my dreams.

—Susan C. Willett—

Home for the Holidays

There's no place like home.
~Dorothy, The Wizard of Oz

Just after Thanksgiving, I awoke to the sound of footsteps in the kitchen followed by the aroma of freshly brewed coffee. Home from college, my daughter, Carolyn, surprised me with a special birthday celebration beginning with breakfast in bed. On a tray adorned with fresh flowers were my favorites: an omelette, hot coffee, and a homemade muffin, along with handmade cards revealing the day's events, including "Picking out a Christmas Tree."

On the way to pick out our tree, I surprised Carolyn and myself by suggesting that we stop at Petco and look at the dogs that were up for adoption. I had been saying that I traveled too much to get a dog, and I was trying to focus on my freelance writing career, but something was nudging me to look anyway. Nevertheless, I confidently announced to Carolyn that we would not be getting a dog that day. We were just looking.

All that changed when I held tiny Ebenezer in my arms. He was a two-year-old Yorkie-Chihuahua mix and he fit perfectly in the crook of my arm as his big brown eyes stared up at me. As I cradled him like a baby and rubbed his tummy, he dozed off, completely oblivious to the chaotic surroundings.

After about twenty minutes of cuddling, I asked the 4 Precious Paws rescue representative, Julie, for more information. She shared Ebenezer's story, explaining that he had been in a hoarding situation with fifteen other dogs. They lived in a small partitioned area of a patio and, at the time of their rescue, were filthy, flea-infested, and in need of heavy medication for parasites. She added that Ebenezer was a sweet dog with a delightful personality. The more I heard and the longer I held him, the more difficult it was to let him go.

After my questions were answered, I remained curious, asking, "Ebenezer seems like an odd name for this dog, especially since he's so sweet. He's definitely no Scrooge."

"Oh, that was just the name we gave him when we rescued him a couple of weeks ago," Julie explained. "We gave all the dogs Christmas names. Jingle is right over there."

"So what was Ebenezer's original name?" I asked.

"His name," she said, "was Toto."

With that, Carolyn broke into a grin and said, "Looks like you found your dog, Mom." I had recently launched my blog called "Tales of Oz," inspired by my nickname "Oz" (for my last name — Osborne) as well as *The Wizard of Oz*.

As I finished the adoption paperwork, I gave Julie my "Tales of Oz" business card, complete with its yellow brick road theme. She smiled and said, "Looks like it's a match made in heaven."

And it was.

Since Toto's arrival, we have enjoyed a smooth transition, and I can't imagine my life without him. My quiet empty nest is now filled with a new energy as well as occasional barking, and my exercise routine has improved with our mile-long walks each morning. Toto is the inspiration for many of my stories as he sleeps on my lap while I write. He even has his own column in our local newspaper called, "Toto Around Town." There's no doubt in my mind that we were destined to meet — not in Kansas, but in Indiana.

And so there is a happy ending for this tiny, lovable dog. Just as Dorothy landed in Oz in her dream, a rescue dog named Toto landed in Oz, too — Oz's lap, that is.

I'm sure Toto would agree: "There's no place like home."

— Julie Osborne —

Interfering

*We cannot live only for ourselves. A thousand fibers
connect us with our fellow men.*
~Herman Melville

I lived in Southwick, Massachusetts, a little municipality with one church, one drugstore, and two traffic lights. After a while, I got to know most everybody since we all attended each other's garage sales, gathered at high school events, and got our cars fixed by the one and only mechanic.

Gossip ran rampant in our little town, but I tried to stay out of other people's affairs. Even if they needed help, I didn't feel right making the offer. I was afraid they would be insulted or angry, not receptive.

Then came the Frank dilemma. Frank was in his late sixties, a Vietnam veteran. His wife had died from cancer ten years earlier and they had no children. Frank's only true friend and companion was his dog, a German Shepherd named Morgan. Morgan wasn't a support dog per se, but he was this man's steady ally and his rock when bad nights haunted Frank. Everyone in town considered them a team and let Morgan come into their establishments. The two were often spotted together at the barber shop, bakery, or drugstore. More often than not, on a hot day, they could be seen swimming in the pond by Frank's cottage.

Then one day I realized I hadn't seen Frank in town for a while. Morgan had been an old dog, close to sixteen, so I began to make discreet inquiries at the grocery store and gas station. It had been a stroke, the clerk at the market told me. Morgan had to be put down. I wanted to knock on Frank's door and tell him I was sorry and ask if he was okay, but I was afraid to interfere.

Frank's loss was unmistakable. He looked terrible and he started shuffling as he walked. No one heard him laugh anymore. His shirts hung loose, and his pants bagged at his knees. My heart broke for him, but I didn't know what to do. So I did nothing.

My work as a court reporter took me fifteen miles away to the city of Springfield. One day, I found myself at the lunch table with Shari, one of the court clerks. She mentioned that she was looking for a good home for her dog Jax because she worked long hours and there wasn't a doggy daycare within thirty miles of her. Jax was almost a year old and full of energy, frisky and playful, and it bothered her that he spent the day alone. Even though she lived in a house with a doggy door to the back yard, sometimes Jax got himself into trouble from sheer boredom by chewing furniture and gnawing walls. As she talked, the proverbial lightbulb blinked on over my head.

Frank needed a purpose, a reason to get up and eat breakfast again. He needed a dog. I told her all about Frank, and she agreed to meet him. I went home happy and sure of my intentions, but unsure how to get the courage to meddle in Frank's life. Maybe he wouldn't want another dog. Maybe it would be too distressing for him. What if I opened up old wounds? I paced around my living room trying to come up with a solution. Whatever I did, it had to be handled gently on all levels.

Every day, Frank waited on his porch for the mail to arrive. Knowing that, I timed it so that my bike and I would be at Frank's property right before the mailman arrived. I waved to Frank on his porch, and then rode my bike up his driveway without invitation. I confided to him that I had a problem and needed some advice. I knew he'd fall for that. He was that kind of guy.

With a nervous hitch in my voice, I managed to blurt out my tale about Shari's dog and her inability to get him properly trained. I asked him if he'd be willing to help her out. He shuffled his feet and looked anywhere but at me. I could tell he wasn't thrilled with the idea, and my hopes dimmed. *This is exactly why I keep out of people's lives*, I reminded myself. But then he mumbled something about sleeping on it, and I rode away thinking, *I just planted a seed.*

A few days later, I accidentally-on-purpose ran into Frank at the coffee shop, and I pulled out my second direct hit: a photo of Jax. I lamented to Frank, as I placed the photo in his hand, that it was such a shame that this gorgeous dog had to be cooped up in a tiny apartment for sixteen hours a day. It was a lie and a terrible exaggeration, but I was committed to this scheme now. When Frank saw that Jax was a Shepherd, his eyes softened. He bit his lower lip in thought while I quietly picked up my coffee and left. I "forgot" to get the picture back.

Two days later, I made sure to ride my bike past the cottage. Sure enough, Frank called me over. He agreed to meet with Shari and the dog, but he didn't promise anything. On the day of the meet-up, Jax bounded out of the car and ran up and greeted Frank like he'd known him all his puppy life. Frank patted him and scratched the dog's ears and said things like, "Well, aren't you a handsome fella, huh?" We sat on the porch and talked "dog" and "military" for over an hour before Frank committed to training sessions three times a week for a month.

Well, the change in Frank was really something to behold, not to mention what it did for the dog. After a few weeks, I got reports of the two of them being spotted all over town with Frank patiently putting Jax through his paces. On the last agreed-to training day, Shari asked Frank if he would adopt Jax. He said "yes."

I'm happy to report that Frank's step became lighter, and he began to smile again. He and Jax went everywhere together: shopping, running chores, even ice fishing out on the lake. It made me laugh to see them seated next to each other on blankets, both staring intently at the dark hole in the ice, patiently waiting for a fish to bite.

A few months later, while riding my bike, I spotted them by the end of their driveway, and Frank beckoned me over. He peered down into my face and waggled a finger at me. "I always knew that dog never lived in no apartment," he said. "I just wanted you to know that." And with that, he gave Jax the command to fetch the newspaper. They walked side by side up the gravel path and in through the front door.

My first foray into meddling in someone else's life hadn't been a disaster, but nonetheless I promised myself I would never do it again. Until I do.

—Jody Lebel—

9

Perfect

Don't give up before the miracle happens.
~Fannie Flagg

After I had to put down Gershwin, my beloved thirteen-year-old Bichon, I became emotionally unglued. I couldn't stop crying. During the nights, I reached out to pat the side of the bed where he had snuggled and slept with me. During the days, I longed to see his wagging tail and hear his low bark.

Jill, my daughter, encouraged me to get another dog, but I told her, "No, I'll never do that. Losing a pet causes just too much heartache."

Fast forward two months later. After many hours of prayer over several weeks, I sent Jill a text message: "I've decided that I'm ready for another dog. The pain of losing Gersh doesn't compare to the years of love we shared together. But I don't want a puppy. I want to rescue another Bichon or a small dog that's a few years old."

Jill texted back: "Yahoo! That's great! I know somewhere out there is a precious little dog that will heal your heart and make you whole again."

The next day, Jill was working at an office where she seldom goes rather than her regular office. As she was leaving in the afternoon, she noticed that Rhonda, a staff member, had several framed pictures of dogs on her desk. Even so, Jill walked out of the building and to her car. But then, as Jill told me later, "It was like I was having a conversation in my head. I heard a voice say distinctly, 'Go back inside and talk to Rhonda about her dogs.'"

Jill went back inside and talked to Rhonda. When Jill mentioned that I had lost my dog and was praying to find another one, Rhonda said, "You should talk to Cassandra. She told me only yesterday that she needs to find a new home for her dog. She keeps the dog in a crate for twelve hours a day while she works. Then when she gets home, she doesn't have the time or energy to spend with the dog who wants to play and cuddle. The dog then spends the night in the crate for another eight or nine hours."

Then Jill talked to Cassandra and learned that her dog was a five-year-old Bichon/Toy Poodle mix, eight pounds of curly white hair. When Jill told me about the dog that evening, I hesitated to commit because quick decisions are not my forte. But after sensing that something more was at play, I couldn't dismiss the tug on my heartstrings. I was ready for a "precious little dog," just as my daughter had suggested.

The next day, Jill called Cassandra and asked if she would be willing to let me adopt the dog. Yes, she would, and she would do it this coming weekend.

I picked up the dog on Sunday afternoon. She's a happy miniature version of my beloved Gershwin, and she even came with the name "Precious." She's perfect.

— Jeannie Rogers —

10

Meeting Earl

All love stories are tales of beginnings. When we talk
about falling in love, we go to the beginning,
to pinpoint the moment of freefall.
~Meghan O'Rourke

was in a lunch meeting with two of my colleagues. The owner of the restaurant, whom I knew well, walked over with a tall, handsome man.

"Excuse me, ladies," Arlene said. She looked at my two female colleagues. "I must ask you to leave." All three of us were taken a little aback. "Not you," Arlene added, glancing at me. She turned to the others. "I have someone here who Jeffree needs to meet."

My two colleagues began snickering as they gathered their purses and stood up.

"Hey, wait a minute," I protested. "Where are you two going? We're not done yet."

"Oh, yes, we are." My boss smiled like the all-knowing Cheshire cat. "You're on your own."

The two women departed, laughing all the way.

Moments later, Arlene launched into matchmaker mode.

"This is Earl. You need to meet and get to know one another," she stated matter-of-factly. She pulled out a chair and pointed at it, indicating that Earl should sit. As soon as he did, Arlene left.

We sat there staring at each other. Neither of us knew what to say. Finally, I asked, "What just happened here?"

"Not really sure," Earl said. "I just moved back to town. I'm a commercial broker, and I sold this restaurant to Arlene and her husband. When I lived here before, I met a nice woman that Arlene knows. I called Arlene to let her know that I had moved back and asked for the woman's phone number, but she wouldn't give it to me."

"Why not?" I asked.

"She said there was someone in the restaurant right now that I needed to meet, and I had to get over here right away before she left. Obviously, that was you."

"Unbelievable!" I said, shaking my head. "I've had people want to set me up before, but never like this."

"Yeah, it's a first for me, too." Earl grinned.

After that, we sat in silence. Every few minutes, Arlene would walk behind Earl, wink, and make a thumbs-up motion. I thought it couldn't get any more embarrassing when Arlene walked up and sat down on one of the empty chairs.

"How's it going, you two?"

We glared silently at her.

"What?" She looked at each of us. "Have you exchanged business cards?"

We shook our heads.

"Phone number? Jeffree, have you given Earl your phone number?"

Again, I shook my head.

"Do I have to do everything?" she admonished both of us, as though we were unruly toddlers. "Jeffree, give me one of your cards."

I knew I wasn't going to get out of the restaurant until I cooperated; I handed over a business card. Immediately, she gave it to Earl.

"You call her, Earl," she instructed him as though he didn't know the protocol.

With that, I got up and excused myself, saying I had to get back to work. As soon as I came through the office door, the two women who had abandoned me began laughing. I got back to work and shortly forgot about the whole incident until a couple of days later when Earl called. I barely remembered him until he reminded me of where and how we met.

"Hey, that was pretty embarrassing," he said.

"No kidding," I agreed.

"I was thinking that we should have lunch."

"Um, thanks, but no," I said.

"Why not?" he pressed.

"You're calling because Arlene pressured you into it. I don't need anyone setting me up on dates."

"No, I'm inviting you to lunch because Arlene is a savvy woman," he said. "Obviously, she sees something you and I don't, and she went out of her way to introduce us. What would it hurt to have lunch and see if we can figure out what it is?"

I thought about that for a moment and then decided, *What could it hurt?*

"Just one thing," I said. "I'll have lunch with you, but not at Arlene's restaurant. In fact, pick a place on the opposite end of town."

We met the next day for lunch. At first, it was awkward, but then we began talking, really talking, about everything. Two hours passed before I realized it.

"Look, I'm actually enjoying this, but I do have to get back to work."

He smiled and asked, "Can I see you again?"

I didn't hesitate. "Of course."

A couple of days later, we planned to meet at a promotional event I was staffing in the evening. As soon as he walked in, I rushed up to him.

"Look, I'm really sorry, but I can't see you tonight," I tried to say, as tears welled up in my eyes. "My dog is really sick. She seems to be dying, and the vet isn't sure why. I waited until you got here so you wouldn't think I stood you up. I have to go over to the clinic now. I can't let her die alone."

"Let's go together," he said.

"What?"

"You shouldn't do this alone. I'll go with you." He placed his hand on my elbow and guided me outside.

We arrived at the clinic in minutes. As soon as we walked in, one of the techs led us into a large room and pointed to a metal crate where I saw Lucy lying on her side. I could hardly breathe; my precious dog was comatose and barely alive.

"Do you want me to take her out of the crate so you can hold her?" the tech asked. I could only nod; I knew if I tried to speak, I would start crying.

I sat cross-legged on the floor, and Earl sat down opposite me. The tech gently lifted Lucy and laid her in my lap. Suddenly, Earl picked her up and lowered her into his lap. He began speaking to her in a low, gentle voice.

"You gotta live," he told her, as he stroked her long, silver coat. "Think of all the living you still have to do. Balls and butterflies to chase. Mailmen to bark at. Bones to eat and bury in the yard. You can't die. You'll break your mama's heart."

At that moment, I fell in love with Earl. He was trying to coax my dog, who he had never met, into living for me. Who does that for someone he barely knows?

We stayed with Lucy for a long time. It became clear that she wasn't going to die as long as we were there. Before we left the clinic, I gave them explicit instructions to call me when Lucy died, no matter what the hour. They promised they would. The next morning, I awoke and realized that the clinic had never called. I phoned them and asked why.

"Your dog is standing up in the crate, wagging her tail and barking for breakfast," the tech said.

I dropped the phone, grabbed my keys and drove like a mad woman to the clinic where I scooped up Lucy in my arms. She showered me with doggie kisses. Then I called Earl and thanked him for saving my dog and giving her a reason to live. We married five months later. That was twenty-six years ago.

—Jeffree Wyn Itrich—

Chapter 2

Miracles Happen

Four-Legged Angel

May the Lord answer you when you are in distress;
may the name of the God of Jacob protect you.
~Psalm 20:1

Surrounded by rolling green hills dotted with horses and cows, the picturesque ranch town of Waimea on Hawaii's Big Island is a peaceful and friendly place. One afternoon, while staying with friends at their house there, my husband and I decided to go for a stroll along the many, mostly traffic-free, country lanes in the area.

We met a beautiful Golden Retriever, obviously well cared for but with no collar. He seemed exceptionally friendly so we stopped to play with him, throwing a stick which he retrieved several times with glee. When we resumed our walk, he followed us, and although I worried that he might be going too far from his home, I couldn't deny that we were enjoying his company. We felt an immediate bond with this adorable dog and even talked about adopting him if we learned that he didn't belong to anyone.

After about twenty minutes, we found ourselves walking along a dirt road in an unfamiliar area, our golden friend still trotting beside us. Hilly grasslands sloped upward beyond a fence on one side of the road, and houses spaced comfortably apart dotted the other. One house, almost hidden by shrubbery and shaded by tall trees, seemed somehow furtive. I shuddered as we passed it and felt an urge to be as far away from that place as possible.

Just then, the door to the house creaked open and five dogs rushed out, barking and growling as they ran toward us. I felt terrified and couldn't move. There was nowhere to hide and no time to run.

All of a sudden, our new friend appeared, like a genie, between the dogs and us. He faced them—all five of them—growling and baring his teeth. I was amazed to see the attacking dogs stop in their tracks ten feet away from him. Our protector held them there while we escaped, scurrying quickly down the road. At a safe distance, we looked back and saw the five dogs heading back toward their house.

But the Golden Retriever was nowhere in sight.

The road was quiet again.

I felt an ache in my heart; I missed our friend already. Instinctively, I knew he was not hurt.

With a feeling of emptiness, we made our way back to the house, hoping the whole way that we would see our Good Samaritan again. But it was not to be.

When I told our friend about the encounter, her eyes flew wide open as she exclaimed, "It was an angel!"

To this day I have no doubt. A four-legged angel protected us.

—Jennifer Crites—

Lost Dog

He performs wonders that cannot be fathomed,
miracles that cannot be counted.
~Job 9:10 NIV

The summer after seventh grade, my friend Rich and I experienced our first "rite of passage"—a fishing and camping trip without adult supervision. My father, whose nickname was Timer, drove us twenty-five miles up into the mountains from our house in the small town of Steamboat Springs. Rich and I were in the front seat. Rich's dog, Turk, a Plott Hound, and Cheeka, our Boxer, were in the back. .

I fidgeted in the front seat. "I can't wait 'til we're at the lake."

"Those brookies better be ready to jump on my line," Rich chimed in, as that was what we intended to do—fish for brook trout.

Dad grabbed the wheel with both hands as we landed in a huge mud hole. "Just remember, you can only have ten fish in your possession at a time," he reminded us. He gunned the engine. The tires spun, but we didn't move. He put it in reverse. Still no motion.

This frightened the dogs and they jumped out the windows of the Jeep and ran into the nearby forest. Turk howled for a few minutes off in the distance, but then all sounds faded. The *chink-chink* of our shovels filled the quiet evening. We dug and dug but to no avail.

"I'll walk over to Round Mountain and see if Bus Nelson is still camped there," said Dad. He gestured to a spot close by. "You boys can throw out your sleeping bags under that bunch of trees. I should be back by dawn."

"What about the dogs?" I said.

"They should be back shortly. I'll keep an eye out for them." Dad set off toward Round Mountain.

At dusk, Rich and I climbed into our sleeping bags. We heard barking off in the distance. A few minutes later, Turk stood over us. He licked our faces and whined as he ran around our little camp.

"Where's Cheeka?" I held Turk's collar as he looked down at me.

Rich and I got up and walked along the edge of the forest with flashlights. We yelled and whistled into the darkness, but Cheeka didn't come.

We climbed back into our bags and tried to sleep. I kept thinking I heard her, but it was only Turk's collar jingling as he moved about. Finally, I went to sleep and dreamed of my lost dog.

At first light, we heard the hum of a vehicle approaching. Rich and I sat up in our bags to see Bus's Jeep bounce toward us. His aluminum boat was strapped to the top. Dad was in the passenger seat.

I put on my pants and shoes and ran to meet them. "Did you see Cheeka?"

"No sign of her, son."

Bus pulled out the tow chain. "Timer, that Boxer doesn't have the nose of a hound. You'll probably never see her again."

Bus's words pierced my heart. I broke into tears and walked away while they pulled our Jeep out of the mud hole.

Dad put his arm around my shoulder. "Do you want to go home or do you still want to go to Percy Lake and camp?" I decided to stay, hoping that Cheeka might find us at the lake.

Before they left us alone at the lake, Bus and Dad gave us more orders and instructions than needed, and Bus lent us his boat for the four days we'd be there. Rich and I set up our tent and then put the boat in the water, but my heart wasn't into fishing.

As Rich rowed us around the lake, I kept thinking of Cheeka, the ugly dog no one wanted at the Boxer Rescue Mission. Her lower jaw protruded so her two canine teeth hooked on things she sniffed. When Dad and I saw her in her crate, she looked up at us with sad eyes that said, "Please take me." We did. She looked so vicious that little kids ran from her when I took her for walks.

When we were in the boat, I thought I saw her run out of the trees along the shore. I looked for her in the forest when I wasn't fishing. I yelled and whistled for her for the whole time we were there.

Dad came for us on our last day. My heart broke when I saw the empty Jeep. "Didn't you see her, Dad?"

"Nothing but chipmunks and squirrels."

"What can we do? We gotta find her."

"Say a prayer, son, and hope for the best."

I went off by myself and sat on a fallen log. "God, if you are real, show me. Let me find Cheeka. If you do, I'll say my prayers every day and help Mom with the dishes 'til school starts."

Every mile on the way back to town, I searched the forest and ravines beside the road. "Stop, Dad! I think I see her."

"Nope, just a stump," Rich said when it didn't move.

I continued to hope as the miles went by. When we arrived home, I was positive Cheeka would be in the front yard.

She wasn't.

Tears welled in my eyes.

Mom came out of the house. "I just got a call from a neighbor up the street. She said she saw a skinny brown dog walk through her yard."

I ran to the street to look toward her house. There, coming down the middle of the street, was a skin-and-bones Boxer.

"Cheeka!" My heart leapt.

She tried to pick up her pace, but she was too weak. She walked into our front yard and collapsed under the big pine tree.

I ran over, knelt, and gave her a long hug. Her stubby tail wagged back and forth.

I did help Mom with the dishes for the rest of the summer, and I still thank God for answering my prayers.

— Gregg Heid —

13

My Heroes

I think that someone is watching out for me. God,
my guardian angel, I'm not sure who that is,
but they really work hard.
~Mattie Stepanek

Many years ago, I was a student at the University of Alabama in Tuscaloosa, where I lived on campus. I had an evening class that was a fifteen-minute walk from my dorm. No one in my dorm was taking the same class and neither were any of my friends, so I walked to and from class alone, returning in the dark.

One evening, I noticed two very large, black and tan Doberman Pinschers following about twenty feet behind me. I have always been an animal lover and I have never been afraid of dogs, so I stopped walking, turned around, and talked to them. They refused to come to me and when I tried to walk toward them, they backed up, keeping their distance. They were not threatening in any way — they did not growl or flatten their ears the way dogs do when they are about to attack — they just wouldn't allow me to get close to them.

For weeks, every time I walked to this particular class, the two dogs appeared and followed me. I was very comfortable with the situation, even though the dogs would not interact with me.

One night, a car with three young men slowly pulled up beside me, paused, and then sped ahead and stopped. The boys were loud and rowdy, and I remember wondering if they were intoxicated. As the young men emerged from the car, I heard one of them say, "Let's get her." As they walked toward me, before I had time to react, the two Dobermans charged at them, snarling and barking. You never saw three people get into a car so fast and pull away!

I spent the rest of the semester looking over my shoulder, hoping to see those heroic dogs again. Strangely, after that one night when I needed their protection, my guardians never reappeared.

—Sandy Alexander Reid—

14

One Sunny Afternoon

Impossible situations can become possible miracles.
~Robert H. Schuller

I pressed my foot firmly on the gas pedal, wondering how much over the speed limit it would be safe to travel. After months of looking for a full-time position, I'd finally gotten an interview. The job wasn't what I wanted, but as a new college graduate I couldn't afford to be choosy. Perspiration dotted my forehead. With only fifteen minutes until the interview and twenty minutes of driving to go, I said a quick prayer before glancing down to turn up the air conditioner. When I looked up again, I saw him.

A medium-sized brown dog had scampered into the road and stood right in front of my car. I slammed on the brakes. The seatbelt squeezed into my stomach as the momentum threw me forward, but my car screeched to a stop just in time. The dog darted back to the side of the road. His fur looked matted and dirty. A broken chain dragged along behind him. A runaway, I thought, and lifted my foot from the brake to let the car coast. The dog continued to walk near the side of the road with his head down, sniffing at every step.

I sighed and steered my car to the shoulder. Someone in a red car honked and whizzed by, apparently in as much of a hurry as I was. But no matter how much I wanted to keep going, I couldn't bring myself to ignore the dog's plight. His chain could get caught in bushes or he might make another dash into the road. If I didn't help him, who else would? I opened the car door and stepped out on rocks that scratched my new tan pumps.

"Here, boy. Come here," I called out as sweetly as I could.

The dog stopped and looked at me with his ears lifted and his head cocked to one side. I held out my hand, wishing for a tempting treat to offer him as I inched closer. He stood still until I reached out to grab him. Then he cut away from me, past a small scraggly bush toward the expansive acres of an open field. There, he began to scamper in circles as though encouraging me to come after him.

Great. The dog seemed to think my presence meant it was time for a game of chase. I gritted my teeth and tried to keep an eye on him while picking my way over stones scattered helter-skelter on the ground.

The afternoon sun burned my face and sweat trickled down my back. The dog didn't seem to mind the heat and continued what he thought was a game, always staying about ten feet away from me. His tail swished and I could see the sparkle in his eyes. I clenched my jaw and kept moving forward until something caught my leg. A thorny bush had snagged the fabric of my pants and held it tight.

I bent down and carefully pulled the cloth away from the thorns. It left a small, gaping hole. Muttering at my luck, I gritted my teeth and stood. I frowned and scanned the field. The dog had disappeared. I called and whistled. Nothing. The entire area was flat with no trees or large bushes to hide behind. I could see for what seemed like miles. But somehow, chain and all, the dog had vanished like a desert mirage. Finally I shook my head and trudged back to the car.

If I couldn't help a dog, at least I could try to salvage a potential job. I nosed the car back into the road and tried to convince myself the interviewer would understand when I explained what happened. Thoughts of the stray dog shamed me into slowing down as I headed toward a hairpin curve not far from where my improbable pursuit had begun. As soon as my car rounded the curve, I saw brake lights and a line of cars. I hit the brakes and screeched to a stop. There'd been an accident. A car was wedged under the side of a dump truck. It appeared the truck had stopped in the road to empty a load of gravel. The car's hood looked like a crushed aluminum can. My eyes widened when I recognized it as the same red car that roared past me only a short while earlier.

The truck driver and car driver both appeared uninjured. They stood next to each other writing on scraps of paper while the faint sound of sirens grew slowly louder. As my white-knuckled grip on the steering wheel relaxed, I looked around, still half-expecting to see a dog dragging a broken chain. Yet there was no sign of him. It was as though he'd never existed. I looked back at the accident scene and a thought struck me. Were it not for a bedraggled brown dog and the grace of God… Suddenly my spine stiffened and gooseflesh pimpled my arms. Had I stopped to save a stray dog or had a stray dog stopped to save me?

My heart pounded as I recalled how fast I'd been racing down the road, distracted by dozens of thoughts. If I hadn't stopped, it would probably have been my car that rounded the blind turn and hit the truck. I closed my eyes and breathed a prayer of thanks. My disappointment over missing the interview melted away. All that remained in my heart was an overwhelming sense of gratitude and peace.

It's funny how even the most trivial of events may prove to have a purpose beyond human understanding. Though I didn't get the job I'd hoped for that day, a much better opportunity came along later — one that changed my career path forever. I know it wasn't only coincidence that brought a stray dog briefly into my life one sunny afternoon. He'd been sent to protect and guide me, a special four-footed answer to a hastily offered prayer. And for that, I'll always be grateful.

— Pat Wahler —

15

Death Cannot Separate Us

Death ends a life, not a relationship.
~Jack Lemmon

Before my husband Bill died, we often talked about whether there was an afterlife. We hoped that there was something beyond this world, and that somehow communication could take place once death occurred. We had plenty of time to talk about these things because my husband's battle with prostate cancer lasted for ten and a half years.

Shortly after his forty-sixth birthday, he was given the news that he had cancer. Neither of us had worried about his prostate biopsy after a positive rectal exam. I didn't know much at all about the prostate, if truth be told. I didn't even know how to pronounce it correctly. What little I did know (or thought I knew) about prostate cancer was that it was something that old men got, and they didn't die from the disease. Boy, was I wrong about that.

I had no idea when the phone rang that day that we were about to embark on a losing battle that would last for more than a decade. One minute, I was a thirty-two-year-old, stay-at-home, home-schooling mother of three young sons. The next, I was a prostate-cancer researcher, advocate and primary support system for a man with cancer.

The first year was a flurry of activity, with hormonal therapy, prostate surgery and its recovery, followed by seven and a half weeks of pelvic radiation. Despite everything that we had thrown at his cancer, we were told it was incurable one year after his diagnosis. They said he had two to four years. Over the next nine and a half years, he fought with all that he had to beat the odds so he could stay with his family and watch his sons become men. Ten days after our youngest son's eighteenth birthday, Bill died.

Five years after his death, I was faced with another trauma that could have easily ended in tragedy. I received a call one morning that our oldest son had been shot just outside Fort Campbell, Kentucky. Living on the coast of Maine, it took me almost twelve hours to get to his bedside. On my flight to him, I prayed a lot, as well as asked my late husband to be with him and keep him safe.

To my shock, when I arrived at my son's bedside in the trauma unit at Vanderbilt University Medical Center in Nashville, Tennessee, he was hooked up to a respirator. He had been shot three times in the back, and his skull had been fractured from a hard blow near the temple. Eventually, his sedation was lifted, and he slowly became conscious. When they knew he would be able to breathe on his own, they pulled the breathing tube from his throat. As soon as it was removed, his first words were "Daddy, Daddy."

Though my son has no recollection of seeing his father during his unconscious state, I cannot help but wonder if my husband heard my plea and somehow acted on it. After a three-week hospital stay and a long recovery over the next year, my son was able to return to a full and active life. I will always believe that my husband was with our son during those crucial hours following his shooting and somehow intervened.

Then, several years later, I had a severe case of the flu that put me in bed for a week. It left me in a very weakened state for nearly a month. My two elderly dogs had died a few months before my sickness, so it was the first time in my life that I didn't have the comfort of a dog beside me when I was ill. At the time, I was living on an island off the coast of Maine where I had provided end-of-life care for my parents who had recently died seven weeks apart. I didn't know many people there, so I felt alone and isolated during my sickness.

More than a week into it, I reached out to my deceased husband in a moment of complete and utter desperation. I looked toward the heavens, lifted my hands to the sky, and said, "Okay, Bill, send me a puppy. You have to send me a puppy." Though I wasn't sure if he heard me or not, I had a sense that a puppy would soon come my way.

The next morning, I opened my e-mail to find a message from a breeder whom I had contacted shortly after my last dog died. I had asked her about upcoming litters. When she had not replied, I assumed she was no longer in business. The breeder's e-mail began with an apology because she had just seen the e-mail that I had sent six months before. As luck would have it, her dog had just had a litter of ten black Labrador Retrievers. Some of the pups were born on March thirty-first, and some had been born on April first.

I had wanted a male, but only one of the puppies was born on the first, the tenth anniversary of my husband's death. I didn't ask which one. Over the next four weeks, I enjoyed viewing pictures of the puppies on social media until the day arrived that I could visit them. I played with them for forty-five minutes before I asked that important question. I had a distinct bond with one of the pups and held my breath hoping that he was the one born on the first. He had been the first to come to me, and when all the others had gone to sleep, he just sat there staring at me. As luck would have it, or perhaps it was divine intervention, the one I felt connected to was indeed the one born on April first.

The breeder had put different colored collars on the pups when they were born. Little did she know that the light blue collar she had put on my pup was the same color used for prostate cancer awareness.

This puppy has been my constant companion and brought me so much joy. I no longer feel alone because he is always by my side. He has been such a wonderful gift, and a continuing link to my husband. Our love was so strong that even death cannot separate us, and I will continue to look for those special signals and signs from Bill.

— Wendy Newell Dyer —

16

Finding Peace

All God's angels come to us disguised.
~James Russell Lowell

heard her tiny body hit the wall before he slammed shut the bathroom door. She sounded more like a child than an eight-pound dog when she cried out. That sound pierced the wall that separated us. On the other side, my heart was pounding in terror.

My stalker was inside my home, raping me. And all I could hear was my heartbeat, his rancid breathing, and my little dog's sudden silence.

I was bleeding from places on my body I could no longer feel. She was whimpering, in the soft delicate way she had whimpered when we first met.

I had rescued her from the colorful alleyways of Venice Beach, on a Sunday evening vibrant with music, laughter, and the other sounds — those of discontent — that fill Los Angeles after dark. She was curled up in a shadowy corner, lying atop discarded debris and broken glass, ignored and alone.

At first I thought she was a large rodent, but it was her huge ears that drew me closer. I saw that she was a tiny dog, trembling from her infected wounds, the worms that had invaded her empty belly, and, most of all — fear.

Had I not found her when I did she would have died right there in that rat-infested alley. Had I not found her when I did, I would have died too — of sadness, self-loathing, and the bondage of memory that kept me prisoner. It was destiny. We were waiting to find each other.

After she recovered at the local vet, she came home to me. The first few months were challenging. She hid beneath my bedroom dresser, never allowing me to touch or cuddle her in any way. I simply slipped a bowl of water and kibble in front of her hiding place each morning, and opened the French doors that led to my gated yard for her to relieve herself. I was content to know that she was safe. It was enough that she had a home, that she was loved, and that she had given me both a challenge and a purpose.

That frightened little dog was a mirror to my brokenness. I understood her lack of trust. I had stopped trusting too after I walked in on my husband naked in the bathtub with the babysitter. I hid from intimacy in darker places than she could ever squeeze her tiny body into.

But one day, after months of hiding, I woke to find her on the pillow next to my own. From that day forward, we were inseparable, until my rapist ripped us apart.

He had a tattoo on his hand of an Om. Ironic, because I had named her Om Shanti. "Om" is a vibration often defined as the sound of creation. And "Shanti" means "peace."

For years we clung to one another. She was my very best friend. She was the only living being who truly saw me, and still cared, without pretense, when I walked into a room. She was the pulsating-with-life reflection of God that I trusted with all of me. She was the wag at the door that welcomed me after long days, and her smile at the end of the leash reminded me that life was still unfolding outside my home and outside my head. She was the friend who licked my tears when life demanded more than I had to give.

When the ambulance arrived, Shanti was freed from the bathroom. The policeman who found her said she was too swift; he tried to catch her but could not. The front door had been left open, and Shanti was last seen chasing behind the ambulance that carried me away on the busy streets of Los Angeles.

When I finally was released from the hospital I spent each waking moment posting signs outside and online in search of my best friend. I couldn't breathe without her, couldn't heal and couldn't sleep.

A month or so went by and I had given up hope of ever seeing her again. I was pulled from a sedated sleep when the phone rang. It was a woman from Boston, 3,000 miles away, who just so happened to be going through missing pet announcements when she read my story. She said the mental image of this poor rescued dog chasing an ambulance led her to call and that she felt compelled to help me search. Her name, she said, was Angel.

One week later Angel called again. "I don't know if it's your Shanti," she said, "but there is a dog with the same huge ears wearing the red collar you described, but without any tags, in a kennel in the city of Downey." Downey was 150 miles from my home. Although I knew it was an impossibility, there was something in the spirit of her voice that gave me hope — that restored a semblance of my faith and propelled me to drive the distance.

I walked into the kennel shaking, and handed the flier and pictures of Shanti to the woman behind the desk.

"There's a dog here that fits this description," she said. "A nurse from a hospital in Los Angeles found her hiding under a bush. But apparently she was headed out here that night, so she brought the dog with her and dropped her off the next morning. If you'll follow me, I can take you back to her. I do hope she's yours. The poor thing is scheduled to be put down by end of day."

As I turned the corner I heard her yelping with excitement. It was her! It was Shanti. I had found her 150 miles from home. She jumped into my arms and I fell onto the floor. She was climbing on my head, wagging every part of her body, and I was laughing and crying at the very same time. We had rescued each other again. And we had both survived to love another day.

The drive home was the very first time I truly exhaled since the trauma. I cried out in gratitude and awe to God until I reached my front door. I immediately ran to the phone to call Angel. When I dialed her number, the automated response said, "The number you have dialed is a non-working number; please check the number and dial again."

— Piper M. Dellums —

17

Chicken Soup for the Soul

Sharing My Friend

Forgiveness is not an occasional act,
it is a constant attitude.
~Martin Luther King, Jr.

Cindy was my best friend. My mom called her a nuisance, but to me, she was a dog with a personality. At eleven, I fell in love with the tiny, curly-haired dog. Cindy was smart, too. I taught her tricks. She would sit by my feet and when I put a stick or piece of carrot by her mouth, I'd say "chew" and she would stand and obey. She loved going for walks with my friends and me. She danced around us as if listening to our conversations about school and clothes and movies we'd seen.

Sometimes, I sat with her in the front yard, letting her explore the soft grass. I'd tell her about my friends, the boys I liked, the test I was about to take in History. Cindy would sit and stare at me as if listening to everything I told her.

Then my uncle, my mother's younger brother, came to live with us. He and his wife slept in my room and I slept on the couch. My mom didn't want Cindy's curly fur all over the living room furniture, so she slept in the utility room in her plush bed. Instead of being beside my bed as usual, she was out of my aunt and uncle's way. I resented their presence and kept Cindy outside with me as much as possible.

But one afternoon, I went to get her from the back yard and she wasn't there. The back gate was partly open. Had Cindy been searching for me?

I looked everywhere around the neighborhood, knocking on doors and asking everyone if they'd seen her. I called her name, my friend who always came to me. This time she didn't come.

"Sorry," my uncle said. "I guess when I went through the gate to check something in my car, I forgot to close it completely."

I didn't want his apology. I cried and searched.

I prayed for her safe return. Then one morning, two days later, my uncle left after breakfast. An hour later he was home, Cindy in his arms.

"She'd been picked up by the pound. I thought I'd check and there she was. Must've pulled her collar off somewhere," he said.

Mom let me keep her beside me all night. I hugged her and told her about everything I'd done since she'd been gone. She licked my hand and listened.

It was two days later before she'd leave my side. She limped a bit, though we couldn't find anything wrong. But she was home.

My uncle felt bad and offered to buy me another dog to keep Cindy company outside. I knew he and my aunt were having a hard time. They didn't have much money. I wanted to hate him, but I knew it wasn't his fault he was living with us.

One day, I came home and found him sitting with Cindy in his lap and talking to her. I listened a moment and wondered how long he'd been telling her his troubles. I guess he was smarter than I thought. Cindy stared at him, looking into his face as she'd always done with me when I talked to her.

I watched them. I thought that maybe Cindy and I could give him another chance.

"Want to feed her?" I asked.

He nodded. I gave him the box of her favorite treats. He fed her and stroked her small head.

"She's a good listener," he said.

I smiled. I already knew that. I guess if Cindy forgave him, I could too.

— Kathryn Lay —

Bryan's Last Gift

We long for an affection altogether ignorant of our faults.
Heaven has accorded this to us in the
uncritical canine attachment.
~George Eliot

t was a dreary March day, and the black clouds that emitted tor-
rents of sideways blowing rain were nature's commentary on the
way I felt. As I sat in my big chair until late in the afternoon, the
thunder boomed and brilliant displays of lightning occasionally
lit up the living room. I fell into a deep sleep but was awakened by a
huge thunderclap and the ringing of my doorbell.

Who could this be? I was annoyed at having to stir from such a
peaceful sleep. I hoped it wasn't one of the neighbors, inviting themselves
over for small talk. Having always kept to myself, I didn't know any of
them very well. And now, after my stroke, was not the time to make
new friends. I hated having to act polite as they yammered on about
the weather, or their kids, or my health.

I made out a familiar silhouette at the doorway, and was pleasantly
surprised to see it was my son, Bryan. I couldn't get the door open fast
enough. After my stroke I moved a bit slower, but he was uncharacteristi-
cally patient while standing at the doorway in the driving rain. Oddly,
he hardly looked wet at all. He stood there smiling like a six-year-old
with something to tell.

I opened the door to receive the biggest hug that I'd had in years,
with all of the exuberance that had been absent since he reached his

teens. No hug had ever felt so good!

I pulled him in and had him sit down. He said he would, but he had to go out and get something. In a flash he was back. Accompanying him was a small dog—not a puppy, but not an adult. It was a cute dog, kind of. As I'm not a dog person, dogs can only be so cute — they are, after all, only dogs!

"You know I don't like dogs," I said, protesting.

The dog looked at me, sniffed at my feet, and proceeded to sniff his way through the rest of my living room. I did not like the idea of a dog walking around my house, but if that's what it took to have Bryan here for a while it was worth it.

Bryan and I talked and talked while the weather outside raged and the dog lay at our feet.

"What's his name?" I asked as I ventured to pet the dog's silky fur.

"It's a she, and she doesn't have a name yet — I was hoping you'd come up with a name."

"Me? You know I don't much care for dogs, let alone name one."

"Let's give her a good name," Bryan said. He gave me the same look he did as a little boy whenever he really wanted something special. I sensed this was important to him.

It seemed like "we" began the naming process, but it ended up being just "me." I settled on "Happy" because she looked like she was smiling.

"And besides," Bryan said, "that's the way she makes me feel." It was clear that Bryan loved the dog, and the dog clearly loved Bryan. They made quite a pair.

So it was settled.

The storm raged on as we talked of times past and looked at old pictures, many of which I had not seen in years. Bryan served as my guide, pulling out dusty old photo albums that were older than he. I relived memories, and fought to remember names, faces and episodes of my life. The journey was amazing. I caught myself petting this little dog that had managed to sit so close beside me that I couldn't help but touch her. Happy was warm and silky with deep brown eyes, almost identical to Bryan's, and she obviously appreciated my touch. I saw a gentleness in her eyes and a desire for companionship that I did not know in my present condition. I allowed her to continue to lie on my feet. It somehow felt natural.

I went to the kitchen to prepare dinner for us. Bryan continued to thumb through the photo album. In the middle of cooking, Happy came in the kitchen. She lay under the table, out of the way, and watched me. I found myself talking to her as I cooked and moved about. She simply watched, and occasionally cocked her head in curiosity.

When dinner was almost ready, I went into the living room and heard Bryan talking... to Happy.

"She's really going to need a friend...."

I didn't know who he was referring to, but I thought it slightly strange that he sounded so serious. I announced dinner and Bryan bounded into the kitchen with the ferocity of a hungry kid, and right on his heels was Happy. We ate what I do believe was one of my finest meals. We sat afterward looking out the living room window and quietly enjoyed the remnants of the storm. Right before the last rays of the sun faded, a muted rainbow appeared, barely clear enough to see.

Happy lay at Bryan's feet, relaxed, but attentive.

I must have dozed off, because the next thing I knew, Bryan was on his feet and announcing he had to leave. He told me not to get up and said he'd lock the door on his way out. I must have been sleepier than I thought, because I didn't get up from my chair. In my half-sleep state, I continued petting Happy's silky fur with her licking my hand in return until I heard the door close. Then I jolted awake, worrying I'd missed giving Bryan one more hug. And, even more importantly, that he had forgotten the dog. How could he have been so absentminded as to leave Happy behind?

I quickly got up and attempted to catch Bryan before he left. But when I opened the door, I saw no sign of him or any vehicle he could have come in.

There was nothing.

Happy stood on her hind legs and looked out the picture window for a while, letting out a long, low whine. Then she came to my side and rubbed her head on my hand to get me to pet her. The look in her eyes told me what I had just realized—my Bryan was gone.

Two days later, two men came to my house to inform me that Bryan had died in an accident four days prior. I found it unnecessary to tell them that their chain of events was not accurate. It was impossible, because Bryan had visited me and left Happy just two days before. I didn't bother to tell them that, because you had to know Bryan to understand. Bryan had always been a most thoughtful boy who would do the least expected thing, and when it counted most! He visited me, bringing sunshine on one of my darkest days, and left me the gift that I needed the most. Happy has been at my side from that moment on.

I cannot say how Happy has changed my life, but the change is obvious and lasting. I get up earlier, and go outside daily, whether I want to or not, to walk my friend. I walk farther and faster than ever. I get more exercise and sleep deeper. Happy and I play together, chasing squirrels and balls. We go to the dog park, where we occasionally take treats to share with other dogs. Happy is the ringleader of doggy-play while I sit and chat with other proud parents of happy dogs.

I now gladly interact with my neighbors, and talk to strangers and children alike. I feel the morning sun on my face, and hear the birds singing in distant fields. I see beautiful flowers, and imagine patterns in clouds. I smile! Happy and I have made friends and acquaintances that I would have never made by myself.

I have once again begun to see the world as a living mosaic of colorful wonder—all thanks to a friend called Happy, made all the more special because she was Bryan's last gift!

—Roberta Marie Easley—

God in the Cockpit

Peace is not the absence of affliction,
but the presence of God.
~Author Unknown

Working in real estate, I'd had the chance to meet and befriend a client who was a property developer. Clarence also happened to be an experienced pilot. He and I had done several business deals together and it was not unusual for him to fly us to see remote parcels of property suitable for development.

One night in late April 1985, I had a dream that Clarence and I were in a plane flying to view some property. A few minutes into the flight I saw engine oil on the windshield of the plane. Looking down in panic, I couldn't see the ground at all. The first thing I saw was the tops of pine trees as they peeked through dense fog, and I knew the plane was going down. Remarkably the next thing in the dream was a clear picture of the actual crashed plane, nose down, as Clarence and I stood back surveying the scene. Miraculously, we had survived.

I woke up really frightened. The image of the plane nose down stayed in my mind. I could not shake the dream. It seemed so real and it had to be a premonition of some sort.

Though the dream continued to bear on my mind, I did not tell my wife. I didn't want to burden her or cause her to worry. I decided, however, that I had to tell Clarence because I did not intend to fly anywhere with him for a while. I truly believed this dream had been a warning, which I intended to heed. I had worried for several days about how to tell him without either insulting him or having him think I was being ridiculous. So one afternoon while he was in the office to see me on business, I finally got up the courage as he started to leave. He was halfway down the hall when I called to him. "Clarence, hold up a minute. There's something I need to tell you." He was standing with one of my other colleagues and he turned back to me. "Yes, Alton? What is it?"

"Clarence, I had a dream the other night that you and I were in a plane crash. It was the most real dream I have ever had. I don't feel good about the dream and I don't think I'm going to be able to fly with you for a while."

Clarence and the other agent started to chuckle. Clarence patted me on the shoulder and said, "Oh Alton, try not to worry. It'll be all right."

Even though he obviously did not take me or the dream very seriously, I felt relieved at having finally told him.

Several days went by and I received a phone call from Clarence telling me about a client who wanted him to build a freight terminal around Daytona, Florida.

"Alton, how about you and I taking the plane down and seeing if we can find something for him?"

I could not believe that after I'd told him about the dream, he still was asking me to fly with him to Florida. I knew then that he really had not believed me or taken the dream as seriously as I did. Not knowing quite how to handle that, I just said, "Well Clarence, I've got a pretty busy schedule for the next few days. Let me look at things and get back with you."

It was really a dilemma. Maybe I was being a little paranoid. He was a good friend and business associate, and he was just asking me to help him find a piece of real estate for a client that I stood to make a pretty good commission from. After serious consideration I decided maybe there was a solution. It had been a while since Eleanor and I had taken any time off — why didn't we drive down to Florida, spend a few days at Epcot, visit my sister Ruth in Melbourne, and then I could drive to meet Clarence in Daytona and check out some properties with him? Clarence went ahead and flew down, and we found a suitable piece of property. Later, I drove him to the airport feeling good about avoiding this flight and what I feared was sure disaster.

About 10:00 p.m. I got a call from Clarence's wife. She wanted to know what time he had left Daytona — she was beginning to worry because she thought he should have been home by then. Cold panic set in. It had been four hours since he'd left Daytona and yes, he should have been home by then. I tried to play it down and not frighten her, so I told her that he'd probably run into some delay at the airport after I left and to give me a call if she had not heard from him in an hour. Turns out there had been a report of bad weather, and he had decided to land at a small airport and complete the trip once the threat of danger had passed. He was fine and I felt relieved knowing now that he had avoided the crash I had dreamed about.

Although the deal closed on our first trip, there were still details like surveys, soil samples and permits. So one morning Clarence called and wanted to know if we could fly down to take care of the things. Feeling confident the danger of the plane crash was behind us, I agreed. Tuesday morning, about 5:15, we left Covington, Georgia and headed for Daytona. Around 5:30 a.m., after we had reached about 5,000 feet, Clarence leveled out the plane. He turned on the cabin lights and we had some of the coffee and sandwiches his wife had made us for the trip. Once settled, he turned the cabin lights back out. That's when I saw it — oil all over the windshield. Just like in the dream. We watched as the oil pressure fell.

We searched for an emergency landing field, but below us was a complete covering of dense fog. We could see no landmarks, no lights, nothing. We turned back towards home to try to get out of the fog. Minutes later the oil pressure dropped to zero and the plane shook so violently that we feared it would break apart. Then the engine locked up, the propeller stopped turning, and the silence in the cabin was deadly. Both of us, however, seemed strangely calm.

"Clarence, remember the dream I had — we've been in these same seats before. And although we crashed, remember we both walked away. Let's just stay calm and try to think of what to do next."

We checked the altimeter, calculating at what point we would hit the ground. This all took less than five minutes—but time seemed to stand still. When we got to about 1,000 feet we saw a break in the fog. All I remember seeing was pine trees. Again, just like I saw in the dream. On its glide path, the plane cut down about eight of those trees and came to rest on its nose in a clearing the other side of those pines. I smelled the strange odor of fresh cut pine and gasoline as it gurgled out of the tank. For the first time, I felt fear.

We managed to get out of the plane and made our way over to a log, where we sat to assess our injuries. We looked back at the plane to the exact same scene I'd first seen in my dream.

I believe God sent me that dream as a warning and a message. I thought I could avert the crash by driving to Florida that first trip. But with that crash, He made it perfectly clear that He, and not I, was in control of my life—in fact, all life.

Several weeks later, a friend asked me if Clarence had been the one piloting the plane. "Well," I responded, "he was the pilot when we took off, but he and I both were passengers when we landed."

—Alton Housworth—

20

Lost and Found

Miracles happen to those who be ieve in them.
~Bernard Berenson

When it comes to being brave, my grand-dog Nessie is no prizewinner. She lets the cat have first dibs at all table scraps. She's never once barked at the postman. Squirrels have taken over her back yard because she dares not chase them up a tree.

Loud noises are what scare Nessie most. She trembles whenever a truck backfires. She goes nuts during thunderstorms. And she's terrified of fireworks. Knowing that Nessie hates Independence Day, my son James and his wife Natalie are always careful to keep her safely inside the house during the firecracker-crazy days of early July.

But one year, assuming that fireworks season was over after the Fourth had passed, they left her outside in the fenced back yard when they went to dinner with friends. Big mistake. They returned home to find spent bottle rockets littering the street beside their house. Nessie, who wasn't wearing her collar and ID tag, was gone. Their black dog had disappeared into the black, black night

It would take a miracle to bring her home.

James called his dad and me before sunup the next morning to tell us the sad news. "Can you come help us look for her?" he asked. Of course we could.

On foot, on bicycle and by car, we searched the area in an ever-widening circle. We talked to friends. We talked to strangers. We hung posters on telephone poles and placed a LOST DOG ad in the newspaper. Nessie's picture was posted and shared countless times on Facebook. We checked daily with the kind folks at the animal shelter to see if a dog matching Nessie's description had been turned in. Every time James received a phone call from someone saying they'd spotted a scared-looking black dog with no collar, we followed the lead. All to no avail.

Days passed. And Nessie did not come home.

Inevitably, the what-if's began. What if she'd been hit by a car and flung into a ditch where no one but the buzzards would ever find her? What if she couldn't find food and water and was wasting away? What if she had a new owner who thought it okay to chain a dog to a tree in the hot sun? There was no end to the horrible possibilities that sprang from our tortured imaginations. When we tried to talk ourselves into believing that a nice family had found Nessie and taken her into their loving home, we failed.

It was after midnight, more than a week after Nessie went missing, when James's phone rang. The caller said he'd been feeding a very friendly and very hungry black dog for a couple of days.

"Female?" James asked.

"Yep."

"About fifty pounds?"

"Looks to be."

"Ummmm," James stammered, his heart beating hard. "Does she, by any chance, have four white feet and a white tip on her tail?"

"She does."

"Don't get too excited," James told Natalie. "This guy lives clear on the other side of the county. We didn't even put up signs that far away. And we've had our hopes dashed too many times."

But this time was different. The dog was, indeed, Nessie. Who was overjoyed to see James and Natalie when they pulled into her rescuer's driveway. The happy outcome that so many people had hoped and prayed for had finally come to pass.

But how?

Nessie wasn't traffic-savvy. Why hadn't she been hit by a car the very night she escaped into the darkness? How could she have travelled more than ten miles and crossed dozens of busy streets and not have a scratch on her? Her coat wasn't matted or dirty. Her ribs weren't showing. How had a dog who'd been pampered all her life managed to find food and water and shelter for more than a week?

And what about the man who found her? He wouldn't have known that the dog who appeared on his front porch was someone's beloved pet unless his buddy had stopped by that evening. A buddy who happened to have seen a LOST DOG poster only because he'd run out of gas and spotted the poster while walking to a service station. A buddy who just happened to have a pen in his pocket when someone or something whispered to him that he ought to scribble the phone number down on his hand.

It was after midnight when Nessie's rescuer made the phone call. What if he'd decided it was too late and that he should wait until morning to call? Would Nessie have headed on down the busy highway in the pitch black dark, trying to make her way back to James and Natalie?

Some folks who have heard this story just shrug and shake their heads. Some contend that we simply got lucky. Others theorize that the stars somehow happened to be lined up just right the night Nessie was found. But we know better.

We know that nothing short of a miracle brought our dear, sweet Nessie home.

—Jennie Ivey—

21

Affirmation

Friendship isn't a big thing — it's a million little things.
~Author Unknown

Marianne was my best friend and she was dying. I had been blessed to be her caregiver. Cleaning up vomit, talking about death, and going to chemo or radiation, or to this test or that appointment every single day for three years had been a joy and never a burden. Marianne and I had prayed, laughed, and cried together every day of those three years and my life was forever changed by the experience.

One night, after presiding over a big, joyous dinner with seven very loud people, of whom I was the loudest, Marianne went to bed and fell into a coma. Hospice was called.

Thirty-three hours later, about nine o'clock on a Saturday night, I went to the bed where my friend lay on her side, struggling to breathe. Overcome with grief, I was at a loss as to what to do. Could she hear me? Could she feel my touch? Uncertain of anything, I went to my friend, who was curled in a fetal position. Ever so solemnly, I placed one hand on Marianne's thigh and the other on her pillow. Then I slowly leaned down and kissed her cheek.

To my great surprise, Marianne opened her eyes, awakening from this coma just to talk to me. "Oh, you finally came," she said with a smile, as though she was the one who had been waiting and not I.

I sat beside my friend on the bed and we talked. "You have been the best possible friend I could have ever asked for," Marianne said.

"I want you to know that I will always love you."

"I'll always love you, too, Marianne," I said as I tried not to cry. "I think you got the short end of the stick on this whole friendship business, though." I tried to laugh, as if I was joking, but Marianne would have none of it.

"Did you hear me?" She squeezed my hand with a strength that amazed me. "I could not have handpicked a better friend." Marianne had written this sentiment in countless cards and letters over the years, but to hear it now was a true blessing. We talked another minute or so and Marianne went back to sleep.

Our brief conversation was to be Marianne's last conversation ever. She never woke up again. Her husband called me several hours later to tell me Marianne had died.

I got through the funeral better than I'd expected, but as soon as I was alone, I crumbled. I cried as I walked my dogs. I cried while I did laundry. I cried in the shower and I cried in my sleep.

Three nights after Marianne's funeral, I went to bed defeated. Not crying, but exhausted by grief and certain I'd never feel okay again. I went to bed early, around eight o'clock. I fell asleep right away.

I woke up to the touch of a warm hand on my thigh. I don't know why, but I had no fear. The clock said 9:14. As I had done to Marianne the night before she died, I lay in stunned silence while my gone-and-buried friend leaned over and kissed my cheek. "I can't stay," Marianne said. "I just wanted you to know I meant what I said: I will always love you. And I could not have picked a better friend to see me through my three years of illness."

I couldn't speak, but I didn't need to. "Marla," she said. "I don't want you to grieve. I just want you to know I meant what I said. And Marla," she went on, "Heaven is beautiful! It's so much more than we imagined! I'm going back now, but I wanted to tell you that I'll be waiting for you. One day, we will be great friends again. So sleep, and don't cry. You'll make your dogs sad." I heard Marianne's sweet laughter and then I was so, so tired I couldn't keep my eyes open anymore and I was asleep again in seconds.

When my alarm went off the next morning, I remembered every

detail of what had happened the night before. Had I dreamed the entire thing? Or had Marianne really visited me from Heaven?

The only proof I had that this event had truly taken place was the way my dogs acted afterwards. For days my beloved pups sniffed and investigated the place on my bed where Marianne had sat while talking to me. They were obsessed with that corner of the bed. Even changing the linens didn't stop their curiosity about that spot.

The message got me through. I stopped grieving and started celebrating the life of my dear friend. I celebrated my own life, too, and the lives of my dogs. No way was I going to let my dogs be sad when Marianne specifically mentioned avoiding that!

I still miss Marianne, but all my memories of our time together are happy ones. I'm certain my two final conversations with my best friend — one just before she died and one just after — had everything to do with turning my grief into joy. To this day, if I ever get down on myself, I remember the things Marianne told me, and I remember that she came back briefly from Heaven to say them once more.

— Marla H. Thurman —

My Very Good, Very Bad Dog

22

It Takes a Village

You can always tell a real friend:
when you've made a fool of yourself
he doesn't feel you've done a permanent job.
~Laurence J. Peter

I got up at the crack of dawn that morning. I expected about thirty people for Christmas dinner, and the meal would consist of a twenty-pound turkey with all the trimmings.

Though the house was clean, dessert was made, and everything was cut, diced and sliced to make the cooking chores go as smoothly as possible, I still had a lot of work to do. My husband, son and I had opened our gifts from each other the night before knowing that this day would be a hectic one.

I wrestled the huge bird out of the refrigerator, dragging it to the sink. As I rinsed it, I noticed that the legs resisted my tugs. It was still a little too frozen to stuff, but I guesstimated that an hour defrosting in my cool office would thaw it completely and keep it safe from the curious cats gathered around my ankles sniffing at the air.

I placed it on my desk and shut the door. Then I busied myself with other assorted tasks, setting my timer so I wouldn't forget the main dish. I threw the tablecloth and placemats I planned to use into the wash, and gave the carpet another once over when I noticed some glitter from the previous evening's gift exchange clinging to the fibers.

The timer went off as I finished layering the scalloped potatoes in the baking dish. I wiped my hands, turned on the oven to preheat, pulled the stuffing out of the fridge and went to retrieve the turkey. As I placed my hand on the doorknob, I heard a loud belch come from behind the door and my heart sank.

I knew what I'd find even before I saw it. Intent on banishing the cats from the room earlier, I didn't notice the dog lying in the warm rays of his favorite morning sunbeam... in the office! I had closed him in with the turkey. I never heard the sounds of his feeding frenzy over the noise of my appliances, or I might have saved the main course. Unfortunately, now, it was too late.

What was left of it lay on the floor resembling the carnage of a wildebeest slaughter by lions in the Serengeti. My dog, Jack, sat licking his lips next to it. He had the grace to look slightly ashamed, but I knew that, deep in his heart, he thought the transgression was well worth any consequence.

I only needed to point to the area of his doggy bed. He slunk by me, head bowed, while his grotesquely engorged belly swayed from side to side. I knew he'd be okay after eating that much. A similar past experience with an entire ham left me feeling pretty confident that he'd expel what he couldn't digest. I could only hope that happened long before my guests arrived.

I approached the remains with tears in my eyes and with some concern. A quick inspection told me two things — the first, that there would be no danger of Jack suffering any mishap from bone shards or splinters, and the second that I couldn't salvage even a wing. Every bone was intact, yet the turkey was picked clean. The rib cage could have been used in a veterinary anatomy class, there was so little meat left on it.

What was I going to do? It was Christmas. There wasn't a store open anywhere, and even if there was, any replacement I'd manage to get would be frozen solid. I had less than seven hours to come up with an alternate plan, and I knew nothing in my own freezer would suffice.

At that moment the doorbell rang. I answered it to find my neighbor and friend, Amy, standing there with a platter of brightly decorated cookies.

"Merry Christmas!" she sang, and I promptly dissolved into a lump of quivering hysteria.

"Oh my goodness!" she cried, pushing past me. She dumped her tray on my kitchen table and pulled me close. "Talk to me," she demanded. My husband and son, having heard my meltdown, rushed into the room from downstairs.

I couldn't speak. I could only make incoherent, choking sounds as I led them to the office to point to the carcass. The cats were circling it, trying to find even a tiny overlooked morsel. My husband shooed them away and immediately discarded what was left. From the other room we heard a gagging splashing noise and I knew Jack had relinquished his feast.

"I have thirty people to feed!" I sobbed. "I can't possibly cancel now," I wailed as my husband scurried off to clean the mess.

Amy patted my back gently, deep in thought. When she spoke, it was with calm firmness.

"You leave everything to me," she murmured. "Keep getting the other stuff ready. I'll call you in about an hour," she assured me.

She whirled around and charged towards the door, averting her eyes from the deposit my husband was cleaning. "Trust me and don't worry," she called over her shoulder. "Oh, and spray some air freshener!" she advised before she disappeared.

She called right on time. By then, I had calmed down enough to put the finishing touches on some side dishes and made sure the meat pies were thawing in a safer place.

"Okay, problem solved," she announced. "We'll be there about four. Don't stress anymore," she said, and hung up without further explanation.

As promised, she showed up with two other neighbors, Sarah and Judy, grinning from ear to ear. She carried a huge foil-covered roasting pan. The other two juggled large chafing dishes. They all walked in as I stood there gaping.

"Ta-da!" Amy exclaimed dramatically, pulling the wrapper off the pan to reveal orderly piles of turkey parts.

"What on earth?" I gasped.

Everyone chipped in," she explained. "All our friends up and down the block donated a leg here, a wing there, until we managed to pretty much come up with a whole turkey and then some," she said, pointing to the extra three drumsticks and two breasts.

"I made gravy," Sarah proclaimed, pulling out a gigantic jar from one of the food warmers.

"And I brought stuffing, in case you didn't make any." Judy offered.

I was speechless. The food smelled delicious and was still steaming, so the girls set up the chafing pans and filled them.

"Keep everything warm," Amy directed. "It's all cooked and the dishes will keep the turkey moist until you're ready to eat. Just tell everyone you sliced it early. "We'll leave now before your company gets here. Merry Christmas."

"Merry Christmas—and thank you so much," I whispered, hugging them all. "You have to tell me who contributed so I can thank everyone else too," I insisted through happy tears, waving goodbye.

As they drove off, my first guests pulled into the driveway. My husband put his arm around me and winked at my son. Thanks to the kindness of friends and neighbors, and polite guests who never questioned the various flavors and extra turkey appendages, our Christmas went off as planned.

—Marya Morin—

23

Pepper's Last Gift

Dogs' lives are too short. Their only fault, really.
~Agnes Sligh Turnbull

Whatever life threw at us each year, come Christmas our family had one constant tradition: our dog Pepper opened our presents for us. When our beloved Black Lab mix had been a gangly adolescent puppy, we had only given her unbreakable gifts to unwrap — things like pajamas and steering wheel covers. She proved to be so careful that we soon gave her any gift that wasn't edible. Every time, Pepper found the seam in the wrapping paper with her snout and held the present down gingerly with her forepaws. Her front teeth pried up the lip of paper with the utmost care. Then she removed every inch of wrapping paper before stepping back to lie in the midst of our gathering. She never bit or scratched the gifts themselves.

Friends and relatives who joined our family celebrations never believed Pepper could be so delicate until they witnessed her talents. Watching our sweet dog unwrap gifts always warmed the holiday, which was often a little bittersweet because college, studying abroad, or work commitments often kept my two sisters and me away.

One year, everyone made it home for a Christmas together. I was back from Ireland, Kaci flew in from Arizona, and Kara visited from college. Mom's jubilance kept her busy baking cookies for us all. Our Christmas season should have been perfect.

It couldn't feel perfect, though, because Pepper's health was deteriorating. Her life had already been longer than we expected — she was fourteen — and yet her mind was still sharp. Her enthusiasm for life made us feel better. But her body could not keep up with her spirit. She'd already shown the usual signs of deafness and stiffness. That year, her hips and back legs started giving out on her. We knew we would soon have to make a difficult decision.

It was likely Pepper's last Christmas, so we decided to make sure she enjoyed it. On Christmas Eve, we gathered around the tree to open an early present. We each took a turn and then called Pepper to open one more. But her tangled legs could not navigate the boxes and shredded wrapping paper on the floor. She stumbled over the obstacles, and soon she disappeared into the next room. She crumpled back to the floor, as out of the way as she could get.

We were heartbroken. Could Pepper even participate in her last Christmas?

Pepper stayed on the periphery of all our holiday activities. Throughout the day, we gave gifts but did not feel very giving. We shared stories over cinnamon rolls that tasted bland. We played games by the tree whose twinkles had dimmed.

That evening, Kaci said what we'd all been thinking: "I wish Pepper could have helped open presents this year."

We all put down our mugs of spiced tea. "Maybe she still could," Kara said.

"But there's none left," Mom reminded her.

Kara jumped up and left the room. We heard her opening drawers and cabinets in the kitchen. She returned with a box of dog biscuits, scissors, and a roll of tape.

"Hand me that green paper," Kara told me, pointing at a large sheet at my feet. She cut a small section from the paper and wrapped a single dog treat in it. She held it up as if she had just struck gold. "Now there's a present for her!"

I knelt on the floor next to Kara and wrapped another dog treat. Kaci and Mom joined in, too. Soon, we had four elegantly wrapped dog biscuits in a row on the floor. We cleared the floor of discarded wrapping paper. We tucked our legs under us as we perched out of the way on the furniture.

"Go get Pepper," we urged Mom. We all bounced like eager children.

Mom went into the next room. "You want to open a present, girl?" she coaxed. In a moment, Pepper stuck her head into the room. Her ears were fully perked with anticipation and curiosity.

She skidded on stilted legs to the row of presents. She sniffed all four in order, and looked back and forth between them. She'd never had such a wide choice of gifts before.

Soon, Pepper selected her first Christmas gift. She nimbly turned the present with her forepaw, just like she was a spry young dog once more. She tugged every last scrap of paper off the dog treat before she chewed it with her customary grace.

Our family swelled with glee.

Pepper licked the last crumb from the floor. She eyed the remaining three presents, then turned to Mom as if asking, "May I please open another?"

"Go ahead, girl!" Mom encouraged.

For the next few minutes, Pepper opened each of her Christmas presents. While she did, she reminded us of the sheer joy of being together. Our family felt whole — not because we were in the same room, city, or country, but because our love bonded us together.

In the new year, Pepper let us know it was time to call the veterinarian. Her passing, while tearful, was peaceful. In its own way, her passing was also a celebration of life, because she gave my family so much love and laughter.

Long after I forgot each of my presents, I still cherish Pepper's final Christmas gift. She taught me that no matter where we each spend the holidays, and no matter what the passing year brings, the smallest act of heartfelt giving can unite our family through our love. For me, that knowledge is the longest-lasting gift of all.

— Zach Hively —

24

The Runaway Who Wasn't the Bride

Dogs are not our whole life,
but they make our lives whole.
~Roger Caras

Weddings have a way of driving a girl crazy. The "real-life" planning for the day she's dreamed about since she was a little girl can turn the kindest, sweetest bride-to-be into a shrill, sobbing, stressed mess if she isn't careful.

I've always been easygoing about things like that. I made it to the eve of my wedding without dissolving into tears over dress choices or seating arrangements. When my DJ canceled a week before the wedding, I took a deep breath and scrambled to find a replacement. When we had torrential downpours the night before the wedding, I told myself, "There's nothing you can do about the weather." We got a little damp going to the church for the rehearsal, but by the time we were all seated for dinner afterward, the laughter was flowing with the wine. I guess as brides go, I was pretty unflappable.

Stacey, my beloved mutt, was a different story. We were planning to leave for our honeymoon directly from the reception, and my grandparents were keeping her while we were away. I had taken her to their house that afternoon. If anything at all bothered me during the rehearsal, it was the memory of her soulful brown eyes giving me the silent guilt trip as I left. But by the time we sat down to our meal,

I had pushed even that aside to enjoy the company of my loved ones.

My father got a call midway through dinner. We were all laughing and sharing bits of food from each other's plates, and I didn't even realize he'd stepped away. When he returned to our little cluster of tables, his face was grim. He whispered something to my mom, and they looked at me. I felt my heart start to pitter-patter just a little.

In addition to Stacey, my grandparents had also offered to house some of our out-of-town relatives who were coming to the wedding. A few them had not yet arrived when my grandparents left for the rehearsal. They had left a key on the back porch so our relatives could go on in and make themselves at home.

"That was your cousin," Dad told me, looking like he'd rather be getting a root canal than share what he was about to tell me. "They just arrived at Grandmom's. When they let themselves in, Stacey darted out. They tried to catch her, but... she's gone."

It took a second for my heart to start beating again. Stacey had been with me since college. She slept at the foot of my bed, and her sweet furry face and wagging tail greeted me each day when I came home. My fiancé loved her, too, and his face grew just as pale as mine. She was part of our family, and embarking on this new adventure without her just wasn't right.

Instantly, our dinner gathering transformed into a search party. Bands of aunts and uncles, cousins, bridesmaids, and groomsmen took to the streets. The rain continued to pour, and the October night was windy and chilly. But no one backed down.

The park near my grandparents' house was suddenly awash with not only rain, but women in dresses and heels and men in suits and ties who traipsed through the mud like an expert search party. My friends and family hunted tirelessly. Our high heels planted themselves firmly in the mud and wouldn't budge, so my bridesmaids and I kicked them off and stumbled barefoot over mucky ground. My elderly relatives forgot their aches and pains and climbed hills, calling endlessly for my dog. Those who weren't searching the park scoured the neighboring back yards. I still wonder what the neighbors thought, looking out their windows on that rainy night to find well-dressed but drenched men and women poking around in their shrubbery.

After a few hours, we realized we weren't going to find her. My mom and sister went home and set about making up signs. I said a tearful goodnight to my fiancé and curled up on my parents' couch. I wept long into the night, finally becoming one of those brides who loses it.

My wedding day dawned crisp and clear, finally free of rain. My head hurt, and my face was pale. I hadn't eaten my dinner, and my stomach was still too queasy for food. My eyes were raw and puffy. This was supposed to be the happiest day of my life, but my heart was heavy. I thought of Stacey out there alone, and my waterworks started anew.

The photographer arrived. Instead of finding a bride in her gown and make-up, he found a tousled, weeping lump of a girl in her flannel pajamas. My mother explained the situation, and he nodded gently and started taking shots of the bridesmaids instead. Mom nudged me into her bedroom, where she managed to get me into my dress. The make-up, however, was an entirely different story. As soon as I'd get on a bit of blush or some eye shadow, I'd drown it in tears and have to start over.

Another knock sounded at the door, and my father greeted my great-uncle. I heard him and Dad talking in whispers, and then Dad uttered a loud "Thank God!" I flew from the bedroom, a ghost of a girl in a long, not-quite-buttoned white gown that matched the color of her pale, sleepless skin.

"She's home," Uncle Don smiled. "I went back to the park at first light and found her. It seemed like she was trying to find her way home. She was wet and hungry, but she's fine, honey. Now go get married." I flew at him and threw my arms around him, laughing and crying all at once.

No bride has ever rushed so much to get ready for her big day. When I walked down the aisle, my make-up couldn't hide the blotches left by my sleepless, tearful night. There was a speck of mud on my dress from hugging the uncle who had just traipsed through a waterlogged park with my dog. But my eyes were shining, and the smile on my face had never been more genuine. Sometimes, even when things don't turn out perfectly, they are still beautiful in the end.

Years later, the memory of my sleepless anxiety has faded. What I have never forgotten is the love of the family and friends who ruined their finery and soaked themselves to the skin helping me search for my wayward pup. Of all the gifts I received for my wedding, their selflessness was by far the most precious. I am forever grateful to the uncle who searched past midnight and still rose at dawn to bring Stacey home.

A wedding is about two people pledging their love, but it is also a reminder that we should cherish the loved ones who surround us and support us through our days. I couldn't have asked for a stronger reminder of that.

—Pam Hawley—

Bitsy and the Pickup Truck

*Being stubborn can be a good thing. Being stubborn
can be a bad thing. It just depends on how you use it.*
~Willie Aames

Every summer, I volunteer as an assistant dog trainer at the free obedience classes my vet friend Rosa teaches. This always leads to more than its fair share of humorous moments, as one can't get a large group of completely novice dogs and completely novice humans together without at least a few hilarious misadventures. One time, the ballroom dance teacher who used the school gymnasium after us joined, quite cheerfully, in a long discussion about the treats Rosa was planning for "Shane's twelfth birthday party," only to be completely horrified when Rosa said she'd had trouble getting enough raw liver at the store. Shane was Rosa's champion Border Collie, not her son, as the ballroom teacher had surmised.

Then there was the time we were tossing tiny bits of hot dog on the floor so the dogs would leave their owners, who would then lure them back with an even bigger and better treat. One first-time trainer with very bad aim scored a direct hit in the scoop neck of my tank top, and the hot-dog bite went straight down into the front of my bra. That would have been embarrassing enough, but then Romeo the Labradoodle decided to put his paws on my shoulders and go after his treat anyway.

Still, the funniest thing that ever occurred didn't happen until after class, when our training was finished for the day and everyone should have been heading home in their cars. It involved a Great Dane named, I kid you not, Bitsy. Teaching a beginning dog class means that you quickly become immune to incongruent dog names. You only have to make the acquaintance of a few Princesses who drool like it's going out of style or Killers who are frightened of their own shadows before you learn how to shrug and just get on with the task at hand.

But even by free-obedience-class standards, Bitsy stood out as being particularly misnamed. He wasn't just big, he was huge, measuring nearly three feet high at the shoulder and weighing close to two hundred pounds. He considerably outweighed his four-foot-ten-inch owner. He even dwarfed the small, quarter-ton pickup truck she used to transport him, making it look like a toy truck into which some optimistic child had tried to fit a much bigger stuffed animal. In short, Bitsy wasn't "itsy" at all.

Bitsy was never destined to be a star obedience pupil. Teaching him to heel was a particular challenge. After many, many tugs at his collar and waves of treats under his nose, his owner finally induced him to stand up and walk with her... for all of three steps. Then he'd sit down again, progressing in steady stages from resting on his bottom to slumping down onto one hip, his hind legs sliding out across the floor. From there the rest of his body would slowly follow his bottom and legs down to the ground, until all two hundred pounds of Great Dane had gently oozed to the floor like a giant melting marshmallow.

This process took several minutes to complete, and it was really quite fascinating and hypnotic to watch. Many times, the entire class would stop training to simply stand and stare. We'd watch the slow-motion ooze until Bitsy was nothing but a spread-out puddle of dog, utterly boneless and completely at ease. After several classes full of fruitless attempts to get him to move once he'd achieved this state, Rosa eventually nicknamed this puddle "Lake Bitsy." She urged the rest of us to ignore him and just keep working around him.

It was certainly a novel way to learn how to heel around obstacles.

Bitsy may not have been our star pupil, but he definitely enjoyed coming to class — so much that he decided he didn't want to leave one day. Rosa and I were cleaning up after class when Bitsy's owner stuck her head through the door, asking for our aid "with a small problem." The moment we stepped out the door, it was plain to see what the problem was: Bitsy was refusing to get into the back of his owner's truck. She had managed, heaven only knows how, to get his front feet up onto the open tailgate, but that was as far as Bitsy would go; nothing would convince him to jump into the pickup bed. He simply stood there, front feet up and back feet down, panting happily while his weight pushed the truck into a definite slant.

Rosa and I tried everything. After giving him a thorough exam to make sure he hadn't hurt his legs or back, we went through Rosa's entire arsenal of dog treats, trying in vain to find one that was yummy enough to tempt Bitsy the rest of the way. We did the same thing with our entire collection of training toys, all to no avail. Finally, we resorted to brute force. Rosa, Bitsy's owner, and I all gathered at Bitsy's hind end. We each planted our hands squarely on Bitsy's furry bottom and shoved forward and up with all our might.

The truck rocked like a boat in a storm, but Bitsy stayed put.

By this time, the dance class was gathering, so we quickly amassed quite an audience: fifteen couples all liberally bedecked in sequins and body glitter, watching us like we were the most entertaining thing they'd ever seen. I can't deny that we made a hilarious impression: three grown women in blue jeans gathered at the base of a tiny pickup truck, all pushing rhythmically on the bottom of an elephant-sized Great Dane who simply stood there with his tongue lolling out, looking around innocently as if he didn't understand what all the fuss was about. Fortunately, several of the dancers were also dog lovers, and with true small-town spirit, they volunteered to help despite their fancy clothes and shoes. They crowded in around us, and with a "Five! Six! Seven! Eight!" we all pushed on Bitsy's butt in unison.

It took three tries, and quite a few ballroom beads and feathers got detached, but it worked eventually. Bitsy was in the truck!

Bitsy's owner opted to have private lessons after that. She paid Rosa to come out to her farm, where Bitsy did eventually learn how to heel, though he never quite managed a non-oozing sit. But it doesn't really matter that I never saw Bitsy in class again. All I have to do is close my eyes, and I can still see him: the rocking truck, the pushing people, and most of all, Bitsy's hilarious, utterly serene face. It never fails to make me laugh and raise my spirits when they are low. Long live Bitsy!

—Kerrie R. Barney—

Making a Good Impression

Etiquette can be at the same time a means of
approaching people and of staying clear of them.
~David Riesman

fluffed up the sofa pillows and glanced around. No ice cream bowls on the end table. No stinky athletic shoes to trip over. No backpacks tossed in the corner. No dog nose prints decorating the window. Yes, this living room could grace the cover of a magazine.

To top off this perfect scenario, the four kids were playing quietly in the back of the house. Fortunately, Sherlock, our English Bulldog, was with them. I heaved a sigh of relief since Sherlock's manners could not be considered genteel.

The front doorbell rang. I knew it must be my guest since friends popped their heads in the back door, yelled "Hi," and came on in. Mrs. Williams would never do that. She was the poster child for proper etiquette. I ushered her in, got her seated, poured some tea, and handed her the cookie plate. So far, so good.

Just as Mrs. Williams reached the high point about her elite women's club and how she wished to sponsor me, I heard movement in the hall followed by snickering. I tried to ignore the commotion, but it became difficult with the bursts of smothered giggling. Mrs. Williams frowned slightly. I concluded either she was childless or had spawned perfect offspring.

As I looked up, Sherlock waddled into the room wearing an old pink tutu stretched around his large, squat body. Topping off his ensemble was a pair of boy's jockey shorts resembling a crown that he wore proudly on his head. Like a professional model, he paraded around the living room. I must admit by now I was having difficulty stifling my laughter. Sherlock stopped by Mrs. Williams and looked up at her with large marble-like eyes. He leaned against her leg and waited to be petted. I could tell from her expression that she was not a dog lover.

With what looked like a shrug, Sherlock padded into the kitchen. He plopped down with his nose pressed against the side of the refrigerator, enjoying the motor's vibration. The culmination of his high-fashion act was a deep burp followed by an enormous escape of gas from his other end.

Mrs. Williams departed.

The kids dove into the cookie plate.

Sherlock snored.

I figured that elite club probably wasn't for me.

— Sharon Landeen —

Guest Appearance

*The great pleasure of a dog is that you may make a
fool of yourself with him and not only will he not scold
you, but he will make a fool of himself too.*
~Samuel Butler

Our neighbor had a wonderful Golden Retriever named Dudley and we often dog-sat for him. Dudley got along very well with our Aussie Shepherd, Gus. They were pals.

On one such dog-sitting adventure, my husband Ron and I were sleeping soundly in the wee hours one Friday morning — 4:30, to be exact. Suddenly, I realized the bed was jiggling. What in the world? Ron slept like a log next to me, unmoving. I shook my head, trying to emerge from my not-awake state of mind. Earthquake? Unlikely in the foothills of Colorado. Windstorm? What could shake the bed?

I went on the assumption that Gus must be leaning against the bed scratching his neck, so I whispered, "Stop it!" I did my best not to wake myself any further from this semi-functioning state, but the bed continued to jiggle. So I whispered again, as if the dog could understand what I said, "What are you doing?" I tried not to wake Ron. How he slept through this jiggling had me baffled.

Then I heard claws scratching the wood floor, causing a spinning, sliding, clawing-for-dear-life noise. Now fully awake, I realized there was a dog under the bed. I reached over the side of the bed, snapped my fingers and whispered firmly, "Come out here whoever you are!" I looked over the edge.

Suddenly, a large Dudley face stretched its way out from under the frame of the bed. I repeated, "Come on, Dudley! What are you doing?" Again, did I think the dog would answer me?

Now the claws were really scratching, pulling, and slipping, unable to grip anything substantial. He was flattened against the floor with his front paws way out to the side. His paws continued this butterfly swim against hardwood flooring as he tried with all his might to get himself out from under the bed.

I began to mutter to myself about the lack of intelligence of the eighty-pound dog who was stuck under the bed that I was blissfully sleeping in just moments ago.

Thinking I had better get my weight off the bed since that was most likely hindering his progress, I knelt down on my bad knees after grabbing my flashlight and attempted to pull him out. Much like trying to assist a breach calf that refuses to come out, I tried to swing his legs under him to get him on his side, thinking he'd come out easier. That didn't work either.

Dudley just looked up at me in the beam of light with his big, sad Retriever eyes. I pulled and pondered how this was going to end.

Ron woke finally, rolled over and said, "What is going on?"

"Dudley is stuck. Under the bed."

Being the helpful guy that he is, Ron started cracking up.

Meanwhile, I was trying to pull on a huge dog to get him unstuck (Did I mention my bad knees?), and Ron was... laughing. Not helping. Totally cracking up.

I realized I was going to have to lift the side of the bed and hope that Dudley could crawl out. It's a king-sized bed.

Ron was still laughing.

I lifted and said through a strained voice, "Come on, Dudley, come out!"

Ron was still laughing.

The only other sounds besides my grunting and Ron's laughter was mad clawing, dragging, and sliding as Dudley finally pulled his large, furry body out from under the bed.

Ron was still laughing, totally out of control, *on the bed*. He was hysterically enjoying this early morning event of trying to obtain a dog's autonomy.

Finally, Dudley was free! He had a plastic newspaper dog toy in his mouth that he must have found under the bed. I'm so glad he was able to save the daily news. He lay unscathed in the corner with the toy between his teeth, happy as a clam, making his Chewbacca noise.

I got to crawl back under the warm covers, joining Ron, who was still laughing. He was holding his stomach and rolling back and forth on his back, hoping he didn't blow open another hernia.

I explained to him what I found when I felt the bed jiggling, which sent him into a laughing fit all over again. That got me giggling. We kept making jokes about what Dudley must have been thinking as I tried to birth him from under the bed. It took us an hour to settle the laughter and try to fall back to sleep.

At least I could rest knowing there were no more dust bunnies under our bed.

We slept late that morning.

— Sandy Nadeau —

Annie and the Fish Pond

Being deeply loved by someone gives you strength,
while loving someone deeply gives you courage.
~Lao Tzu

The minister agreed to marry us in my mother's living room so Steve wouldn't have to stand up in front of "all those people." We dressed up for the occasion, went out to dinner, and spent the night at a small country inn. One year later, with a new life and Annie making us a family, it was time to celebrate again.

The sun was warm but the hills and fields were still deeply blanketed with snow. We were moving into the little house set well back from the road and barns at the farm in the Laurentians where we would manage a flock of sheep, several chickens, and a trout pond. It was the country life we'd sought — two suburban kids escaping "real" jobs, the hustle and bustle of city life, and the noise.

In our new oasis of peace and quiet, there was no need to talk as we unpacked. The windows were open and the breeze that blew in would have flapped the curtains had there been any. A candle, scrounged from one of the many boxes strewn about the kitchen, graced the table for later. We had gathered large, brown eggs from the hen house to scramble for our anniversary supper. Everything was ready when the precious silence was shattered.

The sound soared like a soprano solo and then stalled at the point of a scream.

Sudden silence again. Steve and I looked at each other, questioning...

then knowing. We recognized the voice. It was Annie. Something was wrong.

More falsetto notes drifted in through the open window.

Only Annie, our pride and joy, had a voice like that. She sang in ecstasy at the sight of you. She howled in agony at your leaving. She yodelled for the fun of it and she had the best nose for trouble of any dog I ever knew.

Her cry for help was unmistakable. Then it stopped. The silence taunted us. We were ready to run as thoughts of leg-hold traps and wild animal attacks caused us to gasp in anguish. Then high-pitched yelps rose again, this time from the direction of the fish pond.

We ploughed down the hill, up to our knees in snow softened by the April sun. The wailing continued like a siren, guiding us. When it paused, we paused, confused, hating the silence. We struggled on, now following dog tracks that circled the pond and then disappeared.

The trout pond lay in a depression between snow-covered banks and was half covered with ice. The open water in the middle was black. It was quiet. We waited, not knowing where to look next. The silence flowed around us, toying with our nerves.

Then a small brown head bobbed into view and a pitiful, water-choked cry reached us.

Annie hated water. We didn't even know she could swim. We watched as she paddled to the edge of the ice and pawed at it. She knew we were there and made no more sounds except for an exhausted wheeze. Her eyes were wide with panic and pleading. She strained to pull herself out of the water but the ice splintered under her weight. She slid backwards and her head vanished again under the cold water.

I was frantic. Annie was drowning while I stood with my hand over my mouth, unable to think.

A boot hit me on the shin. A second boot landed beside the first. Steve's jeans lay in the snow, coins and keys spilling from the pockets. His heavy flannel shirt settled in a heap. I watched him hop on one foot, then the other, as he tore off his socks. He glanced around, not meeting my eyes, and shed his underwear.

He high-stepped through the rotting ice at the pond's edge, fists clenched and shoulders hunched against the cold. He hesitated as pond muck engulfed him to the ankles. He paused, I think, to calculate the potential appetite of hibernating trout before plunging in. With water up to his neck, preserving his modesty for the moment, he reached the dog's collar and towed her to safety.

On shore, Annie yapped and cavorted. Her voice echoed around the hollow where the pond lay. Heart hammering with relief, I shushed her.

In the silence that folded around us once more, I stared as Steve retreated, bare-backed and bare-footed, through the snow to our little house, and the warmth of an anniversary candle and scrambled eggs.

—Joanne Darlington—

How Not to Jog

If you can look at a dog and not feel vicarious
excitement and affection, you must be a cat.
~Author Unknown

"So you're going for a run?" This from my husband the skinny engineer and non-runner.

"Yes. I thought I'd take the dogs."

"All three of them? Is that wise?"

"I don't know if it's wise or not, but that's the plan." This from me, the elementary school teacher who's trying not to slip into the disappearing waist, puffy thighs, flabby abs, end-of-youthful-figure zone, and who only started running recently.

I grab the leashes. The kind made of slim cords that extend with a flick of a button from a thin plastic handle. The dogs start slobbering. Jumping. Vibrating. Whining. They won't sit still while I put on their collars.

"Can you help me?" I ask my husband. He's watching me with an amused grin on his face.

I should explain here about the dogs: two Labs, Nate and Duke; one Border Collie, Jessie. They aren't exactly sterling choices for a peaceful afternoon jog. Two have never been to obedience school. One flunked out. And I rarely even take them on walks.

But we are all collared and leashed and ready to go. I've even done my pre-jog stretches. "I'm going to get a good workout today," I tell my husband. "I can feel it. Lots of cardio-building, thigh-busting exercise."

He smiles again.

"Okay, open the gate." I hold onto the leashes with a death grip, two handles in one hand, and one in the other. The three dogs hop and yip and foam at the mouth.

"Are you sure?" my husband asks.

"Yes, I'm ready."

He slides back the latch and begins to open the gate.

Larry, Curly, and Moe nose through and take off like rockets, dragging me behind them.

The wind rushes past my ears, and I hear the faint sound of laughter behind me.

Okay. This is not the plan. "Whoa!" I yank back hard. All three dogs jerk to a stop. Jessie, the meekest of the three, sits down and looks slightly guilty. "Walk!" I say, forgetting that this is supposed to be a quiet afternoon jog.

"Have fun," my husband hollers after me.

"We will!" I wave and smile. And the dogs jerk me onward.

We half-walk, half-trot down our long driveway. Then we turn left, onto a winding blacktop road, and settle into a brisk jog, the boys in front setting the pace.

My normal route is down this road, which runs past hayfields and then into an area with pristine woodland on either side, and back again. A nice two-mile jog full of the clean-air smells of the country. Unless you come across roadkill. That roadkill being a mashed-up skunk.

Now there's something about dead animals that I realize is terribly interesting to dogs. Especially mine. Before I can say, "Don't even think about it!" all three dogs are wallowing in the remains of the dead skunk.

I scream. I jerk. I stomp. I scream some more. The dogs run circles around me, tangling me in the thin nylon cords of their leashes, always going back to the skunk.

A pickup truck headed our direction stops beside me as I'm untangling myself. "Need any help?" the elderly driver asks.

I shake my head. "No thanks. I think I've got it under control." The dogs wag their tails when they hear the man's voice. They whine and try to jump on his truck, like the man is their long-lost owner, and

I'm just a ranting stranger. "Cut it out!" I yell. The man drives away.

I reel in their leashes as short as possible, and we finally leave the dead skunk behind, but not the smell. It lingers in the fall air and makes me gag as the dogs jog in front of me.

We're almost to the end of the road, where the woods are thickest and where I plan to turn around and head back, when I hear a noise in the bushes beside me. A loud, crashing noise.

The dogs hear it, too.

They stop. Ears prick high. No more panting. They all three stand like statues, staring in the direction of the noise.

And then it's there. A deer. A large deer. A large running deer.

My dogs take off. Straight for the woods. I pull back on their leashes and scream, "No!" I dig my heels into the soft leafy soil.

They keep going. "Stop!" I holler. Whatever made me think I could take three large, powerful, slightly overweight dogs on a collective jog? I must have been crazy.

I'm skimming across the ground now, leaning back, digging ruts with my feet, and they're still pulling me. Through weeds and briars.

I sit down for leverage. They keep running. Now I'm bouncing along on my bottom. I feel dirt sliding up under my shorts. My backside starts to burn. I bump across the ground, screaming. But I don't dare let go of the leashes.

"It's gone," I yell. "The deer is gone!" But the dogs don't believe me.

Finally, my feet hit a fallen limb, and we stop. The dogs are shaking all over. So am I. My heart is pounding, I'm drenched in sweat, and I think I have enough dirt in my shorts to plant a small garden.

I stand, rearrange the leashes, and take a quick look around. Then, as discreetly as possible, I yank down my shorts and dump out the dirt. I find a few biting fire ants mixed in with the dirt. And I think I have stickers in my butt.

I pull up my shorts. "So much for a nice peaceful jog," I say to the dogs. "Thanks a lot. I hope you're happy." They wag their tails at me like they are extremely happy.

I limp home with the dogs. They strain against their shortened leashes, and my arms feel like they're being yanked from their sockets.

When we get to the dead skunk, though, I'm ready. We walk far around.

At home, I turn the dogs loose in the backyard. I will bathe them in tomato juice later.

I drag myself inside.

"How was your jog?" my husband asks, looking over his newspaper. "Dogs do okay?"

"My jog?"

He nods.

"I wouldn't be lying if I said it was interesting."

"Yeah? Get your heart rate up?"

"Yep. Did that."

"Feel like you got a good workout?"

"Oh yeah." I rub my hand across my backside and feel the prick of splinters. "Except…"

My husband sniffs in my direction. "What's that smell?"

"Meet me in the bathroom with a pair of tweezers. I'll explain everything then."

— Sharon Van Zandt —

Bolo

Remember that it's never too late and you're never too
old to get the body you were born to have.
~David Kirsch

My daughter is a runner. When she was a baby, she didn't just learn to walk; her first steps sent her running. I ran with her, or rather *after* her, to guide her past obstacles, but I was never built for running. It was obvious by the time she was eight that she could run circles around me and nearly everyone else. I used to call her my "deer." Not dear, but "deer" — she was that fast.

She was on the track team in school and never walked anywhere if she could run there instead. Of course, she was lean and sleek. Even in college, she had time for her morning run. If she was the family Greyhound, I was the family Pug.

She lived with her intended, a very nice fellow she met in college. The wedding was nearly a year away, but they could not wait to begin their life together and got a little apartment off campus while he finished his master's degree.

Since I'm a widow, Jenny and I used to have dinner together once or twice a week when her beau had a late class or a paper to research. But college and our separate to-do lists left her little time for leisurely eating. And she had races to prepare for. She asked if I wanted to go running with her, which made me laugh.

"Run?" I chuckled. "I haven't run since I used to chase you all over the neighborhood. I'm 20 pounds overweight and out of shape."

So, she didn't ask me again. She was training daily for a fall marathon.

One Saturday, she called and said she was going on a run with friends, who were also training for the marathon. "Lonny will be studying for an upcoming exam, and there's no one I can get to take out Bolo. Could you?" She was referring to her dog.

Bolo was her fiancé's dog. He was part Boxer, part something else, probably more "something else" judging from the haphazard way he was put together.

"When I come home, I'll bring Chinese," she said, bribing me.

It worked.

"Be sure to get his leash on him before you open the door," she warned. "Bolo means 'Be-On-the-Lookout-For.'"

Yeah, yeah.

I got to her place, re-met Bolo, and then my daughter was off on her run.

Bolo slept on the sofa while I cleaned up the breakfast dishes. Then it was time to take out the dog.

"Come, boy, want to go for walkies?"

He sure did. He was dancing, prancing and slinging drool from his floppy jaws. I got out his leash, glad it was a sturdy one, and prepared to clasp the hook onto his collar. He was wiggly, but I thought I had managed to clip the leash onto his collar. I opened the back door at the same instant that I saw the leash had only snagged a bit of his neck hair, not the collar. Before I could do a thing about it, he was out.

"Bolo!" I yelled, but he was gone like a flash. That huge pony of a dog was galloping down the walk. I yelled again, but I could just as well yell the sun out of the sky as stop that racing dog.

There was no way I could catch him. He was at the corner of the block and across the street into the small park before I had gone 100 feet.

"Bolo out again?" a boy on a bike asked.

"Yeah," I gasped back, running faster than a 40-something, overweight woman should ever run.

"I'll help," he said, grabbing the leash and pedaling toward the park.

I was gasping by the end of the block. *I'm going to die right here,* I thought.

"Bolo on the run again?" a man, mowing, shouted. I nodded. I was too winded to speak.

"Try down by the lake," he said. He shut off his mower and took off after me, passing me as we crossed the street. "Sometimes, he likes to play in the water," he called back as he raced ahead at a pretty good pace for a guy who looked to be in his fifties.

The boy on his bike, the able 50-year-old man and the puffing woman strung out across the park, chasing after the dog.

"Bolo!" the boy called.

"Bolo!" the man repeated.

"Puff-puff," I gasped as we neared the lakeshore.

Sure enough, Bolo was splashing happily in the shallows of the lake.

The man caught up to him and held him as the boy brought forth the leash and clipped it on his collar.

I thanked the boy, who nodded and whizzed away on his bike without so much as one hard breath.

"I've run my first and last marathon," I puffed out between gasps.

The man laughed. "You're about a block from where your daughter lives."

"I was taking Bolo out for his walk. My daughter is training for a marathon."

"And he slipped away. Yes, he does that now and then. Are you Jenny's mom?" he asked.

I said I was, and he told me what a funny, joyous, bright girl my daughter was. He was right. I could have added that I was once like that.

I thought about that as the nice man, David, walked me back to my daughter's place. Bolo behaved nicely once on his leash.

We stopped and continued to chat.

"Jenny said she'd bring Chinese on her way home," I said. "You know how they pack so much food in those little boxes. I'm sure..." I started to say, and then realized what I was doing. I know I blushed. I could feel the heat on my face.

"I'd love to," David replied.

"My daughter said she'd be home around six."

He waved and went on to his mower, and I walked Bolo back to my daughter's apartment. Every bone in my legs, knees, and back ached with that sudden wild dash… yet, there was a new sort of exhilaration, too. Was that what running did?

I doubted it, but for once I felt free of my dirge, the sameness of my life. I would never be a runner, but maybe a nice, brisk walk now and then… Who knows where that could lead?

— Nancy Lee Davis —

Sibling Rivalry

The reason cats climb is so that they can
look down on almost every other animal.
~KC Buffington

Like many young couples, my husband and I were looking for something to nurture but weren't quite ready to start a family. Into our lives came Smoky and Sparky, gray and black littermates. They were aptly named since my husband was a fireman. It was so much fun having two kittens together. Their antics were hysterical, and we were never short of entertainment.

We got these two while we were in an apartment, but soon purchased our first home, a small bungalow. The cats were now able to play in the yard as well as the house. Not long after, we added Sheba to the mix, a rambunctious white German Shepherd. Sheba loved to chase the cats around the house and often singled out Smoky for her torment. Maybe she did it a little too often for the frisky young feline. Maybe she was a little too rough about it. Either way, Smoky must have been fed up, given what she did next.

One beautiful sunny day, I had thrown open all the windows and was enjoying the fresh air. The curtains waved softly in the breeze, birds were singing, and all was good. Working around the house, I suddenly heard incessant barking coming from one of the bedrooms. "What is that dog up to now?" I thought. "Is she torturing one of those cats again?"

I walked briskly into the bedroom, ready to scold her and get her away from whichever cat she had cornered. I was stopped short by the sight in the window. Smoky was on the outside, hanging onto the screen with all four legs sprawled out from her body. Initially, I thought she had gotten herself stuck trying to get in, and I was about to go outside to rescue her.

It only took a moment to understand what was really going on. Sheba had her front paws up on the windowsill and was barking furiously into Smoky's face. The cat remained suspended and motionless in the middle of the window for a couple of minutes. All the while, the dog was going nuts.

It occurred to me that she was doing this on purpose, knowing full well that the dog couldn't get to her. It was as if Smoky was taunting Sheba like a child chanting, "Nah, nah, nah, nah, nah! You can't get me!" I laughed out loud and cheered her on, now unconcerned that the screen might get wrecked from her claws. I'm convinced she hung there as long as she could take it. Then she extracted herself, dropped down and walked away. Point made.

I leaned close to the window and observed Smoky heading to the back yard. I'm pretty sure I detected a proud strut, not just a regular walk. I imagined her saying, "Humph, that'll teach you to mess with me!" After all, cats rule, dogs drool.

— Carolyn Barrett —

32

Wedding Night Blues

Be all in or get all out. There is no halfway.
~Author Unknown

It wasn't supposed to happen that way. On my wedding night, as the drenching rain soaked my ecru lace wedding gown and my carefully coiffed hair wilted in the storm, I ran through the back yards of my neighbors crying, "Honey! Honey, come back!"

I could feel them staring behind their curtains, wondering how what was supposed to be the best night of my life had turned out so badly. I imagined how my carefully applied make-up was probably giving me raccoon eyes and wondered if the grass stains would come out of the bottom of my once-lovely gown.

"Honey!" I was almost screaming now. "Honey, please come back! Please!" I could feel their pitying eyes as my pleas became more desperate, and the rain pounded down on my back.

It was just after midnight on our wedding day.

The minister had declared us husband and wife much earlier that evening inside the small Baptist church where my betrothed had once attended Sunday school. We made it through the vows, and when my new husband gazed at me, there were tears in his eyes. Tears of joy, I assumed. There was a brief moment of concern when we were lighting the unity candle and I caught my veil on fire, but quick action by my betrothed smothered it out.

The typical Florida summer rain had started its drizzle before we even left the church. "It's good luck when it rains on your wedding day," everyone told me as we tried to dodge the rain and headed to the hotel where the reception would begin.

It was a glorious gathering of our closest friends and relatives, with an open bar. We made the rounds of the tables, danced to the deejay's tunes, which we had selected together, and then laughed and cried as we got ready to leave.

My bridesmaids had loaded my car with boxed gifts and cards, and we planned to drop them by my house — now, our house — before we went to the hotel where we would be spending our wedding night. Our flight out to San Francisco wasn't until the next afternoon, and a honeymoon in the wine country awaited us. I looked forward to sleeping in through the morning.

The house was only five minutes away from the lovely, turn-of-the-century hotel where we'd hosted the reception, so we figured we'd leave the gifts there and go home to take out my dog. That would hold the little Australian Shepherd until the next morning, when my friends were coming to take her to their house.

I unlocked the front door and held it open as my husband carried in a stack of boxes wrapped in glittery white and silver paper. As I stood in the doorway, my honey-colored Shepherd dashed past us into the rain.

By the time we put the gifts on the dining room table and ran after her, Honey was gone, nowhere to be found. And that's why my husband and I spent the first hour after our wedding reception — tired, wet and more than slightly drunk — running around the neighborhood, calling desperately for the dog named Honey.

Finally, we cornered her, filthy and wet, and smelling — well, like wet dog — and brought her back into the house. We wiped her down with a towel as best we could and then went on to our hotel. We flew off to our honeymoon the next day.

But from the time we began our married life in the little Lake Worth neighborhood where I owned my first house until we moved together, along with the dog, an hour north to Port St. Lucie, I imagined I could feel the pitying eyes of the neighbors, who were probably still imagining that I was chasing my new husband that rainy wedding night.

—Sue-Ellen Sanders—

Who Rescued Whom?

33

When Hope Found Me at the Beach

Dogs are miracles with paws.
~Attributed to Susan Ariel Rainbow Kennedy

The clouds were as murky and gray as my thoughts. Brooding about life and deeply preoccupied, I collected some things and pointed my car toward the ocean. I trusted the beach to make everything clearer for me, and I wanted a dramatic, solitary view. On a dismal weekday like this I hoped to find everything I needed at the jetty at Fort Stevens.

I drove for miles without seeing a car before I finally pulled into the parking lot. I was the only person there. Note that I said the only "person." I was, however, not alone. A ragged dog looked hopeful as I parked. Ears up, eyes searching, he looked expectant, wanting to recognize me.

Hoping.

A stiff, steady wind whipped the beach grass, and the rail thin dog hunched against the cold. There wasn't enough meat on his bones to block the chill. He limped slowly toward me. I stepped out of my old Cadillac, and he picked up his pace to greet me. A battle waged in his soft brown eyes, a war between despair and optimism.

A battle was going on inside me, too. My drive had been full of murky thoughts and dark emotions. But I wasn't going to share my darkness, and it looked like too many people had already snubbed this wayfarer — I reached out to the dog, and he came to me.

I looked closer; his feet were swollen and the insides of his thighs were chapped and pink from salt water and wind. His elbow was scraped and covered with fresh blood.

I walked toward the lookout, my destination, to watch the waves break against the great rocks. He followed. There were three short flights of stairs. I took them slowly; he climbed beside me haltingly, limping.

I searched the horizon beyond the violent waves for answers. He stood quietly at my side. The harsh wind whipped the surf into froth. My long hair blew wraithlike; his fur tossed wildly.

I slowly descended the stairs, and he kept pace. I headed for the shelter of my car, and he followed, stopping only to sniff at a trashcan, but he found no food. I turned and saw him trying to eat the sharp-edged beach grass.

I looked at him and called out "Hope!"

It was my grandfather's name.

The dog came. I opened my passenger door, pushed the seat forward, and invited him in. He hesitated, wagged his tail, and stepped in gingerly. Then he stepped back out. He kept looking around, like there was someone still expected, like my car was the wrong car.

But there was no other car.

He stepped in and out half a dozen times, each time staying longer. When a white-haired man walked by my car on the way to the lookout, Hope growled a warning. "Good protective dog, ma'am," the retiree said.

"He's not my dog," I answered.

We chatted and he said coyotes lived in the park, and the fresh blood on Hope's elbow would be like a magnet. I had to do something, so I invited Hope into the car, and shut the door. I rested my hand against the back of the passenger seat to keep it from flopping back and scaring him. The kindly man followed me in his truck. I made it about twenty feet before Hope decided to claw his way out of the car. I stopped and opened the door and he hopped out. But how could I leave him?

I couldn't.

We coaxed Hope back into the car. More determined, I drove off and just let him claw the door. I opened the window, and drove faster. Hey, my car was old anyway. Hope relaxed enough to curl up on the floor and rest.

Going through Astoria, he sat up. He faced me, and I spoke gently. He studied me, and I rested my hand against the back of the passenger seat. Then he quietly lowered his chin into the crook of my elbow, sighed, and closed his eyes. In moments he was asleep.

All that remains to be said is that I found Hope at the beach one day. More accurately, Hope found me.

The truth is, he rescued me as much as I rescued him. I can't say what would have happened that day if Hope hadn't been there to meet me, but I can tell you my beach bag didn't have a towel and a sand bucket in it.

I believe God sends us what we need. If a person had tried to talk to me on that dark day, there's no way I would've listened or turned aside from my self-destructive path. But to suddenly be presented with an innocent dog in dire straits? That was a call I could never turn away from.

I've heard people discuss whether angels have wings or not. I think it's a matter of dressing for the occasion. I'm of the opinion they appear from time to time on stone bruised feet — with doggy breath. And I promise you, one angel rested his chin in the crook of a deeply depressed person's arm — at just the right time.

— Christy A. Caballero —

34

Mica's Miracles

For every mountain there is a miracle.
~Robert H. Schuller

"Thirty-seven... thirty-eight... thirty-nine... Yay, Mica! Woohoo!" Mica's excited barks rang out in the frozen stillness. Atop Blackhead Mountain in January, I stamped my feet and clapped my hands to stay warm and also to celebrate Mica's amazing accomplishment. Making it to the summit of Blackhead is no mean feat, as the trail ranges from steep to wickedly steep to holy-cow-you-have-got-to-be-kidding-me steep. At the summit, she planted her feet and pointed her nose skyward and barked thirty-nine times — once for every mountain she'd climbed since our beginning more than a year earlier.

Mica, a Belgian Malinois, came into my life in May 2012. I already had a pack of rescued dogs of my own, but when I heard that a senior dog had been dumped at a shelter, I turned to Iske, who was reading the computer screen over my shoulder. "Look, Iss," I said, "a dog your age, abandoned at the shelter. We'll foster her and help her find a family of her own." Iske's tail thumped against my chair as my heart raced and my eyes filled. Iske's approval meant a lot. After all, I may have adopted her, but she rescued me. Through a brutal breakup and single parenthood, illness and eviction, financial troubles and relationship meltdowns, Iske had been my rock. Rescue, I learned from Iske, is a two-way street.

Now it was time to give back, and Mica was clearly in need. She had spent the past eleven years bored, frustrated, lonely, angry, and frightened, alone on the end of a chain. Her potential went utterly unappreciated, the neglect all the more piercing due to her incredible athletic ability and intelligence. After eleven years, her family moved from their home and disposed of Mica as if she were just so much trash. From that first glance at her photo, there was no talking sense to me. I would make sure she was safe and comfortable, no matter what. A few e-mails and a transport miracle later, Mica arrived at my home.

Mica had a tough time adjusting to her new home. She refused to be petted, walking away from all affection. She didn't know any commands, pulled dreadfully when on the leash, and sought distance and solitude at home. She was not aggressive at all — just stiff and aloof, sad and uncomfortable. She missed her family and all that was familiar, as awful as it was. We loved her from the distance she maintained and hoped her heart would heal enough to let us in.

After being with us for a few weeks, I decided to take her into the Catskill Forest for a short hike. She had learned her name and came when I called her, so I weighed the risk against the potential joy hiking might bring her. After a half a mile or so on the trail I took off the leash. She pranced away and sniffed the ground. Then she raced, paws flying, leaping over fallen logs, wagging and barking, along the next three miles of trail. At the lookout, she posed upon a rock and surveyed the layers of hills dropping away towards New Jersey and beyond. And everything changed.

Mica's miracle unfolded over many more hikes. She tasted freedom and she loved it. Hiking became a way of connecting with me, as she came to trust that I would give her the freedom she valued above all else. She'd been with us just over six months and had settled in nicely when a run-in with a porcupine resulted in a vet visit. The vet and I examined every centimeter of her body with a fine-toothed comb, seeking any stray quills. And that was when we found it: a small ugly bump on her belly.

The bump grew quickly and surgery was scheduled. When I took Mica in for her post-op checkup, the vet sat me down and spoke in that horribly quiet tone reserved for the worst of news. Grade 3 mast cell sarcoma, very aggressive subtype, no clear margins, and in his brutally honest opinion—"six months at the most." We discussed all the options and he shook his head slowly, petting Mica's soft ears. "Just take her home and make her happy," he said. "Anything else will ruin what little time she has left. Just make her happy."

In the face of such heartbreaking news, I did what any reasonable person would do. I adopted her. No more foster status, I felt that for whatever time she had left she deserved to die with my last name, a full member of this family.

And then I took Mica hiking. We committed to completing the Catskill 35—the thirty-five highest mountains in the Catskill region. If Mica could live long enough to hike them all—and then repeat four of them again in the winter—she could earn a certificate and patch for doing so. Hiking the 35 gave me a goal that structured our hikes. It gave me something to focus on besides her cancer. It gave me hope. And it gave her profound joy to be loose and running free up and down the mountains of the mighty and ancient Catskills.

We took it mountain by mountain, hike by hike. I kept a tally sheet next to the computer, filling in the dates as I uploaded photos. Doing anything thirty-five times takes time, and I fussed and worried over Mica as we hiked the list. Her pack mates came along to lend a paw. At first I thought we'd never make it to the winter hikes. Predicted to survive six months at most, we hiked often, logging miles and mountains in good order. And miraculously, Mica did not sicken. She did not show any signs of illness or discomfort at all. In fact she looked vibrantly well. It would have been amazing for any senior dog to hike and climb at this level of intensity, but Mica bravely trotted up those mountains at age twelve with terminal cancer, thirty-nine times. I got choked up at least once on every hike, burying my face in her neck and tearfully telling her what an amazing girl she was.

We hiked with the forest ranger and we hiked with my human friends, but mostly we hiked alone, just Mica and her canine sisters and me, up and down mountain after mountain. We gained hope. We got more and more excited as the number of remaining climbs shrank. And then the day was upon us: more than one year after her surgery, we were making that final climb. From a hopeless and pitiful creature on the end of a chain to barking her thirty-nine barks upon the summit of Blackhead Mountain, Mica's spirit has shown me just what a miracle really is.

It's been six months since Mica finished. Her certificate hangs above my desk, testimony to her courage and strength. We still hike regularly, working on a new list now. At her last vet visit, we got more bad news: the shadow we saw on the X-ray is lung cancer. Not a problem. Mica and I know what to do. "The mountains are calling and we must go."

— Halia Grace —

35

One More Day

Until one has loved an animal a part
of one's soul remains unawakened.
~Anatole France

Experience fostering retired racing dogs led my husband and me to believe we could handle anything. Yet nothing prepared us for what padded into our lives the day we adopted Ray.

Steve and I had inquired about a sleek, handsome boy who sported a black-and-white tuxedo coat. Retired due to injury, he had transferred into foster care almost immediately. Within two short weeks of house training, he pranced through our door.

Ray had no other place to go. Behind his sweet face lurked a dark and damaged soul. An atypical Greyhound, Ray possessed an aggressive nature. Wide-eyed and fearful, his strong prey-drive kicked into overdrive during his foster care with other pets, and he created havoc. Desperate to find him a home and not deliver Ray to the farm, the adoption agency rushed him to our door when we offered to adopt. Our experience with Greyhounds and a home without children or other animals made us perfect candidates, and we were his refuge of last resort.

Ray pranced around our house. He tried to understand the enormous world he now lived in, a strange one compared to the confined quarters he had known for so long. Adjustment would take time, but his inexperience, and apparently ours as well, made coexistence interesting.

Patience and training with any new pet is important, but with Ray, it was vital. He tested our limits and tried our patience in every way possible. He did not respond to commands, love, encouragement, or food. He had no idea what we expected of him. In fact, he had no idea that he was a pet, or that he even had a name. Like an alien from another planet, he had no concept of life in our world. He had known only the racetrack, so he sped around our back yard with a crazed look that shouted, "This is what you want from me — to race and to win — right?" And so a new and challenging journey began for all of us.

In a large, scary world, fear manifested in bursts of rage. Ray's hostility coupled with separation anxiety and antisocial behavior were a recipe for disaster. He literally threw himself at the window whenever anyone approached our home. In a canine frenzy, he scratched at windows and doors whenever we left the house. Concerned for his safety and the condition of our home, we crated him. But he resisted and attempted to bust free, so leaving our home became increasingly problematic. The stress we encountered as a result of the stress our dog endured overwhelmed us.

Then things got worse.

We had adopted Ray in the heart of the recession. Two weeks after welcoming him into our family, I lost my job, and then Steve lost his. Now three worried individuals paced anxiously through the sanctuary of our loving home. Our burdens consumed us. Steve and I no longer had any idea how to alleviate the mounting bills or threats to our sanity. Still, we focused on the positive. Time not working provided additional time to teach Ray about life in a house.

Eight weeks after adopting our dog, we hung our heads in defeat, ready to send him back. Ray had consumed our attention 24/7, showing minimal improvement and unabated anger. He attacked the window blinds for obstructing his view, the coffee table for daring to be in his way, and the baby gate for barring his entry. By the end of the second month with Ray, our frazzled nerves had stretched to the breaking point. We discussed alternatives and realized we had only one: returning Ray to the adoption agency, where he would most likely be put down.

"Do we call first thing in the morning or give him another week?" I whispered to Steve. His eyes filled with tears. He shrugged. The question tormented us. We decided to give Ray one more day and then make the call. We saw no other option. Ray was too aggressive to enroll in obedience training and too unpredictable to leave home alone. He'd shown slight improvement — at last, he knew his name — but little will to change, and his aggression persisted. The quality of life for all of us had deteriorated. Something had to give.

I knelt down beside Ray that night, hugging him tight. Tears stained my face as I whispered into his ear. "Please, Ray, please try harder. You must be good tomorrow, or we'll have to send you back. We want you to stay, but you have to want it, too!"

As if my words had struck a chord of meaning deep within him, the next morning Ray's attitude was transformed. Calm and mindful, he came when called and responded to commands. He still had a long way to go, but now exhibited a willingness to learn and behave. All that training had sunk in. Steve and I breathed easier each day that Ray improved. If he was willing to keep trying, we owed it to him, and to ourselves, to do the same.

Within a month, we had found work, and Crazy Ray no longer tore at doors, windows, and blinds when we left the house. We trusted him home alone, knowing no harm would befall him or our possessions.

Like training, socialization played a huge role in his development, and Ray evolved into a socialite. When he padded through the pet store door to attend a meet-and-greet, it was like Norm walking into a bar of welcoming cheers. Everyone would call out "Ray!"

Ray grinned at the smiling faces, and other dogs rushed forward, dragging their owners along to ask, "So, how's Mr. Personality today?" The group recognized the change in our dog, and pats on his back for all that he had accomplished felt like a tribute to all of us.

After retirement, Ray still needed a purpose in life, and he found it in guarding our home and being a loyal, loving companion. He also provided comic relief with his never-ending funny faces and attempts to pilfer food. In the process, he earned a few nicknames: Corned Beef Thief, Baklava Bandit, and Strawberry Stealer.

Sweet Baby Ray entered our lives at a time when we needed him most. We taught him how to thrive in our world, and he taught us how to focus our attention on something tangible and valuable, rather than on failure. We three became a family. Ray learned to open up and love, and with a huge heart, he loved us with all of it.

Despite a difficult beginning, Ray's time with us ended too soon. Losing him to illness at age seven tore a hole in our souls that still hurts, but we remain grateful for our time with him. Ray taught us a great deal about endurance — to never give up on ourselves or those we love — and to give new members of our family a chance to find their place.

— Cate Bronson —

Making a Difference

If there are no dogs in Heaven, then when I die,
I want to go where they went.
~Will Rogers

t was a crisp fall morning when I suddenly awoke from a deep
sleep. I looked over at my husband, snoring slightly, and nudged
him not so gently. "I was thinking about starting a Labrador
Retriever rescue."

"Why?"

That one-word question made me stop and think, really think,
about where this crazy notion had come from.

"I think I'm being called to do it." It was as honest an answer as
I could give.

"Then go for it. Can we talk more when I'm fully awake?"

That was eleven years ago. As I reflect back on all that has happened
in my life since then one thing remains constant. I saved lives and I
will forever be changed because of it. In 2000, I founded a Labrador
Retriever rescue. I had never visited an animal shelter and had no clue
that Labs were one of the breeds of dogs most likely to be euthanized.
Who would want to give up a Lab?

I was pretty clueless as to where or how to start this venture, so
the computer became my friend. I Googled and searched and then
made more phone calls than I care to remember.

One call I made was to our local animal shelter. I made an appointment to meet with Cheryl, the head of the Humane Society. Her job

was to pull as many animals from death's door as she could. I was excited about meeting her and seeing the dogs.

When Cheryl and I met, I noticed an edginess about her, even a slight distrust. I assumed correctly that this saving-life business was just a short-term interest for most volunteers. They would start out strong, last a couple of weeks, and then get too busy. I think Cheryl had already me sized up in her head. I'd prove her wrong.

The first time I walked down the corridor of the kennels, I was in shock at the number of dogs in this high-kill facility. My excitement quickly turned to disbelief at these conditions. It was staggering to realize that most of these potential pets would die on what became known as Terrible Thursdays, when the gas chamber was fired up.

I walked a little further and happened upon kennel #25. What I saw took my breath away. There he stood, a gentle giant of pure chocolate love. The look on his face was so full of hope, I couldn't turn away.

I asked Cheryl for a leash and we took the big guy outside. I'll never forget how he stopped to sniff the flowers and lifted his head to the air as if to absorb those moments before harsh reality came back. We continued walking around (well, he was walking, I was just trying to catch up) and came upon an old stump. I sat down on it, and this beautiful chocolate boy sat down right beside me. He was just precious. Those velvety triangular ears that only a Lab can have were sheer perfection. Any passerby would have thought we were long lost friends.

I was stunned that a dog this gentle and loving would be stranded at a place like this. I knew one thing — he wasn't going back in there. He'd just have to come home with me.

I made my decision and filled out the paperwork. As we stood to go in, a family pulled up and parked. Without one moment of hesitation a little girl threw open her car door and rushed over to us.

What's his name?" she asked.

"Hershey," I said. I had no clue what his name might be, but I couldn't let him go nameless.

"He is so sweet, and I like his name." The little girl and Hershey were drawn to each other.

The little girl's parents came over, and we were all gathered around oohing and aahing over Hershey.

Cheryl came out to observe the scene. She gave me a thumbs-up. I realized I had just made my first save.

"Are you a Lab rescuer, ma'am?" the father asked.

I hesitated for just a moment before answering. "Why, yes, I am. And it appears you have found yourself a new addition to the family."

The father chuckled but there was sadness, too. "It appears to be love at first sight. Our daughter, Olivia, has leukemia, and she has wanted a dog for so long. She loves dogs and chocolate, so I think Hershey is just what she needs."

Tears began to well up in my eyes. I turned away before anyone noticed. Olivia and Hershey explored the grounds together. Unlike the way he'd tugged when I held the leash, Hershey was very gentle with Olivia. If she stopped, he stopped. It was truly magical. Only once did Hershey look in my direction. Already, he was completely devoted to that little girl.

The family adopted Hershey on the spot, loaded him up, and prepared to go home. I cried like a baby. Hershey's tail never stopped thumping. He had found his Heaven.

I can't describe the feeling of rescuing an animal. It is addictive and selfless in the same breath. I went on to save nine hundred and ninety-nine more Labs in the two and a half years I was blessed enough to have my rescue. A divorce left me no choice but to close my doors and dream of one day opening them again. It is a calling. When you wake from a dead sleep to embark on a dream you never even knew you had, you don't ignore it, you simply take that bull by the horns and go full force. There isn't a day that I don't think back and smile and tear up remembering details about each experience. It is hard to say who comes out on top, the rescuer or the rescued. Each gains something so special in the process. I used to tell people that a little piece of my heart went with every Lab I rescued and every one I couldn't.

Olivia died two years later. She was nine years old. Her parents told me Hershey never left her bed those last few weeks of hospice, and he was there when they buried her.

We can all make a difference if we hop on a wing of faith and let it guide us to where we are supposed to be. I learned to make the most of every situation, even those that seemed tco difficult to handle. This lesson was taught to me by a precious little girl who knew her time on this earth was limited, and by a chocolate Lab who had every reason to give up on the goodness of people, but didn't.

— Lisa Morris —

You're Home Now

It is only with the heart that one can see rightly. What is essential is invisible to the eye.
~Antoine de Saint-Exupéry, The Little Prince

I didn't want to take Sasha back to the shelter. When she sat down on the river trail and gazed at me with her brown-sugar eyes, I understood that she didn't want to go back either. We had a bond, but I couldn't seriously keep this dog, could I?

"What do you think, girl?" I asked. "Are you my dog?"

Sasha and I had known each other for all of twenty minutes. We were taking a half-hour walk together from the Humane Society and back. I started volunteering with the dogs a few months before because I was living in a rental that didn't permit pets. I expected every dog to steal my heart, and I figured I would want to take them all home. But it turns out that dogs are like other people's children: I am happy they exist, and I want them to have loving homes, but I'm relieved that most of them are not mine.

Sasha was different, though. She was incredibly gentle, and she softened my resolve. She also displayed a submissive side, as if she'd been mistreated earlier in life. She needed a mellow home and someone to cuddle her more than she needed forty acres and a pack of playmates.

Now, I finally lived in a house that allowed pets. There were no logistical hurdles blocking me from adopting Sasha.

I walked her back to the Humane Society. "You're home now, girl," I said. I handed her leash to one of the kennel techs and left her there.

I drove home and reasoned with myself. My life was in no shape to care for another creature. Thirty years into life, I was finally taking care of myself. I was living on my own, had found an exceptional therapist, and landed a full-time job pursuing my passion. This was *my* time, and I wasn't going to give it up to another creature.

Or that's what I told myself. Obviously, I couldn't really let go of the thought of adopting Sasha because she came up first thing at my session that week. I offered my therapist all my logical explanations for not adopting Sasha. Then I expressed the emotions that are always percolating under our logical explanations.

"I'm also afraid I'm just putting off the hard work of owning a dog," I said finally. "I'm doing all this great work with myself, finding out who I am, and taking care of myself. If I get a dog, aren't I giving myself an excuse not to focus on me?"

I anticipated my therapist would do what therapists do — invite me to talk about what I'd just expressed, walk me deeper into the emotions, circle me around the underlying issues like a squirrel around a nut until finally I cracked into the truth.

Instead, she asked me one simple question: "What does your heart say?"

Her brevity startled me. "Say about what?" I asked.

"Do you want a dog?" she said. "What does your heart say to that?"

"Yes," I said. "Yes, I want a dog." And I meant it. My heart space had swelled when I presented it with that simple yes-or-no question, and I could only trust the response that made me feel free.

"There you go," she said. "You can trust your heart on these things."

I really could trust my heart, couldn't I? I had just felt it, physically, in my body. Her simple statement sounded like something I'd read on a hundred tea-bag tags. Those little sayings always sound nice, but they don't usually land. But this one — "You can trust your heart" — had an experiential component. I felt in my own chest what it was to trust my heart.

It was open and easy. There was no other way to live. I could listen to my heart. And my heart said I should go back to the shelter and see if Sasha was there.

That weekend, I made a beeline for Sasha's kennel. She was gone. Maybe she'd just moved. I asked one of the kennel techs about her. "She went home this week," he said.

My heart sighed. Dogs come into our lives for reasons. Sometimes, they come in to teach us about ourselves throughout a lifetime. Sometimes, they teach us valuable lessons on a thirty-minute walk. Sasha had come into my life for a reason, and then she found her home.

I walked a few dogs that day, and none of them spoke to my heart. I knew what it felt like to have my heart hum, though. I knew I didn't need to seek out a dog. My heart would tell me when I found the right one.

I tested that theory about a month later. I walked a dog named Wally. He was another chill dog, very gentle on the leash and comfortable with me. When I returned him to the shelter, I told the tech that Wally had done great on his walk.

"Wally did great?" the tech repeated.

"Oh, yeah. He was awesome," I said.

"Wally," he said. "Wally did great?"

"Totally." The tech's response baffled me, until I saw Wally in his kennel before I left. The shelter had clipped a sheet over his door to block his view because he was barking at everyone who walked by. He was throwing himself against the sides, miserable in his space. This was a different dog than the one I had just walked.

"Bye, sweet guy," I said. "Good luck finding your home soon."

And that was the end of that. Or so I thought. But Wally kept wiggling his way into my head that week. I'd find myself thinking about him while I was hiking to work and making dinner. He'd done well with me — me! — when he had not done well with anyone else in three weeks at the shelter.

I'd seen for myself how much living in a kennel stressed him. I'd also seen how relaxed he was while walking with me.

About mid-week, I finally heard my heart pounding against my ribs. It declared, in its outdoor voice, "Go walk that dog again."

I could trust my heart. Absolutely. The trick, though, was to actually listen to it. It had been sending me this message all week. My mind kept getting in the way, questioning my heart's decision-making abilities. But my heart knew what my mind could not comprehend. My heart knew love when it found it.

This time, when I returned to the shelter, my dog was still there. I took Wally for another walk, just to try out our connection one more time.

Then I walked him back to the Humane Society. "You're home now, bud," I said. I handed his leash to one of the kennel techs and added, "Wally's coming home with me today."

—Zach Hively—

Bed, Bath and Way Beyond

It is a happy talent to know how to play.
~Ralph Waldo Emerson

Volunteering wasn't my cup of tea. The thought of giving up my precious time in exchange for nothing didn't interest me. But then, at the ripe young age of fifty, I unexpectedly found myself unable to work as the result of a medical condition. Suddenly, I had way too much time on my hands.

The first year or so of my forced retirement was spent mostly sitting for hours alone feeling sorry for myself. The second year I spent my time cleaning out more closets, junk rooms and cubbyholes than I'd ever realized one home could have. There were times I was so bored with life that I actually contemplated knocking on my neighbors' doors to beg them to let me clean their forgotten spaces. The "postal lady" dreaded seeing me sitting on the porch when delivering the mail. I so longed for conversation I'd talk with her about anything that popped into my mind. The librarians at my local library called me by name because I'd spent so many hours bothering them.

By the time the third year rolled around I was still moping a bit, but with the tidiest garden on the street, the most organized pantry shelves, and the cleanest nooks and crannies on the block, I realized the thing I'd valued most in my life I'd been squandering.

One Sunday afternoon I saw an advertisement in the newspaper asking for community volunteers at the local Humane Society shelter. I'd always loved animals, and having lost my own best friend and beloved

Pit Bull a few months prior to my sudden illness, the idea of working with dogs that needed homes seemed a perfect fit. There was no time to waste. After all, if I procrastinated they'd surely find someone else to fill the open slots. I dashed off an e-mail to the shelter letting them know of my interest and before the day was up had a return e-mail telling me where and when to "report for duty."

After sitting through a two-hour orientation, my reluctance to volunteer was back in full force. Each volunteer was asked to complete a three-hour stint in "Bed, Bath and Beyond," a fancy title for scrubbing food bowls and litter pans and washing trash bins stuffed with dirty, smelly laundry. Who knew animals could dirty so many blankets in one day? But with all the determination I could muster I told myself to relax and enjoy the task at hand. After all, this was only the beginning of a long list of volunteer opportunities available at the shelter, a way of weeding out those not truly interested in giving their time. Once this task was complete I'd be promoted to bigger and better things, right?

With all the diligence and enthusiasm I'd become famous for at the shelter, I went right to work. There was never a dull moment and always a new animal that needed love and the reassurance that it would soon find its new home. There was the occasional shy, grown cat that just needed company while it waited for its new owner to arrive. There were dogs of all sizes and breeds — some excited, some scared, some wanting to play, others simply needing a bit of space while they adjusted to the new surroundings.

One blustery January morning I pulled open the shelter doors, punched the volunteer time clock and went to work. As I'd come to learn, no day is considered normal at the Humane Society, and this one was no different. I began by washing dishes and shoving a load of laundry into the washer — a rather mindless task I'd actually come to enjoy, especially after seeing firsthand what a benefit it was to the paid staff for a volunteer to do the "grunt work" so they could spend more time teaching the animals basic commands in preparation for their new owners.

With the laundry packed away and the dishes drying, I made my way through the shelter in search of a "newbie," a dog or cat just introduced to the shelter that needed a bit of extra tender love and care. I found an unexpected surprise. With her lipstick mouth, spotted floppy ears, and paws that seemed perfect for a dog four times her size, she was packed in a twelve-week-old package of energy and excitement, with hazel eyes that screamed, "You need me, you just haven't realized it yet!"

Just looking at her brought a long-forgotten smile to my face. Around and around the pen she ran, chasing her tail until she fell over from dizziness. She would grab her tail between her teeth and growl at it like it was an enemy she'd finally conquered. I laughed, and the sound of my own laughter startled me. It had been years since I'd laughed out loud.

I stood watching the puppy for what seemed like hours before I finally reached in and pulled her to my chest. She sniffed, wiggled her way up my shoulders to my face, and began licking me with her warm, wet tongue. After a while she calmed, laid her head on my chest and stared into my eyes. Then she closed her eyes tight and sighed as if to say, "I'm at peace now, you're here." She knew it before I did. We needed each other.

A fresh zeal for a changed life can often be found in the strangest places. Mine was found in the eyes of a pup I named Hazel, and I would have missed the opportunity altogether had I not been willing to give of the most precious thing in life — my time.

— Lisa Fowler —

Dropped from Heaven

Alone is impossible in a world inhabited by angels.
~Author Unknown

had just come home from the hospital. As I stepped out of the car, I was assaulted by a pair of huge paws and a wet, lapping tongue. In less than a minute, I was sitting on the driveway, receiving the biggest tongue licking of my life! My heart immediately belonged to that dog. In spite of our search for his owner, no one claimed him. It was like he had been dropped from heaven, and maybe he was.

Sam did more than change my life; he became my guardian angel. My convalescence from a serious illness was supposed to take place at home, under the care of my husband, a first class petty officer in the U.S. Navy. Louie had been given thirty days emergency leave from his ship for the sole purpose of caring for me. I was so thankful as Louie cooked, cleaned, and took care of our two young daughters.

My doctor had spoken to Louie's commanding officer, personally explaining my illness and need for constant care. The commander assured my doctor that Louie would get the leave. All that my husband had to do was check out from the ship Monday morning. So when Louie left for the ship, we were both certain that he would be home by noon. I could take care of myself for a few hours, and I could use that time to get to know my new puppy.

Mid-day came and went, and Louie did not come home. Then it was two o'clock. Perhaps he had to finish up things. Four o'clock arrived. Then five, and six, and seven. Finally, the phone rang. It was

Louie. He was on the ship, and it was leaving. His emergency leave had been canceled, and he had only a moment to call and say goodbye. My husband was sick about it, but he had no choice in the matter.

What many civilians do not understand is that emergency leave for a service member is at the commanding officer's discretion. So, sick wife or no sick wife, Petty Officer Lewis was ordered back to duty. The ship went out to sea, and I was alone.

I don't remember much about that week. I was sick, helpless, and afraid. My young children did the best they could for me. Neighbors came and went, but the only thing I remember is Sam. He never left my side. I stayed on the couch, except to go to the bathroom. I don't know if I ate or drank. But I can still feel the pressure of Sam's body leaning against me, and I can still feel the scrape of his tongue on my face. He hovered near me every moment. At one point, when I began to lose consciousness, Sam barked wildly and licked my face, bringing me to. He made me laugh, and I clung to the reality of Sam.

God took care of everything. I needed someone, and God sent me Sam. In time I recovered, and our family was reunited. Sam remained a member of our family for years. Though it's been nearly twenty years since I last hugged that blessed dog, Sam will always be a part of my heart. I'm certain that Sam is frolicking in some snowy part of heaven, looking forward to seeing me again.

—Jaye Lewis—

Misty's Thanksgiving

I think dogs are the most amazing creatures;
they give unconditional love. For me,
they are the role model for being alive.
~Gilda Radner

My husband and I purchased our first home about six years ago. We had fallen in love immediately with a bank-owned, three-floor log cabin in a lake community that was part of the Pine Barrens. I recall standing on the porch of our dream house alone with my husband after the Realtor left. We promised the universe that day that if we got the house, we'd rescue one dog that needed it most. It would move in with us the same day we moved in and become part of the family.

We didn't want a puppy; we wanted an unwanted dog, a large one. Those are the ones that usually get left behind in the shelters, anyway, but I wanted a large dog. It would be a companion for the kids and me because my husband worked far away during the day. The dog would watch over us.

I reached out to a rescue group, and we started the paperwork. They approved us and were very excited to have adopters like us. Three days before moving day, we got the call. They had rescued a twelve-year-old German Shepherd on Death Row. She had heartworm, suffered from malnutrition and had lost most of her chest hair. According to them, she certainly wasn't what most adopters considered pretty. She wouldn't need much—just a home to live out her days. We fell in love with Misty before we even met her.

Moving day came, and just as the last truck was unloaded, the rescue arrived. Friends watched eagerly, excited to meet Misty. She was more beautiful than I could have imagined. She moved with a senior grace, her cloudy eyes taking in her new home and family. She was underweight at eighty pounds, but she was aware of where every inch of her was. She was led over to where my infant daughter was stretched out, cooing on a blanket. We held Misty while she sniffed the baby's head and then gingerly lay next to her without touching her blanket.

That evening, my husband set up Misty's new dog bed in the living room. The baby was asleep in her crib, and I passed out on the mattress on the floor. I felt a large body moving next to me, but was too tired to wake up. I snuggled into the dog's warmth, her breath soft against my neck.

I have never seen my husband more emotional than that night. Misty had curled into bed next to me, cuddled up against my body. I could hear my husband's breath hitch as he looked at that poor girl — so full of grace, warmth and love — who appreciated her new family as if we'd always been hers.

My husband covered us with an extra blanket and then lay beside her on the hard floor, petting and comforting her all through her first night with us.

Misty was given the best of everything — home-cooked meals, a seat on the sofa, and all the love this family could muster. She enjoyed the companionship of her doggy brother and sister as much as she adored her human brother and sister.

By Thanksgiving, we were well situated and preparing for our first holiday in our new home. We invited friends and family.

A day before Thanksgiving, I had begun cooking a series of three turkeys so we'd have enough food for everyone. I left the first one cooling on the back of the stove as I stepped out for a short break to have coffee with the neighbor.

Misty, who'd never taken a thing from the counter, must have found that turkey too much of a temptation. I couldn't even be mad at her when it was my own fault for leaving temptation within reach.

When I returned, there were only a few bones remaining, scattered about the kitchen. She slunk under the table, acting as if she was about to be beaten, quivering, shaking and whimpering.

My heart broke; she was terrified by her own behavior. Someone in her past had abused this sweet, gentle girl so horribly that she had wet herself in fear. I spent over an hour gently coaxing her from under the table, comforting her. I will never forget how she finally emerged and buried her big head against my chest, sighing and whimpering. I held her tightly, stroking her coarse fur and kissing her, promising her no one would ever hurt her again.

She recovered and was given all the turkey and apple pie she could eat that Thanksgiving. Every guest greeted her with love and told her what a wonderful girl she was. It was as if, in hearing the story of the turkey, every friend and family member pitched in to give her the lifetime of love she'd missed in just that one day.

Unfortunately, Misty's time with us was short. She passed in my arms the following fall.

To this day, the kids still miss her. We built her a memory garden, and we visit her there. She touched us in her short time with more than a lifetime of love, and we will always be thankful for that.

— Nicole Ann Rook McAlister —

41

Chicken Soup
for the Soul

The Tale of Tabby

*You cannot do a kindness too soon, for you never
know how soon it will be too late.*
~Ralph Waldo Emerson

It was a cold and rainy October day in 2003, when the animal shelter where I worked received an elderly, emaciated, blind, virtually hairless Cocker Spaniel. We did not hold out much hope that the dog we named Tabby would find a home, but we were committed to helping her anyway. Because Tabby was a stray, she had to be held for a period of time to ensure that her owner wasn't looking for her. Based on her condition we were fairly certainly that no one would be coming forward to claim this poor little wretch of a dog.

Tabby received treatment from the attending vet and was then bathed, fed and settled into the quiet of the administration building, where we felt she would be less frightened and better able to heal. I should explain that the admin building was in an old house and therefore retained a sort of homey feeling. Tabby quickly endeared herself to our staff, who noticed that she appeared to be deaf as well as blind. She slept very soundly, and at about fourteen years of age, she liked her naps. She also quickly learned her way around the building and its various offices. With time and care she gained weight and grew in a luxurious coat of soft cream-coloured fur.

Despite or maybe because of her various challenges, Tabby had a great attitude. She high stepped along walls, feeling her way and never missing a beat. She boldly navigated obstacles, recovering from any missteps quickly. The one concern we had for her successfully being placed into a home was that she was easily startled, particularly when asleep, which caused her to nip. Tabby would require a special home in many ways, including one that did not include children who might be accidentally injured.

The days turned to weeks and then to months and Tabby settled into a comfortable routine. She seemed to like everyone she met, but she claimed a couple of our staffers as her own special friends. Her ability to know when one of these folks arrived on the shelter property was nothing short of remarkable. We attributed it to her keen sense of smell as we had no other explanation. Tabby would bark and bark until her person came to say hello. She insisted on being acknowledged and only when she had her fill was her person allowed to carry on. Tabby would then happily go back to napping.

When winter began to turn to spring and not a single person had asked about adopting Tabby, we assumed she would live out her days with us. She was happy and our staff loved her. Her life at the shelter was good, even though we normally hoped for a home for every animal.

The promise of spring began to turn into the long days of summer when a mom named Loretta came by the shelter with her three children, including her son, Andrew, a young boy who suffered from seizures. It was this boy who had noticed Tabby on the shelter website. What drew him to her was the note on her profile explaining that she had special needs. As a special needs child, he identified with Tabby and insisted they pay her a visit.

With three active young boys, including a toddler, this well-meaning family hardly seemed like the ideal fit for Tabby. They were shown other more suitable dogs to consider for adoption, ones that did not startle easily and sometimes nip. The child who somehow seemed fated to be Tabby's boy would simply not hear of it. He would not leave without his dog and as far as he was concerned, Tabby was that dog.

After having a long and very frank conversation with Loretta about our concerns that Tabby might nip a child, we reluctantly suggested that the family try fostering Tabby before making a permanent commitment, fully expecting them to call us the next day asking to bring her back. Call us they did, but only to tell us they loved her and wanted to adopt her. Tabby had, indeed, nipped everyone in the family, but no harm was done and they took it all in stride. They agreed to continue to foster her for the next week. At the end of that week, mom and son were at the shelter when we opened to sign all of the adoption paperwork. Tabby was officially their dog, or perhaps more importantly, Andrew was Tabby's boy.

This story could end here and be one of a thousand happy shelter memories, but Tabby's tale was not yet finished. Through tears, Loretta told us about the bond that had developed between her special needs son and his special needs dog. Where once Andrew suffered from four or more seizures a day, he had not had a single one since Tabby came home with them. He was no longer afraid to go to bed at night, as he had no fear of the terrifying seizures that would wake him from sleep. So concerned was he for Tabby's needs that he did not think about his seizures at all. It was clear that this once lost, broken little dog had not only found a happy home, a family and a child who loved her, she had found a purpose.

We heard from Tabby's family fairly frequently. Her boy went almost two weeks without having a single seizure. His mother attributed this to Tabby's presence. Although fewer in number and further between, the seizures did eventually return. Then something truly magical happened. Tabby began to alert Andrew before each seizure. This allowed him to prepare by getting into a safe place and position.

So Tabby, our little wretch of a dog, a dog with so many challenges and few options, a dog that most other shelters would have euthanized, found her perfect home with a boy who needed her as much as she needed him. Tabby, our blind, deaf, fourteen-year-old Cocker Spaniel, had not only found her perfect home, but her perfect job, where she enriched, enlivened, encouraged and inspired a young boy. Together these two indefatigable spirits marched bravely on.

Unfortunately, Tabby's age meant that her time with her boy was shorter than anyone would have liked. They supported and cared for one another for two years until Tabby closed her eyes for the final time. Andrew and his family mourned her passing, but also cherished their time together. The bravery she inspired and the selfless nurturing shared between them are memories that live on, as does her spirit, forever etched in the memories of those who were touched by this remarkable dog.

— Tammy Zaluzney —

What I Learned from the Dog

Cabin Life

*Deny yourself the connection to the wild places
that your soul craves and the fire inside you
will slowly turn to ash.*
~Creek Stewart

When I was a child, I had a teacher who played the sounds of the forest during our nap time. It was relaxing to hear bubbling brooks, light breezes in the trees, and wildlife calls.

Many years later I adopted my first dog, a German Shepherd coyote mix who came from the woods. Because my townhome was not ideal for him, I searched for a place I could bring him that suited him better. I found a rental cabin in the Blue Ridge Mountains.

Baxter and I spent many seasons exploring the surrounding woods, admiring the wildflowers and watching clouds of ladybugs swarming like tiny tornadoes as they passed us on our trek. I learned to identify tree frogs, golden flies, and peacocks from their sounds.

Baxter was a wild one, but also fiercely protective. He always stayed close by, and I never had a flutter of fearfulness with him there.

He was from those woods. He was part of that wildlife. Before coming to live with me, he'd been hit by a truck. A Good Samaritan rescued him from certain death. No one would adopt him due to his injury and wild nature. Then we met and became best friends. But deep down, I always knew he belonged to these woods, more to the woods than to me.

Eventually, he and I brought our other dog on vacation with us, a yellow Lab that I often called My Sunshine Girl. Her favorite pastime was sitting on the screened-in porch snoozing while I spent the day nearby on a swing reading. Once, I found a copy of *The Phantom of the Opera*, and I read it from dawn to dusk as I lay on that swing lazily, completely content with my life under blue skies.

I've been to that cabin as thunderstorms threatened. I've stayed there on moonless nights when it was so dark that you couldn't see your own hand directly in front of your face. I have woken up there as early morning mist has risen from the depths of these mountains like hallowed spirits. There have been bone-chilling days when I sipped piping-hot coffee while watching the sun come up over the horizon. I have decorated a Christmas tree while nibbling on homemade treats and listening to holiday music before watching a classic Christmas movie.

I have taken hours-long bubble baths in sweet silence there, spending some quality time with my own thoughts. There have been days I cooked like a pro and then sampled my efforts while happily sipping on a favorite glass of wine or, even better, a glass of sweet orchard cider. Later, there would be a good movie to watch while cuddled up under several blankets, sometimes sitting beside a roaring fire that I proudly started myself with kindling I'd collected and the logs that were piled up outside for guest use. At night, I'd fall asleep with the stars so clearly visible overhead in that dark mountain sky. Sleeping well is never a problem there.

I have visited this cabin in good times and bad. It's been a sanctuary when I've needed it, like when Grandpa Ben passed away. I've been to these woods seeking refuge from exhaustion and sudden illness, to recover and rest. I've come to celebrate milestones in my life and to have a porch party with friends. Other times, I've gone there to mourn the passing of a friend. I recall sitting on the porch that Baxter and I shared for so many seasons, reading *Chicken Soup for the Pet Lover's Soul* with tears streaming down my face since I had just released his ashes in his favorite place. And yet there was a smile on my face.

Sometimes, when I return to the cabin now, I am overwhelmed by too many memories, but then I imagine the familiar pitter patter of his paws and I realize he'll always be there with me. This is our place, available when I need it.

The cabin is my church, my sanctuary and my escape. When I leave the cabin, it often rains, just lightly, as if the woods are sad that I have to go. But as I look over my shoulder, at what's fading from view behind me, I always whisper, "I'll be back," because this is where my heart is, and this is where my spirit feels most free, at Mile Marker 13, Highway 5, in Northwest Georgia.

— Tamra Anne Bolles —

43

Tang's Christmas Miracle

*Animals' instinctive spirituality enables them to
interact with their Creator and with creation
in ways that can truly be called miraculous.
Animals have a talent for bypassing the
mind and going straight to the heart.
~Allen and Linda Anderson*

Sometimes I think I should have named my dog Casper instead of Tang. He's a small grey and white mix of Shih Tzu and Poodle with the personality of Casper the Friendly Ghost. He's not just friendly; he is sincere. Whenever we go for a walk, he stops to greet every dog, cat, squirrel and person we meet. He loves all people young and old, babies in strollers and people in wheelchairs. He loves Canada Post letter carriers—even those without cookies in their pockets.

Tang expresses his love of life in a very vocal way. He has a special greeting where he raises his head to the sky and howls happily. Translated from dog language it means, "Joy to the World!" Nine years ago while brushing Tang's teeth I discovered blood in his mouth. My husband and I took him to the vet even though we only suspected a gum infection. The vet thought so too—at first. The antibiotics failed to reduce the swelling, and we returned to the clinic. Dr. Hall, a canine dental specialist removed the suspicious mass, and had it biopsied.

The news was devastating. Cancer. Tang was only five years old. Dr. Hall informed us that Tang's best option was radical surgery. Tang needed one third of his lower jaw removed. "Afterward he may require radiation treatment or chemotherapy," Dr. Hall said. "It might give him another couple of years. Without treatment, he will have only a few months."

Dr. Hall was honest enough to admit that the surgery was beyond his skill. He made an appointment for us at the Ontario Veterinary College in Guelph. Tang, he said, was a little trouper. At the OVC hospital, Dr. Alexandra Squires was confident she could perform the surgery successfully. But trouper or not, we were terrified to proceed. How was Tang going to eat? What would he look like with his jaw removed? What if the cancer had spread? Was it worth putting him through all this pain and suffering just so we could have him a little while longer? Were we being selfish? We did not want Tang to suffer.

Tang's response to all of the poking and prodding, X-rays and tests was a great big happy-bark song of joy. He was nervous, but he trusted us. He even trusted all of the different specialists who examined him. And for each of us there was always that howled song of joy.

By now it was mid-November. The city was decorated for Christmas. I knew I would soon have to go Christmas shopping and write cards, and there was also our annual Christmas party to organize. My husband was asked to be the chair of the anthropology department at his university. He wished desperately to decline. We were too sad. All we could think about was losing Tang. But my husband agreed to take the job of department chair. And I did not want to disappoint the students who looked forward to the annual Christmas fest in our home. We began to prepare for Christmas.

On the day of Tang's surgery heavy snow was falling. We made the drive to the hospital in just over an hour. We left Tang in the arms of one of the veterinary assistants. He twisted his little head to watch us leave, his soft round eyes curious rather than frightened. I recall thinking that this might be the last time I ever saw him. We drove home in a horrific storm, a salt truck flinging salt onto our windshield to mix with the flying snow. It was black that night — in so many ways. The highway was a booby trap of ice and blinding weather. We made it home to a cold supper and then bed. We couldn't sleep.

Tang's surgery was successful, but he wasn't out of the woods yet. He stayed at the hospital for three nights. The veterinary students were wonderful, and the girl assigned to Tang stayed by his side twenty-four hours a day. She called every evening to update us on his condition. When the doctors decided he could eat on his own, they let him come home. We picked him up on a snowy afternoon. His eyes looked bright. His mouth had been reconstructed and there were stitches in his jaw. His tongue protruded halfway out of his mouth. He wore a white cone around his neck and a morphine patch on his back.

My husband and I exchanged horrified glances. What had they done to our dog? What had we done? I remember saying afterward that I would never get used to seeing Tang like that.

Tang's jawbone was sent to the pathology lab to be tested. The pathologist was away at a convention for three days, and the wait was agonizing. By the time he contacted us our nerves were raw. But the news was good. The outer edges of the bone were clean, no sign of cancer. The following week we returned to the OVC hospital to have Tang's stitches removed. The waiting room was cheerfully decked out in Christmas lights and ornaments. A young woman sat beside me with a cage containing two ferrets. She was worried. The ferrets seemed overly large around the belly, and I asked if they were pregnant.

"No," she said, tearfully. "They have adrenal disease." Her grandfather had driven her to the hospital (clearly he loved his granddaughter) but he wore an impatient expression on his face that said "they're only animals."

Tang thought otherwise. The girl was called into the examining room with her beloved ferrets. Tang trundled over to the grandfather, and, despite the stitches under his mouth, gave his defining happy howl of joy. Even Grandpa couldn't stay grumpy with Tang around.

"That dog never stops wagging his tail," he said, cracking a smile.

By the week before Christmas all the stockings were hung. The Christmas tree was decorated, and red and green lights spiralled around the conifers outside. We welcomed the students into our home. As everyone sat down with a glass of holiday cheer, Tang greeted each and every one of his guests, tail wagging, his snout raised to Heaven howling his special song of joy.

Heroes come in many forms and I am thankful to the veterinarians who have devoted their lives to saving pets. But it was Tang that reminded us of what Christmas was really about. It wasn't just about finding the perfect gift, or cooking the perfect turkey or decorating the most festive house. It was about showing kindness to others and appreciation for the ones you love. That small furry package of joy showed us what it takes to have strength, how to find hope and courage, and how to believe in miracles.

— Deborah Cannon —

Back in the Saddle Again

The essential joy of being with horses is that it brings
us in contact with the rare elements of grace,
beauty, spirit, and fire.
~Sharon Ralls Lemon

Was this what menopause was all about? I'd known there would likely be hot flashes. A thickening waistline. Mood swings. What I hadn't figured on was falling into an ever-deepening funk as I moved further and further into my fifties. I'd scold myself when I'd become weepy for no reason. I had nothing to be unhappy about. I had a wonderful husband, three happy kids who are on their own, a roof over my head, shoes on my feet and no worries about where my next meal was coming from.

It wasn't that I didn't have enough to keep me busy. I had a too-big house to clean and a too-big lawn to mow. A garden to tend. Meals to cook and dishes to wash. I volunteered at church and at a neighborhood elementary school. On top of all that, my husband and I lived on a small farm. Though the cattle, goats and chickens that we'd once cared for were gone, we still had horses, cats, and Sophie, our three-year-old Boxer mix who clearly relished being a farm dog.

But Sophie's waistline was thickening, too, and I knew it was my fault. Did I feed her too much? Yes. (Somehow it made it easier to justify my own overeating.) Did I exercise her enough? No. (Most days, I had no desire to walk through the woods behind our house or around the pond in our pasture. Surely, Sophie didn't either.)

We did, however, climb the steep stairs to the hayloft in the barn every morning. I'd cut the rough twine away from a couple of hay bales and toss them, flake by flake, down into the horses' manger. Then Sophie and I would descend the loft stairs and make our way back to the house. We were both out of breath by the time we got there.

Pathetic. It was clear that Sophie and I needed to find something to bring physical fitness — and, along with it, zest — back into our lives. But what?

On a sunny morning in early April, we headed to the barn as usual. And as usual, our three horses stood in the pasture and followed us with their gaze. But on this day, they didn't sprint to the barn. Instead, they dropped their heads and tore at the new-green grass that had, seemingly overnight, begun to poke through the pasture's brown stubble. When I got to the loft, I saw that the hay I'd tossed out yesterday still littered the barn floor.

I knelt down and threw my arms around Sophie's neck. "It's spring, girl," I told her. "No more hay chores!"

Sophie wagged all over.

"How about if we take a walk?"

More wagging.

As we began our first loop around the pond, I noticed that Sunny, our palomino gelding, was following us. I stopped to scratch between his ears and discovered that his mane and forelock were matted with cockleburs. "You poor thing," I told him, "let's take you to the barnyard and get you cleaned up."

Sunny stood patiently as I combed the burs out of his hair. He lifted his feet so I could use the hoof pick to clean out the dried mud and rocks. He practically grinned when I began rubbing the curry comb over his coat. As he grew cleaner and I grew dirtier, I noticed myself humming and wondering how long it had been since I'd groomed this horse. More than that, how long had it been since I'd ridden him? Or any other horse for that matter.

Two years at least. Not so long ago, I had ridden almost every day. But I'd fallen out of the habit. Allowed other things to get in the way. Let myself and my animals get fat and lazy. Perhaps the time had come to change that.

Except that you can't just jump on a horse and ride him as if he's a bicycle. It's important to make sure he's in decent aerobic shape. Free of leg and foot problems. And safe to ride. (A horse that's used to being a pasture ornament just might morph into a bucking bronco!) I needed to work Sunny on a lunge line for at least a couple of weeks to make sure he was sound. He seemed to have no objection. In fact, he seemed to enjoy our daily sessions. As did Sophie, who romped and played the whole time Sunny and I were working.

When it was clear that Sunny was ready to be ridden, I lugged his tack out of the barn. I draped the saddle blanket over a fence rail and beat the dust out of it with a broom. I cleaned the saddle and bridle and reins with saddle soap and rubbed them with Neatsfoot oil until they gleamed. I polished the bit until it shone like new. Then I got Sunny tacked up. He looked beautiful. And, as crazy as it might sound, happy.

The time had come to untie Sunny from the fence post and climb onto his back.

My fifty-five-year-old heart was beating hard. Was I too old for this? Were my muscles still strong and limber enough to mount a horse? Could I keep my balance once Sunny started to move? Did I remember how to use my hands and legs and voice to make him stop and go and change directions? There was only one way to find out.

I put my left foot in the stirrup, grabbed a clump of Sunny's perfectly coiffed mane with my left hand, and sprang off my right foot into the saddle. It felt good. No, not just good. Wonderful. I relaxed my grip on the reins and squeezed Sunny's sides with my legs.

"Giddy-up, fella," I said.

And with that, Sunny and I headed for the woods, with Sophie following close behind. We rode for more than an hour that day, taking in the sights and sounds and smells of spring and having a perfectly marvelous time. I collapsed into bed that night with every muscle in my body groaning. They were groaning even louder the next morning. But no matter. As soon as my housework was done, I headed straight for the barn.

I whistled once. Here came Sophie. I whistled again. Here came Sunny. Both of them ready — just like me — to put a little fun back into our lives.

—Jennie Ivey—

The Wisest Woman in the World

To conquer fear is the beginning of wisdom.
~Bertrand Russell

The September I entered first grade, I'd just lost my beloved friend and companion of two years, our neighbor's English Bulldog named Duke. He had died from heat stroke during an extremely hot summer's day. The delightful, new experiences of school helped eased the sting of his passing somewhat.

Then one day not long after school started, I was walking home when a black Cocker Spaniel darted out of a yard near the corner of our street. I stopped and turned to him, and saw a side of dogs I'd never experienced. Growling and barring his teeth, he began to circle me.

Startled but deciding this dog simply didn't want to become my friend, I once more started for home. The moment my back was turned, he seized my ankle. His teeth locked into my flesh.

I screamed and kicked, and he released me. Shrieking, I ran toward home, the black curly ball in hot pursuit. Just before I reached our drive, he gave up and set off at a gallop back up the street.

Bursting into the house, so incoherent that for a few moments my mother couldn't understand what had caused my bloody ankle, I fell into her arms and sobbed.

Later, with my wounds cleaned and bandaged, I told her the story. "He bit me, Mommy. He grabbed me and it hurt." By then my words reflected more my sense of betrayal than pain or fear. One of the creatures I loved most in the world had attacked me, had caused me pain for no reason. "I'll never, never trust another dog as long as I live."

"Never is a long time, sweetie." My mother stroked my braids. "And that was only one dog. You can't judge them all by one that made a mistake."

I presume my mother must have called the Spaniel's owners, because from that day on, the dog, Robin, was tied in their back yard whenever I passed on my way to or from school. I was still afraid though. What if the rope broke? What if he came after me again? I dreaded passing that house.

I must have had nightmares about the incident because I recall my mother gently waking me to tell me it was all right, that Robin was safely tied up at his house.

But the trauma only worsened. I refused to visit my grandfather on his farm because he had a St. Bernard/Collie mix named Buster, whom I'd formerly loved and couldn't wait to see each Sunday afternoon.

My fear grew so debilitating that my mother had to walk with me past the dreaded corner house each morning and meet me before I came to it each afternoon. My days in school were haunted by a black horror named Robin. I couldn't concentrate. My teacher contacted my mother.

"Gail, you have to get over this fear," she said the following afternoon as we walked home from school together. "You remember my friend Emma who lives two houses beyond Robin's?"

I nodded, dread already rising. Where was this conversation going?

"She has a lovely black Lab named Chips." I tightened my grip on her hand. "She's invited us to stop by this afternoon and meet him."

"No, no, Mommy, please no!" I stopped and stared up at her, begging with all my heart and soul. "I hate dogs. They're bad. They want to hurt me!"

"Not Chips." My mother smiled gently down at me. "I promise. Have I ever broken a promise to you?"

"No…"

"Then trust me now. You know I'd never take my darling girl anywhere she might be hurt, don't you?"

I hesitated, then slowly nodded.

"Good. Let's go. Emma said something about baking sugar cookies this afternoon."

Moments later we stood on Emma's front step. My heart was pounding as my mother rang the bell. Footsteps approached, the door opened, and there stood Emma with a big black dog slowly wagging his tail by her side. Sweat broke out over my body.

"Opal, Gail, how lovely. Come in, come in. I'm just taking the last batch of cookies from the oven. Chips, sit."

Obediently, the big dog dropped to his haunches and sat watching us, tongue lolling out of his mouth in what probably was a canine grin but which I only saw as fang baring.

"Hello, Chips," my mother said. To my surprise he raised his right front paw. As my mother laughingly accepted the greeting, my breath caught in my throat. He was going to bite her. I wanted to lunge forward to save her but I was frozen by fear. A moment later we headed down the hall with Chips following at a respectful distance, tail still slowly wagging.

We sat in the kitchen. I had milk and cookies while my mother and her friend drank tea and chatted. Chips lay on the floor leaning against the back door. Our gazes met. His tail beat faster and his mouth opened wider. Could it be he was smiling, the way Duke used to? But Duke's mouth was wider and his teeth were all crooked and funny looking. This dog had big, straight, white fangs. But he did appear to be friendly. Maybe he wasn't such a bad dog after all.

I slid off the chair and stood staring at him. His tail wagged just a notch faster but not too fast. Not like he was getting excited or ready to rush at me. I took a step closer. He remained lying by the door, watching me. I took another step and held out my hand. Chips hesitated, then eased forward to sniff. When I managed to hold fast, he licked it.

My terror melted. I sat down beside him on the floor and offered the last of the cookie I held in my hand. He took it with such gentleness that I've never forgotten the touch of his soft, wet muzzle on my fingers.

Only then did I realize that Emma and my mother had stopped talking and were watching us. "Chips is a good dog, Mommy." I stroked the soft fur. "A really good dog."

"I know, sweetie, I know." She smiled.

My love of canines was restored. At that moment I believed her to be the wisest woman in the world.

These days, with four dog books (two of them award-winners) to my credit and a lifetime of wonderful canine associations behind me and continuing, I give thanks to my mother for her clever insight. She saved me from crippling fear and from losing out on all the wonderful opportunities dogs have given me throughout my life.

— Gail MacMillan —

Where Have You Been?

We derive immeasurable good, uncounted pleasures,
enormous security, and many critical lessons
about life by owning dogs.
~Roger A. Caras

Maggie was our first and last dog. As a family, we had our share of unfortunate pets. A rabbit that kicked up shavings in great plumes as it scurried away from our daughter's hands. A cat that sulked behind the kitchen cabinets, and a desiccated goldfish that we scraped off the dresser, discovered a weekend after its tragic leap for freedom. However, my wife Katherine never gave up hope that somewhere, out there, was a pet that suited our family.

After reading an advertisement for a sweetly tempered rescue dog, Katherine traveled up a winding mountain road in the verdant hills of western Virginia to fetch her. Unfortunately, that sweet dog had a temperamental stomach. When she traveled back down the winding mountain road, she vomited the entire way.

Katherine would often surprise me with an impulsive adoption. Maggie was no exception.

"She didn't cost anything, Bill," Katherine said.

"A pet is an investment," I countered. "Nothing is free."

To say that Maggie was sweet-tempered may have been a marketing ploy. When I met her, she cowered, her black-and-tan body shivered, while her tail retreated between her legs. She stood eye level with our daughters, whom she would run from, scared silly by a pair of girls, ages six and four.

We fretted over another poor pet choice. It was clear that Maggie had been mistreated by her previous owners, and we worried that she might never recover. We decided to give her a week.

In the cool of the morning, I would sip my coffee, watching Maggie dart to the far corner of the yard and tremble beneath the girls' trampoline. I'd crawl underneath and tug on her collar, and she'd crouch down as if she could somehow disappear into the dirt. "Come on, girl." She would peer into the den, where the girls were playing, and when they looked at her, she'd scurry, nails clawing to get a purchase on the hardwood floors.

As the end of her probation week approached, Maggie must have sensed that her fate would soon be sealed. She placed a paw next to me on the sofa. I looked at her timid, brown eyes and patted the cushion. "It's okay, girl. Come on." Slowly, cautiously, she inched a paw forward and then another. It was a Herculean effort, as she wiggled her body, her legs shaking, one leg up, one leg down. Then, she placed her head on my lap.

"There you are," I said while rubbing her soft head, and looked over at Katherine who was wiping her eyes.

From that point on, her metamorphosis was astonishing. When sunset's glow painted the walls orange, she waited by the front door for my workday return, and when the girls placed a homemade newspaper hat on her head and draped a scarf around her neck, she sat still, looking quite miserable. Other times, she would playfully chase the girls around in a circle, crouching down on her front legs with her rump high in the air, her tail curled up into a C — Miss Maggie the Courageous. When she caught them, she would lick their faces while they laughed uncontrollably.

"Maggie, stop!"

We were shocked the first time we heard her bark, a deep woof that echoed. When the girls were playing softball in the front yard with a group of neighborhood kids, Maggie situated herself in front of our elder child, acting as a canine speed bump to trip the boy who was running toward her.

What I Learned from the Dog |

On our annual trips to the beach, I'd take curves gingerly to keep from upsetting her tender stomach, but invariably, she'd start puking. Each of us was so in love with her that we stomached the stench of vomit so that she would never again smell the inside of a kennel.

When I accepted a job in Massachusetts, after the company I worked for in Virginia went belly-up, we called for Maggie, "Come on girl, let's go!" Up she jumped into the van, good girl. One morning she was in Virginia and the next, she was sniffing a frozen, foreign yard. Her adjustment was far smoother than ours. Maggie's love remained steadfast. Our marriage crumbled.

The move shifted something I had buried deep inside, making me temperamental and depressed. Seven hundred miles and twenty-odd years was enough distance for the aftermath to bubble up. Katherine discovered that, like it'd been the case with Maggie, my previous owners had mistreated me. I came out to my parents when I was nineteen years old, revealing to them the true nature of the beast. But, they pushed me back into the closet, forced me to obey their religious rules. After two decades of marriage, Katherine rescued me.

"Bill, I have to ask you this now, or I may never. Are you gay?"

"I've tried not to be."

"Oh God," Katherine muttered. "I told myself to be ready for the answer. After all these years, how do I give you up now?"

When Maggie and the girls left me and returned to Virginia, I slunk into a basement apartment, a cheap rental in Waltham, Massachusetts. Many nights, I would come home and shout, "Maggie, I'm home," before reality struck me. The empty spot by my outstretched hand yielded not a soft head to rub, but a hollow emptiness.

Still, a piece of me was in Virginia with the girls. Maggie acted as my surrogate, the one who let their heartbroken tears roll onto her warm hide and nuzzled their sweet faces; the one who listened without judgment or reproach. When I visited, Katherine would stand motionless in the doorway, holding on to Maggie's collar, until she wiggled free and bolted toward me. I'd crouch down, letting her lick my face, and she'd whimper, as if to ask, *Where have you been?*

As with grief, there are stages of a divorce: denial, anger, hate, bitterness, indifference, and acceptance. We experienced them, much in the way we had collected ill-fitting pets with their nasty yellow teeth and a bite that induced pain and regret.

We fought over the mundane and argued about money. We were petty with our insults and name-calling. We became cold and distant. When my phone rang and Katherine's number appeared, I braced for another round of bitterness, another nasty bite.

"Bill, Maggie's sick."

That was what it took to shift us into the acceptance stage. I wrote a check for Maggie's final care.

Shortly after that call, I returned to Virginia, traveling up and down those winding mountain roads to fetch my daughters for Christmas. When Katherine opened the door, I crouched down before I remembered, and as I glanced up, in the gloaming winter light noticed the empty spot next to Katherine's waist. I rose and then slowly, cautiously, placed my head on her shoulder.

"There you are," Katherine wept. "Where have you been?"

Our investment in Maggie matured, and so had we.

— William Dameron —

47

Lesson from Larry

Cats will outsmart dogs every time.
~John Grogan

I've wanted a cat for as long as I can remember. Now that I'm thirteen, I finally have one. His name is Larry.

Actually, my whole family, except for Dad, has wanted a cat for a long time. About a year ago, Dad finally gave in, and he and Mom went to the animal shelter. They brought home three-month-old Larry. My two younger sisters and I jumped for joy. At first, Larry trembled constantly because of our two large Labrador Retrievers. It wasn't long, though, before he taught us an important lesson.

The day was bitterly cold outside. Our family of five, along with our two dogs, was snuggled near the warm fireplace watching TV. The dogs, who weigh about ninety pounds each, were sleeping calmly together in their new dog bed after a long day of activity. Their eyes were closed, and they were snoring peacefully.

Larry had been keeping a watchful eye from atop his cat post. All at once, he jumped off his high perch. He bounced off the floor, raced over to where the dogs were sleeping and swatted them sharply, like a human swatting a fly. Larry was ready to fight, his claws out, his muscles tight. Larry wanted the new dog bed for himself, possibly because it was next to the warm fireplace, or maybe he just wanted to snuggle into the fluffy fur.

The second Larry attacked them, the dogs jumped up and yelped. Both raced off their bed and out of Larry's way, their tails between their legs.

We couldn't help but laugh. What had just happened? Had our cat just kicked two ninety-pound dogs off their bed? Perfectly placed next to the warm fireplace, Larry fell asleep and had a wonderful nap. No one bothered him, not even the dogs.

We learned an important lesson from Larry that day, which we won't soon forget: Size doesn't matter. If you want something, go for it.

Thanks, Larry.

—Brook-Lynn Meijer, age 13—

48

Think Like a Dog

Those who find beauty in all of nature will find
themselves at one with the secrets of life itself.
~L. Wolfe Gilbert

I was excited to take my rescue Beagle to the river the other day, as it's within walking distance of our new home. Having spent her first six years in a cage, Georgie had never seen a body of water, and I wanted to get there before sunset to watch her experience it.

I was growing increasingly impatient about all the stops her little Beagle nose required. She inspected the grass, dirt, and trees, and licked whatever was stuck to the road. These were all new discoveries for her, and she took her time studying them.

When I accepted that it was fruitless to hurry her along, I whipped out my cell phone and began texting. I thought that I needed something to do while Georgie was slowing us down.

Then, for some reason, I heard the cicadas, and I remembered that the sound of cicadas is my favorite sound in the world. That awakened something buried within me that yearned for the simple pleasures that had been replaced by technology.

I made a conscious decision to be present, and to enjoy the journey *to* the river, just like Georgie. The journey was just as wonderful as the final destination would be, and it took that little Beagle to remind me.

Now, I admired the intricacy of the flowers and the wonder of the winding ivy on our path. I felt the occasional warm raindrop on my skin from a gray sky threatening to burst at any moment. I smelled the asphalt, the grass and the flowers, and the dirt and the air. I treasured each one equally, as if discovering them for the first time. I took note of the colors everywhere that people would claim I exaggerated if I were to paint them on canvas.

I tripped over my feet and stumbled in some holes, and I was damp with sweat and rain. A few mosquitoes circled my head and landed on my sticky arms. As we neared our destination, I realized something even more important: It didn't matter if we even reached the river. Why must there always be a destination?

Georgie had no idea that we had a destination. She was present for the journey, and she savored every bit of that sweet experience. There was no race and no finish line.

Now I'm not sure who rescued whom.

— Lauren Mosher —

49

Princess's Posse

*An effort made for the happiness
of others lifts us above ourselves.*
~Lydia M. Child

I went to veterinary school later in life. Due to the fact that I had to hold a job during the day, when it came time to log numerous hours in an internship, my choices were limited. Finally, at the last possible moment, I was taken on at an urgent care/emergency veterinary hospital located deep within the inner city. The facility was open 24 hours, 7 days a week. Nights were long and heart wrenching. Most of our clients did not have the means to pay for the care their pets required. They often came to us far too late, when nothing could be done to save their pets. Clients would spread out meager sums on the counter and beg for whatever services that precious amount would buy. Most nights I dragged myself home at 3 a.m., exhausted and heartsick.

One night started about the same as the others but soon became very special. An elderly woman arrived carrying her small Poodle wrapped in a bloody blanket. She said they had been out for their evening walk when a large dog had attacked her Princess. A man came and pulled the large dog away. She had grabbed Princess and come straight to us.

The Chief of Staff and I took the small bloody blanket to the exam room.

We were expecting the worst. No movement or sound came from

the bundle.

As we peeled the bloody layers away, a small white Poodle emerged. She was alert and looking at us. There was a lot of blood, but as we examined her we grew more excited. "There are a lot of lacerations, but nothing major has been damaged! I think we can sew up this little gal!"

He formulated his plan and what the estimate would be for our client. My mission was now to speak to Princess's mom.

I brought her into the office. "The good news is," I said, "that it looks far worse than it is." I then told her the bad news — a several hundred-dollar estimate for Princess's care.

She asked, "How long would I have to pay that bill?" I immediately began my rote speech that we had no payment terms, that payment must be made in full at the time of service, etc.

"That's not what I meant," she said. "How long tonight?"

I felt a glimmer of hope.

"How long do you need?' I asked. She wanted to know if she could stay in the office and use our telephone to make some calls. She handed me two crumpled twenty-dollar bills and gave my hand a squeeze. "Is that enough to start? Give me a little time to get some people down here."

I relayed the information to the Chief of Staff. He had given Princess some pain medicine and cleaned her up in order to get a better look. His decision was to prep Princess and let her owner have some time to work on a few things.

Shortly afterwards, chaos ensued and we became very busy. Our receptionist walked into the exam room, waving a twenty-dollar bill over her head, and said, "Some lady just gave me this and said it was for Princess. What am I supposed to do with it?" Before we could answer we heard our bell ringing nonstop at the front desk. A woman and three children were there. I went out with the receptionist. The woman handed us $30, and each child opened his hand and dumped a fistful of change on the counter. "We brung that for Grandma and Princess," the little boy said.

Next came a young woman who handed me four credit cards. She said that each one had about $20 left on it. Her direction: "Fill them up for Princess and Grandma." The funny part is that after they made their contributions they stayed. Our little lobby filled. Where it was usually deathly quiet or the only sound you heard was crying, it was now filled with joyful greetings and phone calls to others to get up here quick to help Grandma. Our receptionist would holler out the current total and cheers would erupt. Our lobby now contained at least twenty people rooting for Princess. The man whose dog attacked Princess arrived and laid a one-hundred-dollar bill on the counter. He wanted to personally apologize to Grandma, so I went to get her from the office. I told her that all of her children and grandchildren were arriving and were in the lobby contributing funds for Princess. She laughed and told me that she had no children or grandchildren of her own. She said, "Everybody in the neighborhood has always called me Grandma — I've always tried to take care of all of them the best I could over the years."

Our Chief of Staff went into the lobby and thanked everyone and said that since our lobby wouldn't hold anyone else, he figured we had enough for the bill! Princess recovered beautifully and she and Grandma bring us treats all the time. My heart swells every time I see them and think of the entire neighborhood that came out to take care of the grandma who had always tried to take care of them.

— Peggy Omarzu —

A Little Magic

A little magic can take you a long way.
~Roald Dahl

Magic was a four-year-old German Shepherd about to be euthanized at the animal shelter along with hundreds of other dogs, at least that is how I remember it. I was editing a news promo for WNBC/New York. The reporter announced that the dogs and cats would be put down if no one came by the end of the day. My friend Rosie and I left work and rushed to the pound to save whoever we could. She got a cat and I asked the shelter worker for the biggest dog they had. His name was Magic.

I was single, self-absorbed, and without responsibilities. I went to rock concerts, hung out with friends at bars, and worked hard. Just a twenty-something who didn't realize I was missing family and community. I had tried volunteering once but the guy on the phone said he needed people to stuff and lick envelopes. That didn't turn me on. In hindsight, it was a blessing. My gluten allergy would have made me a *Seinfeld* episode. You know the one, where Susan, George's fiancée, dies from licking envelopes?

So I brought Magic home. When I stepped out of the elevator, my neighbor smiled and said, "You did a mitzvah!"

"A what?"

"A mitzvah! You did a good deed without asking for anything in return. It's a good thing."

There wasn't a lot of trust at first. Magic would take the food out of his bowl, bring it in front of me and eat it one nibble at a time. My co-workers were pretty sure I was crazy and that this would be a huge mistake. But slowly Magic and I got to know each other. We became best friends. For the first time, my apartment felt like a home. We walked together through Central Park every morning and night.

My friends invited me to parties, but I just wanted to be home with Magic. Our lives were happy. For the first time, I was content. Unfortunately, Magic didn't like being left alone during my working hours. To remedy the issue, I tried doggie day care, a dog therapist and running to tire him out. In the end, I realized he was lonely.

Enter Whiskey. She was a pit bull/boxer mix, scarred from the dog fighting streets where guns and hate were rampant. Her name was Kissy, but that wasn't working for me. So I renamed her Whiskey. Magic and Whiskey fell in love and our home was complete. At least I thought so.

The neighbor below did not agree. He worked nights and had a loft bed. The pitter-patter of their feet and playing irked him. And, it turned out, my landlord did not allow dogs. Paying $1,600 for a studio apartment on the Upper West Side with duct tape holding the plumbing together suddenly lost its appeal. I didn't realize it but my "babies" and I had grown out of our home — and essentially New York City.

Since the age of seventeen I had dreamed of heading out west. Land to hike, spacious homes and thoughts of friendly people filled my head. I was discontented with my job, my lack of social life and the constant noise of the city. I made plans to leave.

I took a trip to Arizona and fell in love. It was perfect. I was at peace. Deadheads, hippies and Allman Brothers music playing at the outdoor bar on a sunny day in Flagstaff made me complete. So Magic, Whiskey and I moved away.

My friend helped me drive across the country, and I found a place near a cousin of mine. It was a three-bedroom house for a few hundred dollars a month in Bullhead City, Arizona. The sunsets blew me away. I couldn't understand why everyone wasn't stopping on the side of the road as the sun went down, releasing an array of colors that painted the sky pink, orange, blue, purple, yellow and red.

I began working at a domestic violence shelter. I wanted to help others. It lasted for a while, but it wasn't enough. I started to travel more, taking odd jobs around the country. Magic and Whiskey came with me everywhere. A friend from Arizona was heading back to Kansas. The Midwest sounded interesting.

A small town in western Kansas became my home. Small towns always need volunteers. And someone who had no obligations besides work was an easy target. I helped at everything—the county fair, the alumni lunch, a local church…. It was social, community-oriented work. And I loved it! It was gratifying. I came home tired yet satisfied. I helped people enjoy themselves. Funny enough, I enjoyed it more than if I had been a guest.

A couple of years later I volunteered for Relay for Life in my area and met my husband. A few more years after that I volunteered at a substance abuse treatment center where I met a woman who later became pregnant and wanted me to adopt her child (a story for another time).

Volunteering has brought me dogs, a wonderful husband and an amazing daughter. And it all started with a little Magic!

— Michele Boy —

A Dying Gift

There is a land of the living and a land of the dead,
and the bridge is love.
~Thornton Wilder

O ut of the blue he said, "I think it's time we get that puppy you've been wanting for so long." He was wrapped in a furry lap robe, sitting in the glider I had moved into the kitchen so he could be near me while I prepared meals. His black hair had turned to silver, his voice had lost its clarity, and the sparkle had faded from the dark brown eyes that had shown his love for me through forty-eight years. I knew that he knew it wouldn't be many more months before the cancer won and the chemo treatments would become ineffective.

For several years I had been begging to have a puppy, but his response had always been, "Not until you retire, because I don't want to be the one getting up in the night with a whining pup!" Now I had given up my job, not because I was of retirement age, but because I needed to be home to care for him while he battled the monster lurking in his bone marrow.

We went the next day to West Rock Kennels and picked out an adorable Shih-Tzu puppy, the healthiest-looking one of the litter. For several days I concentrated on choosing the perfect name for this adorable little distraction. Precious? Fritz? Piddles? At the suggestion of my sister, I finally settled on Skoshi, the Japanese word for small. While part of me wasted away along with my dying husband, Skoshi provided a silly kernel of delight that kept me going.

The diagnosis had come as a complete shock in the summer of 2002. During a routine checkup at our local clinic, his primary physician noted an unusual spike in a blood protein and referred us to a specialist for further follow-up, never mentioning the dreaded "C" word. As we drove up to the professional building in Robbinsdale, Minnesota, our hearts skipped a beat as we read the words "Humphrey Cancer Center" in bold design above the door. After further tests and consultation with an oncologist, it was confirmed. He had multiple myeloma, the technical term for bone marrow cancer, considered to be one of the more difficult cancers to treat.

As the months went by, we had many conversations about his impending departure, and he made lists of the important things I should know how to do when he was no longer around. To put his mind at ease, I assured him that I would be fine and that he needn't worry about me.

One day, in October 2005, a clinic appointment for a blood draw indicated that his chest cavity was filling up with fluid, and he had to be hospitalized. The doctors planned to remove the fluid the following morning and advised me to go home and get some rest. Sleep did not come. I prayed and committed the man who had been my best friend and lover for so many years to the Lord's care, asking that he be spared further suffering.

The next morning I rushed back to the hospital and found him somewhat confused. I reminded him who his visitors had been the previous day — grandson William, son Bruce, daughter-in-law Jeri, Pastor Tim. Then a strange look came across his face, as he said, "Oh, Marg, I feel so dizzy, so dizzy!" He lost consciousness, as I frantically ran into the hallway, calling for the nurse. Within minutes the once vibrant man I had loved since our teenage years lay still and silent, as I lay my head upon his chest and wept. The inevitable day had arrived.

I was strong and resolute throughout the week of making plans for his memorial service. Our grown children came to be with me. Together we chose music that he had loved, flowers to grace his casket, and special friends to take part. The last time I looked on his dear, familiar face, I wanted to climb into his burial bed and go to eternal rest along with him. But I greeted friends and relatives with a smile. I watched proudly as his children eulogized him, his granddaughters read his favorite Scriptures, and his seven grandsons carried him to the family plot to take his place alongside his mother, father, and grandparents, where one day I will finally lie beside him again.

Kicking aside the dead oak leaves as I walked the circle of my driveway in the late afternoons, I called out to the sky, "Where are you? Do you see me? Do you know my heart is broken?" My husband was finally free from the cancer's pain and suffering, but I never dreamed being left behind would hurt so much. As I walked, Skoshi faithfully watched and waited from the kitchen window. Day after day, spent from crying, I went inside to the joyful, wiggling, tail-wagging welcome from Skoshi, who needed my attention.

Friends called me from time to time to ask how I was doing. I always replied with a lie, "Oh, I'm fine. It's hard, but I'm doing fine." Funny how we want everyone to think we can handle situations that have rendered us immobile, unable to cope. I continued attending church, my one refuge, but as I sang the beautiful praise songs, the tears would not be denied and would soon stream down my cheeks. I felt a compulsion to destroy things that once held meaning to me, but no longer did. I stood in my living area and contemplated ripping all the books off the shelves and slamming them around the room. When I went to my closet to dress in the morning, I wanted to pull the clothes off the hangers and stomp on them.

I could sense that my children were becoming concerned, especially my daughter who began calling every night just to chat and make suggestions.

"Mom, maybe you should make an appointment with your physician and ask about taking an anti-depressant?"

"Mom, I'm worried about you."

"Mom, have you thought about seeing a counselor? Take down this number; he's a good one."

Most days I wanted to stay in bed, turn my face to the wall and never get up. As I lay there on a dark December day in 2005, Skoshi, curled in sleep behind my back, began to stir. He stretched, stood up and found his way to my pillow. As he licked my chin, I finally realized I needed help. I gathered that precious little dog into my arms, the last gift of love my life partner had given me, and murmured, "Thank you, my beloved Gordon," into Skoshi's furry little body. Once again, even in death, he had come through for me. Skoshi smiled at me, as Shih Tzu are known to do. Then with all the courage I could muster, I picked up the phone and dialed.

— Margaret M. Marty —

Chapter 6

Best Friends

52

Man, Dog, Boat

A man is not old until regrets take the place of dreams.
~John Barrymore

I stood at the kitchen window watching Papa as he sat in the old, aluminum lawn chair staring out at the lake. Ralph, his old black dog, lay on the ground at his side, his eyes following Papa's gaze. Papa's hand absently stroked the head of his old companion as they dreamed the dreams of old men and old dogs in the evening sun. "He does this day after day?" I said to Mama.

She nodded, sadness filling her eyes as she looked to me for answers that I didn't have. "I don't know what to do for him. There is a longing in his eyes that I can't fulfill. A longing for the past." She sighed. "The past can't be brought back to the present. Once days are gone, they are gone forever."

"I'm going down to talk to him," I said.

Mama took Papa's old brown sweater off a peg by the back door. "It's getting chilly outside," she said, handing the garment to me. She poured a cup of coffee into Papa's cracked green ceramic mug that I made for him in third grade. Silently, she held it out to me. My heart melted a little at her tenderness toward the stubborn, old man.

I called out to Papa as I drew near, and he turned in his chair, eyes glowing with delight as usual when he saw me. His beautiful azure-blue eyes looked out of place in the gaunt, wrinkled face of an old man who had spent many long days outdoors in all kinds of weather. Every time I saw those eyes, I wished that I had inherited them instead of Mama's brown eyes. I handed him the cup of coffee and then wrapped the sweater around his shoulders before bending to kiss the top of his head. "What are you and Ralph thinking about all these hours you spend out here?" I asked.

"We're not thinking," he said softly. "We're wishing."

I dropped down in the grass beside his chair. "Wishing for what?"

He sighed. "For the impossible, I suppose."

"You always told me that nothing was impossible if you wanted it badly enough and were willing to work hard enough for it," I reminded him.

He chuckled softly, but there was no amusement in the sound. "But Ralph and I have come to learn that when you reach our age, some things actually are impossible."

"What is it that you want so badly that you spend all your days thinking about it?" I asked.

Papa looked away. "You're going to think I'm a foolish, old man."

"It doesn't matter what anyone thinks," I said. "It's your dream, and you should have it. Maybe I can help you. What do you want?"

He grinned, and his amazing eyes sparkled at the thought of his dream becoming a reality. Just seeing the shine in his eyes made me want to give him what he longed for before I even knew what he wanted. He leaned down and scratched behind Ralph's ears, and Ralph gave him a contented grin.

"Ralph and I want to fix up the old boat in the shed and go out on the lake again." Papa looked out at the lake, and his eyes saw things that I couldn't see. "Ralph and I used to spend all day out on the lake, fishing, drinking beer and eating bologna sandwiches. We'd start for home when the sun went down, totally satisfied with ourselves and with life. And before Ralph, there were other dogs. Good dogs that spent their lives on the lake. But Ralph was cheated because I grew old and had the heart attack while he was young. Ralph deserves one more day on the lake even more than I do." Ralph raised his head and looked at me as if he were imploring me, too.

At first, Mama was appalled at the idea of Papa fixing up his old boat and going out on the lake again. "He's almost eight-five years old.

I'd worry every minute he was gone," she said.

"Mama," I said. "You worry about him sitting in his lawn chair staring out at the lake every day. Worry is worry. And we are all going to die doing something. Isn't it better to die doing something we love rather than die longing to do something we can't do anymore?"

Once Mama gave in, I enlisted my husband and a couple of nephews to help renovate the old boat. The boat was sound, but it was old, and the paint was faded and cracked. The motor was good, but to be safe it was taken in for an overhaul. My two nephews spent several weekends sanding and painting the boat. I replaced the faded and cracked seat cushions. We didn't want the boat to just look okay. We wanted it to be special. We wanted Papa to be proud of the boat as he and Ralph went out on the lake again.

As we all worked together, we were happy to be making an old man's dream come true. We didn't tell Papa that the goal was to have the boat ready by his birthday. We always brushed him off when he asked when the work would be done.

On the day of his birthday, we all gathered at Papa's house early that morning. He was surprised when we all showed up as he was finishing his breakfast.

"It's too early for cake," he quipped.

Then he noticed the cooler that one of my nephews was carrying. "What's this?" he asked, puzzled.

"Beer!" my nephew said.

My other nephew held up a large lunch tote. "Bologna sandwiches, cookies, and dog biscuits."

I stepped forward. "New sunglasses to keep the sun out of your eyes."

My husband grinned. "A new hat in the same colors as your boat." He popped it on Papa's head. Papa's mouth flew open. Mama stepped forward and hugged Papa.

"Happy birthday, honey. You and Ralph are taking your boat out on the lake today."

Papa batted his eyes and fought to hold back tears. It didn't matter because by then all of us were crying. Soon, we all stood by the lake and watched as Papa and Ralph drove away, Papa waving and laughing, looking happier than I had seen him look in a long time. Mama turned to me.

"Look at him. He doesn't look like an old man, does he? Being happy makes him look young again."

I hugged Mama. Papa and Ralph spent many days after that out on the lake where they were always just a man and his dog. They were never old when they were on the lake. They were just happy. Ralph didn't live long after Papa died. He spent most of his remaining days lying in the sun at the edge of the yard gazing out into the lake — remembering, I am sure, the days he and Papa spent together out on the lake.

— Elizabeth Atwater —

53

Brave, Crazy or Both

The biggest adventure you can ever take
is to live the life of your dreams.
~Oprah Winfrey

rave, crazy or both — that's what my family and friends thought when I announced I would be embarking on a search for a new place to call home. But after a lifetime of doing what I thought others expected of me, I needed neither their permission nor their blessings.

So on September 14, 2015, I literally drove out of my old life and into my new one, without a clue as to what that life would look like when I found it.

I had packed my memories into a storage unit and the rest of my life into my Malibu with a roof bag. My only traveling companion was my dog Bella, a nine-year-old mixed breed who resembles a short, fat Collie. With six months of reservations in various places, the two of us hit the road.

Driving out of the tiny town in South Dakota where I'd been living was the most frightening moment of my life for many reasons. I was terrified of being alone. I hated driving. I'm directionally challenged. And my beautiful dog was a high-stress traveler who always needed to get out of the car at inopportune times.

To make sure I had time to rethink my decision, the only stoplight in that tiny town turned red. I spent that eternal minute waiting for the light to turn green, asking God to give me a sign that I was going to be okay.

That's when I learned that God has a sense of humor.

For the next hour, every girl-power anthem ever written played on the radio, one after another. Cher told me to "believe in life after love." Beyoncé reminded me that girls "run the world," and Rachel Platten sang her "fight song." All the songs one would want to hear when some courage was needed came on. Finally, I looked up through my tears and said, "I get it. If Katy Perry says I'm a firework, I'm a firework! I can do this!"

For the next ten months, Bella and I checked out possible new places to live. We investigated towns we knew and places we'd never been. We stopped in Boulder, Colorado, where I had my first tofu pizza. We spent time in high-altitude Park City, Utah, where I nearly had a heart attack climbing the eighty-eight stairs to the cottage I'd rented. There were some scary moments in Reno, Nevada, that led me to lie to a hotel clerk. But when our only other option was spending the night in our car, my fib that Bella was under their dog weight limit seemed forgivable.

After a few weeks on the road, our scheduled month-long stay in Northern California was cut short by an encounter with a vacation rental host who has since been dubbed the "Crazy Viking." When I told my "super host" his accommodations were not up to my expectations, he began to rant at me. As he spewed his angry words, I found myself trying not to giggle in a scene that would've had me dissolving into tears in previous years. I recognized each of his many intimidation tactics and felt my courage grow when none had his intended effect! I stood my ground bravely while he threw a grown-up hissy fit on his front porch.

By facing down the Crazy Viking, I realized I was no longer the shy, scared girl I'd once been. And the blessing-in-Viking-disguise turned out to be what happened afterward. My replacement travel plans led me to a reunion with old friends and meeting two lovely new ones, all of whom were *actually* super hosts for this weary traveler.

My journey was filled with unexpected ups and downs, often

leaving me agreeing with those who had thought I was crazy to do it. Yet, I also felt as if I were being guided. At last, I was learning to listen to the inner voice I had ignored for so long.

My journey covered thousands of miles, twenty-two different beds, and a host of life-changing events over the course of ten months. Today, I'm no longer traveling or terrified. My final destination turned out to be Palm Springs, California, a unique village that spoke to my heart and that I'm thankful to call home every day.

Before I started my travels, I didn't think there was another option for figuring out where I wanted to live. So, I didn't really have an opinion about whether what I was doing was brave or crazy. In hindsight, I can say it was a little of both.

During my travels, one of my daughters made me a gift that said, "Home is where my mom is." And as I look at it today, I realize that finding a home wasn't nearly as important as finding myself.

— Mary Guinane —

Saved

Follow the light of your intuition, and keep
away from the darkness of convention.
~Michael Bassey Johnson

I almost didn't go to work that Saturday morning because of Hootie, our fifteen-year-old Terrier mix. I told myself I was being silly; there was no cause for concern. Hootie was old, but he was in good health and showed no signs of separation anxiety. He and our Doxie mix, Roxanne, had the run of the house, plus a dog door to the back yard.

Besides, my husband Lee and I were home with them most of the week, and only left them on weekends when we sold our artwork at an artisans' market in San Francisco, a half-hour away. They were always fine when we returned home around seven in the evening, overjoyed to see us and demanding their dinner.

Still, I worried about Hootie that Saturday and felt an urgent need throughout the day to get home early. "We need to be home by four o'clock," I told Lee. "I have no idea why, but it's important."

Lee and I packed up our displays early and arrived home shortly before four. Roxie greeted us at the door, leaping and twirling and barking with joy. Petting her, I looked around for Hootie, my worry intensifying as I hurried down the hall to find him.

He stood in the doorway to our bedroom, strangely quiet. "Hootie," I said, in a questioning voice, as he gave a subdued little greeting and took only a few unsteady steps toward me, before suddenly stopping, turning sharply to the left, and keeling over onto the floor.

Reaching down, I lifted his little body and placed him gently on the bed. His eyes were wide open and to my horror he threw his head back and cried out as though in great pain. Yelling loudly for Lee, I bent to soothe Hootie, who cried out again I thought he was going to die right there in front of me.

By the time Lee rushed into the room, with a frightened-looking Roxanne at his heels, Hootie had gone silent and lay still on the bed. "Get the Rescue Remedy," Lee said, bending over the bed. Fighting panic I backed from the room. "Come on, son," I heard my husband murmur. "Breathe."

Returning with the calming homeopathic medicine, I saw Lee take a deep breath and blow air into Hootie's mouth, filling his lungs, again and again. Several breaths later, Hootie stirred, moved his head.

"Yes! He's got a heartbeat again," Lee said, just as our little old dog opened his eyes and looked up at us. Limp with relief, we squeezed Rescue Remedy into his mouth and gave him low-dose aspirin. By evening he was his usual bouncy self, gobbling his dinner like he hadn't eaten in weeks and demanding a Greenie for dessert.

Exhausted by the strange turn of events, we all piled in bed at nine-thirty, with Hootie curled between us and Roxanne's little head resting on his hip. Thanks to my premonition and Lee's quick action, Hootie had survived his heart attack. I couldn't stop petting him, running my hands over his furry little body, realizing how close we'd come to our final parting.

— Lynn Sunday —

55

Operation Christmas Puppy

The dog was created specially for children.
He is the god of frolic.
~Henry Ward Beecher

Mom and I bumped into each other, our arms loaded with plates, as we raced to clear the table on Christmas Eve. "Fifteen minutes!" I yelled to the kids, who were jostling to claim the mirror in the bathroom.

Dillon flew into the kitchen. "Can you help me with my tie?" I gestured for my husband to handle it.

"I still need you to do my hair!" Faith wailed.

Dumping the casserole dishes on the counter, I turned to my mother. "Would you put the ham in a Ziploc bag while I curl her hair?"

Exactly fifteen minutes later, we somehow managed to buckle into the minivan with the children in their Christmas outfits and the leftovers in the refrigerator.

"Why isn't Daddy driving with us?"

"He has to go to work for a little bit." I backed out of the drive. My husband and I had a special surprise for the kids, one we had no intention of blowing before the big reveal.

Our children loved dogs. We joked that Faith was obsessed with them. Her favorite stuffed animal was a puppy, and she shared a special bond with my parents' Cocker Spaniel. When Faith was a tiny two-year-old, we decided to add a dog to the family, but the rambunctious Golden Retriever proved too feisty and three months later we sold him to a farmer with two preteen boys. It had crushed our little girl, and we promised ourselves we'd consider another dog someday. Now our children were finally old enough to handle the responsibility of one, and we were determined to make the event special.

I pulled into the church parking lot and escorted the kids to a classroom for their rehearsal. Both sets of grandparents joined me in the pew, and my husband arrived right before the service began. Our hearts were moved by the children's retelling of the story of a baby born in Bethlehem. All too quickly, the children sang the final hymn, and my husband gave my hand a quick squeeze to let me know Operation Christmas Puppy was underway.

Our friends bred miniature dachshunds, and they had six puppies ready to leave their mama. At exactly nine weeks old, the friendliest female in the litter was about to be introduced to her new home. My husband had picked up our new addition right before church, but he needed to take her outside to do her business and get her in a special gift box before I took the kids home. I had no idea how to stall the children that long!

We kissed the grandmas and grandpas goodbye, and I slowly drove away.

"Can we please open one present tonight?" Dillon begged from the back seat.

"We'll have to ask Dad, but I think that would be okay." My spirits soared, thinking of their reactions when they opened the gift waiting for them.

"I can't wait to change out of this dress," Faith said. "And I'm hungry. I was too nervous to eat much dinner."

Both kids were more than ready to go home, get comfortable, and anticipate the next phase of Christmas — the presents. But would my husband have enough time to get the dog situated? I was running out of options when inspiration struck.

"Look at those pretty lights." I pointed to a yard with twinkling white reindeer. On a whim, I turned into the subdivision next to it. "Let's drive around and admire the displays."

"Aw, Mom, do we have to? I just want to go home."

I ignored them and crawled past the houses with multi-colored lights. We drove through another subdivision, and I popped in a lively Christmas CD. Too soon, the tour ended.

"Mom, we've seen enough lights."

I still had time to kill. The stoplights didn't help. Where was a red light when I needed one? I remained stoic, keeping the minivan at a good five miles per hour under the speed limit.

Out of options, I finally entered our subdivision, and Dillon pressed his face to the window when we passed our home. "You passed our house!"

"I just want to see the lights behind us." I made sure we drove down every street, praying I could safely return home soon.

Thank goodness my husband's car was in the driveway. As soon as I parked the van, the kids raced to our porch and scrambled inside, ignoring the Christmas tree on their way upstairs to change. I quietly asked my husband if everything was ready. He grinned.

"Hey, wait," my husband called up the staircase. "Don't you want to open one gift?"

Thump, thump, thump. Still in their dress clothes, they charged down the steps into the living room. "Really? We can open one?"

That's when they saw it. The huge wrapped box with the big red bow on top, sitting in the center of the room. Would the puppy bark and give it away?

The package remained quiet, and the kids hesitated as they neared it. "What is it?"

"I bet it's a PlayStation," Dillon said.

"It's too big to be a PlayStation," Faith said in her superior tone.

"It could be one."

"Well," I said. "Open it and find out."

Faith tore at the paper, but Dillon lifted the box. To their surprise, the top lifted right off. They peered inside and gasped.

Seconds ticked by in silence. The shock on Dillon's face kept him from speaking. Then Faith looked at us, her eyes brimming with tears, and she whispered, "A puppy. Can we pick it up?"

My husband assured her, yes, she could pick it up. Tenderly she lifted the precious black and tan dog. With a small sob, she cradled the tiny body to her chest. I got teary-eyed watching them. Then she passed the calm bundle to Dillon, equally awed.

For ten minutes our house existed in hushed pleasure. The cinnamon scented candles, lights on the tree, and soft Christmas music playing in the background created a kind of wreath around us. The children set the puppy on the floor and pointed to her fluffy bed, which she launched into as if she knew it was hers.

We named our Miniature Dachshund Sophie, and she's been a treasured member of our family since that special Christmas Eve. We might have taken the long way home, but the kids agreed it was worth it for Operation Christmas Puppy.

—Jill Kemerer—

56

Into Her Arms

In all things of nature there is
something of the marvelous.
~Aristotle

"Hey, Bonnie! Your leg any better?" I asked my Aussie/chocolate Lab mix when we came in the door. Her bobbed tail wiggled and her long brown body squirmed closer. She looked at me with her one green eye. The other was blind and a nasty purple.

"Oh, you're still limping. I don't know how you manage to get yourself so banged up — first your eye all those years ago, and now your leg."

"Would you all come into the kitchen?" Dad asked. His voice was choked.

"I've just gotten word," he said. "Your Uncle Alan passed away a few hours ago."

The words hung in the air like daggers. They could only hurt me if I believed them — but the truth slowly sunk its cruel blade into my heart.

The next few days were endless in their tears, heartache, and worry. Always in my thoughts was Paige, my sixteen-year-old cousin whose father was now dead.

When I saw her, she said nothing. When I visited her home, she said nothing. Her face was pale, her blue eyes expressionless, and her blond hair pulled back. Saying nothing.

On my way out their door, I froze when I saw a picture of Alan's dog, Annie, hung on the wall. The beautiful chocolate Lab had died four years before, but suddenly memories flooded my vision.

My bearded Uncle Alan, middle-aged, slim, average height... his calm voice growing excited as he rewarded Annie.

"Sit, Annie. Stay." He placed a treat on her velvety muzzle.

"Catch! Good girl, Annie! Shake... good. Roll over...."

They nuzzled each other, Alan caressing her soft brown fur, her long tail wagging. I imagined I saw them together again — together, happy. I knew Alan was in heaven. I knew that he and Annie were reunited.

"You know, I never liked that dog," Paige said. I turned, wiping the tears from my eyes.

"Dad sure did love her," she went on. "It was awful when she died, after he rescued her, trained her, and kept her all those years."

"Yeah, I know," I managed.

"You remember how he buried her on the hill? He'd always told Mom to bury him on that hill. So we're going to, right alongside Annie."

The day of the funeral dragged painfully by. Paige's friends surrounded her the whole time. She spoke to them, and they received her hugs and tears. I gave her one hug and drew away, realizing I wasn't needed and longing to do anything for her. If I could ease her pain, then somehow my own would shrink.

But she got through fine without me.

Days afterward, I paced, cursed myself, racked my brain for a way to cheer up my cousin, to say I was there. Not that she needed me — she had her other friends.

But things came to a head when Bonnie's blind eye got worse.

"Come here, Bonnie. Come here!" I chirped.

She came eagerly, still limping. I rubbed the white hourglass on her chest and scratched her brown ears, silky as rabbit fur. Her eye was oozing. I reached for the phone.

"Bonnie, you're going to hate this, but we've got to get this taken care of, even if you're going to fight the vet like a demon."

We dragged her to the vet, snapping and growling, but finally the sedatives kicked in and the vet removed Bonnie's blind eye.

"It was ruptured," the vet told us. "And causing a lot of irritability and pain. We've sewn the socket up, but it's swollen."

The medicines knocked Bonnie out and made her act drunk. She stumbled and fell, couldn't eat, couldn't drink. She couldn't bear for us to leave her. She looked scared, her heart rate was high, and her legs shook uncontrollably.

Thanksgiving came amidst all the confusion.

"It's important for us to be together — especially now," Mom said. "So we invited the family over. We'll move Bonnie to the bathroom and let her sleep."

"When do you think she'll come out of it?" I asked.

Mom sighed. "It won't be for a while yet."

Thanksgiving filled our home with vines of orange and yellow leaves twisting around the banisters, maroon cloths draped over tables, wood and glass polished, stone hearth swept, burgundy curtains drawn back to let in the light of the November sun. The smells of pumpkin, potatoes, turkey, and apple pie perfumed the air.

Everything was ready, including Bonnie, who we carried away to the bathroom. She was so weak she couldn't stand, and it was painful to watch her — barely able to open her eye halfway.

I dreaded seeing Paige. Much as I longed to, it would be so awkward not knowing what to say.

All the family tromped in. They piled their muddy boots and designer clogs in a corner and got in line for food.

The entire time, something was missing. Alan was gone. I missed the heated political discussions where we all agreed with each other, but pretended we didn't. I missed him competing with Dad in *Guesstures*, pulling Paige's hair, hugging my aunt, laughing at Grandpa's jokes.

We sat in the living room, the adults on the plush couches, wicker chairs in an uneven circle. Paige sat with her back against the hearth, her knees drawn up to her chest, blocking out those around her, her face mournful. Why was there nothing I could do? If only I could help...

I couldn't stand it any longer and went to check on Bonnie.

"Hey, you're awake!" I laughed. She was alert and standing at the door, triangular ears perked up, looking as well as ever.

"You must've smelled that food! Let's get some exercise."

Instead of going to the kitchen like I expected her to, she bounded into the living room, straight to Paige, to whom she'd never shown personal preference before.

Bonnie's stump of a tail bobbed furiously, her nose cuddled into Paige's neck. Paige looked surprised as her hands went up to Bonnie's sides.

"Go lie down, Bonnie," Mom commanded.

"No, no! She's fine, really," Paige said.

And something happened that warmed me all over.

Paige smiled. Really smiled. That sweet, happy grin that Alan said he loved to see. For the first time since his death, I saw joy in my cousin's face, and quick tears came to my eyes when Bonnie plopped into her lap like it was the most natural thing to do.

Thank you God, I prayed. Even though I couldn't help her, Bonnie could. She knew Paige was hurting. I guess wise words and glorious deeds aren't needed — just being there is all that matters.

Bonnie wouldn't be lured away from Paige for food or toys, and that in itself was a miracle. The sight of an old, torn-up, bob-tailed, one-eyed, limping dog comforting a mourning girl who didn't even like the animal reached into my very core — that was the miracle.

For a moment in the history of this hurting world, two creatures came together and offered each other comfort, the solace of a kind touch and having someone to hold. Those few moments made a world of difference in the lives of all who witnessed it.

As the hum of afternoon voices drifted around us, Paige sat there with one arm encircling Bonnie's chest. Maybe she was thinking of the love her father had shown his own dog. I don't know. All I know is that the smile never left her face the rest of the day.

— Alandra Blume —

57

A Splash of Insight

*The ability to be in the present moment is a
major component of mental wellness.*
~Abraham Maslow

I was stumped. The question posed on social media wasn't difficult, at least for most people, but it was like being hit with a bucket of cold water for me, shocking me into a realization.

What do you do for fun?

I couldn't come up with a single answer.

Had my existence become so empty? Living alone, with an office in my home, work time had overflowed like lava, consuming more and more of my days until there was no boundary safeguarding my personal time. It was all work, all the time.

The worst part was that, at the end of the week, I could not successfully justify it. What had I accomplished? Ryder Carroll says, "Inevitably we find ourselves… spreading our focus so thin that nothing gets the attention it deserves. This is commonly referred to as 'being busy.' Being busy, however, is not the same thing as being productive."

I was not productive, and I was not happy. However, I was endlessly busy.

Something needed to change. I had no idea how to make it happen or where to begin. That is, until a four-legged fluffball entered the picture, upended the status quo, and made it clear that there was so much in the world yet to be discovered.

Dogs had always been a part of my life. For this next dog, I had specific requirements. My someday dreams included doing some traveling in my RV, visiting new places, and meeting new people. I needed a dog that would be happy with that. My last dogs had been Jack Russells, bright and energetic, but needing a lot of stimulation and challenges. Besides the Terriers, I'd owned Labradors and Belgian Tervurens. They were all lovely animals, but each bred with a purpose. They had active, outside-focused motivations and were driven to stalk, retrieve, or herd.

I wanted a dog that had been created to be with me. I wanted to know that, when she cuddled next to me, she was fulfilling her purpose and was satisfied. After much research, I settled on the breed: Havanese.

When I got my puppy, she was eleven weeks old and the smallest dog I'd ever owned. She weighed a mere four pounds and moved like a wind-up toy. I wanted to start her off right, as a socialized pup who was comfortable around other dogs and humans, so I took her to weekly playdates hosted by a local dog trainer.

I remember walking into the room, my tiny puppy cradled in my arms, and watching the rambunctious puppies jumping, running, and roughhousing. My eyes began to fill with tears. "I can't do this," I mumbled, turning to go.

"Wait." One of the puppy moms stopped me. "Just sit here beside me and let her stay in your lap."

I sat next to her. Her pup was a Cavalier King Charles Spaniel about the same age and size as my Trixie. Both our puppies were a little shy. However, my initial panic eased, and I returned week after week. In a short time, Trixie was running around, dodging the bigger puppies and finding a spot on a piece of equipment or a box where she had height equality. She was having a blast.

Then Ziggy came.

He was also a Havanese, three months older. Before long, Trixie and Ziggy were obsessed with each other, wrestling without a sound and ignoring the other dogs.

It wasn't long before Ziggy's mom and I decided we could hold our own playdates since our puppies only had eyes for each other. The first time we met at Jane's house, we drank tea and watched the puppies tumble nonstop for nearly three hours. It was Zen-like for me, calming and mesmerizing, taking me to a new level. When I left that day, my stress level was nonexistent, and I felt like I'd had a relaxing two-hour massage.

Our friendship grew, and we found we had more in common than just our good taste in dogs. We both wanted to visit places in Montana and the surrounding areas, and we both liked to cook. That led to a regular and sacrosanct tradition of Friday playdates. We'd try new recipes while the dogs entertained each other, or we'd take day trips with them.

Trixie and Ziggy will be five years old this year, and our pack of four has had many adventures. We've expanded our travel time, taking the RV on extended trips to Yellowstone, Glacier National Park, Canada, and shorter jaunts around our state. We share an interest in birds and other wildlife, and we've photographed bears, moose, eagles, and waterfowl.

The dogs, true to their natures, are happy to be part of the activities and never fail to bring us joy and laughter.

We keep a running list of new places to go, things to see, and recipes to tackle. I find the planning to be just as much a delight as the actual events. My weeks no longer pass by, indistinguishable from one another, without meaning. My Fridays are my oasis, a place where the whole day is simply about having fun and celebrating being alive.

As I recall my past habits, I realize I am accomplishing as much, if not more, by changing my focus from being busy to being present. That question, that splash of cold water, made me aware of how much I'd been missing by not carving out time for the things that really matter.

Now, I treasure every minute. By creating clear boundaries and giving myself designated time for fun, I have an easy answer to that question that once baffled me: *What do you do for fun?*

Where do I begin?

— Lynn Kinnaman —

It's All About the Dogs

You can usually tell that a man is good
if he has a dog who loves him.
~W. Bruce Cameron, A Dog's Journey

"If anything ever happened to your mom, I'd be devastated," my dad confessed. "But if something ever happened to Sadie Mae, I don't think I could survive."

"Dad, never tell Mom that!" I shrieked.

Sadie Mae was his German Shorthaired Pointer. I grew up knowing that it was all about the dogs. There was Pixie, Chrissy, Seymour, Brandy, Charlie, and, of course, Sadie Mae.

And somewhere behind the list of dogs were the kids: Sherrie, Connie, and David. Dad could never remember our names, but why should he? He knew all the dogs' names. We knew where we stood — our pedigrees couldn't measure up to those of our housemates. Our human plans were often altered to accommodate the "doglings" because they always came first.

According to my father, kennels were no place for "human" dogs. And pet sitters never lasted very long because the dogs made sure they trashed the house to remind all of us who was really in charge.

I remember when my parents drove me to Whitworth University — my freshman year — and dropped me off at my dorm at 5:00 a.m. so Dad could get home to his dogs. I knew then I was not my dad's favorite "child." After taking a few psych classes, I understood that my family was a "little" crazy, particularly my dad.

I married and had children, and it wasn't all about the dogs. In fact, we never had a dog while our two boys were growing up. They had our full and undivided attention. And they bemoaned the fact that all their friends had dogs and cats and other pets (hamsters, rabbits, and goldfish).

When our older son graduated from Donegal High School in Mount Joy, Pennsylvania, in the year 2000, we sent out save-the-date invitations to our entire family. Since we lived on the East Coast and everyone else lived on the West Coast, it took some planning. We rented a venue, had the event catered, and all the family from my husband's side and my side planned on attending. I could hardly believe it when I heard that my mom and dad were coming and leaving Sadie Mae in a kennel.

Due to a scheduling conflict, we had to have the party the day before graduation. It was going to be a combined family reunion/high school graduation. Everything went as planned: The food was delicious and everyone raved about the leather photo album that I put together of Jeremy's childhood through high school years.

The next day, we planned a lovely brunch before we headed to the graduation, where Jeremy was to receive a scholarship award. That morning, I received a call from my mom. She said, "Dad won't be attending the graduation."

"What?" I questioned. "Is Dad sick or something?"

"No, nothing like that," Mom explained. "Your dad needs to fly home to be with his dog."

"But *you'll* be staying for graduation, won't you?"

"No, dear. I'll be flying home with your father. I hope you understand," Mom said apologetically.

I hung up the phone and sobbed until I realized there was no reason to cry. It had always been about the dogs, so what was my problem? I had grown up with this.

We said our goodbyes, Mom and Dad got on the plane, and Jeremy graduated with honors. And we had a great time anyway.

There are things in every family that one has to either accept or reject. I chose to accept the fact that my dad would never change, and

I had to make a decision to accept his behavior as crazy, but normal for him.

It's been seventeen years since Jeremy's graduation. We have another family reunion coming up and, again, it's all about my father's dog — Charlie — who doesn't like children.

So we've arranged for my other son and his wife and toddler to stay at a nearby hotel. That way Dad won't have to kennel his beloved "Charlie Girl." At eighty-seven, that's out of the question for him.

It will always be about the dogs.

— Connie K. Pombo —

How I Found My Running Partner

Beware of the chair!
~Author Unknown

One morning I started to sweat. Profusely. Just sitting down. I would have attributed it to hot flashes, but I knew those were years away. The accompanying pain in my left arm was what made me ask a neighbor for a ride to the emergency room.

The heart attack was minor in nature, but a major scare. Who knew that a size 2 forty-year-old who ate plenty of veggies, hated junk food, and only ate lean meats would be a candidate for heart problems? After one night of observation in the emergency room I headed home.

My doctor blamed my sedentary lifestyle for my new health problems and told me I needed to get some daily exercise. He said that because I worked at home, I lacked the need to go out, walk around an office building, walk at lunch, run for trains, and all that. I simply walked from my bedroom each morning, headed to the kitchen for coffee, and walked about 35 feet to my office. Sometimes still in my jammies.

He told me to start running. Slowly at first, maybe 50 feet, stop, walk, rest, run another 50 feet. He told me perhaps I could run each day with my husband, an accomplished headstrong runner who could do five miles a day without even breathing hard. I knew for a fact that my husband would never allow me to accompany him and slow him down, but I was ready to promise my doctor anything in order to stop the lecture.

The following day, Karen, the neighbor who had driven me to

the hospital, came over to check on me. I told her I had my marching orders, or rather, my walking orders. Karen knew how much I detested exercising and laughed at my predicament.

Then she said, "I have an idea! Roxy loves to go to the park!" Roxy was her nine-year-old Lab, and we were crazy about each other. I frequently took her for her afternoon walks when Karen was away on business. "With my travel schedule, I can't take her as often as I'd like. Why don't you take her?"

Before I could answer, we heard some barking. Our yards were connected by a two-way gate that Roxy had mastered. As we watched her padding across the lawn and up my back stairs, we were astonished to see that Roxy had somehow managed to find her leash and bring it with her! As she pranced through the kitchen door, she proudly wagged her tail as she dropped the leash at my feet, and extended her paw in a "high five."

"How did you get her to do this?" I asked Karen. The entire episode smelled of conspiracy! Karen, however, couldn't stop laughing and swore up and down she had nothing to do with this!

I picked up the leash and headed out the front door with Roxy in tow. She led me down the block to the park where she promptly took off like a wild bronco! Up, down, around bushes and trees, other dogs, other owners, hills, dales and doggy hydrants. I couldn't even get her to slow down enough so I could take her leash off! And she seemed to know exactly what she was doing. She had this all planned! I finally begged for mercy as I sweated, gulped for air, and headed to the bubbler.

As I walked her home, Roxy was calm and kept glancing over at me with what looked like concern. She would slow down, look up, and when I nodded to say, "I'm fine, girl," she'd pick up the pace a bit.

The following day I had a deadline I was certain I wouldn't meet. Being a freelance writer, this was my life. As I worked diligently, I heard Roxy barking out back. This was nothing unusual — Roxy loved to bark at the neighborhood squirrels and kids coming home from school. But something made me get up this time and go look.

Sure enough — here came Roxy, leash in her mouth, heading up my kitchen stairs! Same time as the day before! I was sure Karen had put her up to it this time, so figuring Karen was hiding in the bushes outside, I called her cell phone, knowing she'd pick up.

"Okay, lady, how on Earth did you train Roxy to do this?"

Karen seemed befuddled. "Huh?"

"The leash thing! She looks so cute sitting here with the leash in her mouth!" I explained.

"She's at your house? Good grief! She must have gone out the doggy door in the basement. I am at the grocery store and she was sleeping when I left!"

I just looked down at Roxy, and I knew. This was her idea. She knew how to help me. And she was doing it.

This routine went on for almost three years. Every day, rain or shine, Roxy showed up with her leash and barked at my kitchen door. I could set my clock by her: 3:00 on the dot, every day.

My doctor was thrilled and I was feeling wonderful. I actually toned up with all this running and chasing and doggy babysitting. I loved spending time with Roxy. It gave me something to look forward to each day.

Even though I wasn't officially "jogging," I was certainly doing my share of running! Maybe without form, but certainly with lots of purpose. Roxy would never let me take off her leash! She seemed to instinctively know I needed to be attached to her in order to get better! Many of our doggy dates ended up with a healthy frozen yogurt at the park, which I lovingly shared with her.

Then one morning my phone rang very early. Caller ID told me it was Karen, and my heart skipped a beat. No one calls at 6:00 with good news.

I picked up the phone and simply said, "What's wrong?"

She was crying. "Can you come over?"

I ran through the backyard in my robe and slippers, not knowing what I'd find. Karen opened her kitchen door for me.

"She's gone. I can't believe it. I tried to wake her for breakfast and she was cold. At least she died in her sleep; she didn't suffer like I thought she might. I didn't want to tell you, but she had a bad heart.

It was a matter of time."

I looked at our beloved Roxy, all curled up in her warm cozy bed, peaceful and quiet — with her leash next to her, ready for our afternoon outing. I couldn't help but think that maybe we managed to keep each other alive a little longer than was meant to be.

That was almost ten years ago. I still run, but this time I have my own Lab, Sally, a gift from my husband.

It's now Sally's job to put me through my paces at the doggy park, and she does a marvelous job. Each day as we walk out the front door, Sally barks once, and wags her tail, looking at the large white urn on the bookshelf. This is where Roxy's ashes are, in loving memory. As I see Sally bark at the urn each day, I can't help but wonder, "Does she know?"

— Marie Duffoo —

60

The Envelope

Rich the treasure, sweet the pleasure.
~John Dryden

My brother Brandon and I had opened all of the packages under the tree. All that was left was an envelope. We knew that envelopes usually contained cards, and if we were lucky they also contained gift cards or cash.

My dad looked almost like he'd forgotten about the envelope as he casually handed it to me. I broke its seal and discovered inside a 3x5 index card with a border of glitter surrounding a poem.

Of course, I don't remember the poem by heart, but its mysterious rhyming message instructed us to go downstairs. We were excited. Maybe we were getting those skis we had wanted.

What we found downstairs was another envelope, containing another index card with a border of glitter surrounding a poem. This poem told us to go to Dad's car. Were the skis already in the car, ready to go?

Nope. There was just another envelope containing another glittery index card. This one told us to go to Mom's office downtown. Neither of us was old enough to drive. This meant we had to implore our parents to hurry up and get dressed and finish drinking their coffee and get going. They took forever.

Eventually, we made it to Mom's office where we found — you guessed it — a glitter-bedecked poem telling us to go somewhere else. This time it was to KATU, the TV station where Dad worked. By now, our curiosity was stretched to the limits of our imaginations. Were we meeting someone famous? Were we going to be on TV? It absolutely didn't make sense to keep skis at the studio — Dad had a desk in an open area shared with the other reporters.

We soon found out, however, that such a desk is a lovely place to keep a 3x5 index card complete with glitter and a poem. The instruction on this poem perplexed us more than any other. It told us to go to an unfamiliar address. Fortunately for us, our parents knew how to get there.

The car stopped in front of the unknown house. It felt like the end of the hunt. My dad handed us the final envelope. The final poem told us to knock on the door and say, "Merry Christmas! Is Humphrey here?"

This is where faith in our parents came in. We didn't know who would answer the door, and we didn't know what a Humphrey was. They shooed us along as they lingered by the car. We peered back to see their smiling faces and built up the courage to knock on the door. As anticipated, a stranger opened. After we recited the greeting, the smiling woman wished us a Merry Christmas and invited us in. We looked to our parents for permission — they were beaming. We were confused. We passed the threshold, and the stranger disappeared down a long hallway. Mom and Dad moved closer to the front door.

While we waited, I examined the room. The yellow, brown and orange couch looked decades old. Across the room, there was a large faded portrait of a well-groomed lap dog. Then I heard a weird sound — like a miniature thunderstorm. And then I saw something coming down the hallway toward us at top speed: a pristine cloud of white fur.

Dad was standing behind us by then. "Merry Christmas," he said. "He's yours." And the woman, who turned out to be a breeder, handed us the puff of fur.

That was the day that Humphrey, a ten-week-old Maltese, became part of our family. It was a gift far surpassing anything I could have imagined — including a set of skis.

— Chelsea Hall —

61

Chicken Soup
for the Soul

Foe or Friend

The only way to have a friend is to be one.
~Ralph Waldo Emerson

As I opened the car door, our new rescue dog Yukon, a Husky/ Shepherd mix, jumped out before I could grab her collar. She ran straight toward our Calico cat Buddy, who arched her back and hissed ferociously.

Yukon tried to stop, but she slid a millimeter too close.

Buddy's front paws flashed forward.

Yukon yelped and jumped backward.

As the days passed, Yukon went out of her way to befriend Buddy. But even though the dog wagged her tail and approached slowly, Buddy's back arched, her tail fluffed, and she growled or spit. The best it got in the next eight years was begrudging tolerance. Buddy seemed to say, "You can live here if you must, but give me a wide berth."

As they aged, Yukon's arthritis made it hard for her to get around. Buddy moved more slowly but kept an eye on the dog. After the cat died, the dog kept right on "smiling" and wagging her tail. Her hobbling got so bad that we thought we might lose her, too. We talked about getting a new kitten.

A few days later, Yukon lay in the center of the pickup seat while my husband went into a friend's house to choose a kitten. He came out with a handful of Calico and sat her down on the seat. The tiny kitten looked around, marched over between Yukon's front paws, sat down, and looked up at the dog as if to say, "Here I am, you lucky dog."

Yukon stiffened. Her eyes got big. She lifted her snout as if trying to avoid the inevitable onslaught. Nothing happened. She turned her head, disbelieving. Then she looked back. The kitten started purring.

At home, the kitten rubbed against Yukon's legs. The dog didn't know what to make of the odd, little creature. But the kitten seemed intent on being friendly. The skinny, little kitten with the flagpole tail and oversized feet just kept loving the big, black, burly dog.

Within a few days, we had figured out that Mischief would be a fitting name for the kitten, and Yukon had figured out that Mischief had come to be her companion. Sometimes, the kitten would walk up to Yukon and swat her nose gently. Soon, Yukon recognized it as an invitation to play and she responded happily. If Mischief slept too long, Yukon would nudge the kitten and start the games herself.

Within a few weeks of Mischief's arrival, Yukon started bouncing around in ways we hadn't seen for two years. Perhaps love and respect had healed her ills. And Mischief earned rich dividends on her deposits of love. The two played together. They napped together. They wandered our three acres together. At night, Yukon curled up in her house. Mischief tucked herself between Yukon's legs, next to her heart.

I marveled at the friendship between the unlikely pair and was saddened about the friendship our earlier cat had missed. Whatever the reasons, she hadn't made room in her life for love, and she was the loser.

Mischief and Yukon's friendship continued to inspire me. One morning when I fed the two in their separate dishes, Mischief ignored her bowl and tramped toward Yukon's.

Uh-oh, I thought. As sweet as Yukon was, she'd whisper a tiny growl if we seemed to threaten her food when she was eating.

Yukon noted movement to her left. She glanced at the approaching Mischief. I could almost see Yukon thinking.

Mischief arrived at the bowl, meowed once at her canine companion, and started eating.

Yukon watched for a moment, and then lowered her head and ate alongside the kitten.

Mischief had gained Yukon's trust by choosing to give love and respect. Together, they reaped happy rewards as friends, not foes. Day in and day out, the big black dog and the little Calico kitten reveled in fearless friendship.

— Helen Heavirland —

62

A Late-Evening Snack

A dog can't think that much about what he is doing;
he just does what feels right.
~Barbara Kingsolver, Animal Dreams

My oldest brother, Dwayne, was a welder. His claim to fame as a welder came from creating an extremely large pie pan. Our community held a Pecan Festival every year. They asked my brother to weld together a pan large enough for their pie to win a spot in the *Guinness World Records* for the largest pecan pie. They won the title and, to my knowledge, it still holds.

Years before welding the pie pan, Dwayne welded a very large smoker. Once finished, he volunteered to smoke the Thanksgiving turkey. "This is going to become a new family tradition," he said. For weeks before the special day, he talked about the perfect temperature, the exact time needed, his use of pecan wood, and his special technique for basting the fowl. We didn't exactly avoid him, but we knew if we were in the same room with him for any length of time, we would have to listen to his "turkey talk."

"I'm smoking the family turkey. I'll cook your turkey, too," he told all his friends. So his buddies brought their turkeys to our house in ice chests. At least six birds were scheduled for smoking. The cooker would barely hold them.

By five o'clock the morning before Thanksgiving, Dwayne had all the birds washed, basted, and cooking on a low heat. "I'll eat out here," he said. "Just put my food on a plate and bring it to the back door." He spent most of the day sitting under the shade tree in his lawn chair, a drink in one hand and his basting brush in the other.

The rest of us prepared everything else. Mom, my sister, and I made pies, cakes, and salads. All we would need to do on Thanksgiving would be to prepare vegetables, reheat the turkey, and make the dinner rolls.

By evening, everyone in the family was bone tired. We decided to go out to eat. "Come eat with us," Dad said to Dwayne.

"I'll go if you can wait a little bit. These birds are perfectly done. Will you guys help me put them on the table to cool? Then I'll take a shower, and we can go eat. When I get back, you can help me load them into ice chests for the guys to pick up in the morning."

So we brought in the perfectly smoked turkeys. Then we went to a local restaurant where we enjoyed a leisurely meal until we realized that we still had turkeys to pack into ice chests before we could go to sleep.

"Look!" exclaimed Mom as we pulled into the driveway. "Larry made it home!"

Sure enough, my younger brother's pickup was parked in front of us. We hadn't known if he'd make it in for Thanksgiving. It had been at least a year since any of us had seen him.

The five of us rushed into the house, Mom leading the way. "Larry, Larry!" she called.

As she walked through the hallway, headed to the kitchen, an enormous Great Dane loped toward her. She stopped, and the rest of us crashed into her, the dog, and each other.

Larry appeared at the top of the staircase. "Hi, guys. I see you've met Sadie. She travels with me to all my jobs. She's a wonderful companion."

"She's certainly big," said Mom as she slid past the dog and continued on toward the kitchen. "I bet she eats a ton."

"She doesn't eat too much. We often share a meal."

The rest of us petted Sadie as we waited for Larry to join us.

"Ohhhh, nooo!!"

Everyone ran toward the kitchen, Sadie included.

My mother stood by the kitchen table, eyes and mouth wide open. Her face was pale. Her finger pointed to the middle of the kitchen floor.

Our little group formed a semi-circle behind her. Sadie sat to the far right, observing everything. Turkey carcasses were strewn around the floor. One lone bird, totally untouched, lay in the center of the table. None of the other birds had survived

Sadie licked her lips, and then looked at Larry with soulful eyes as if to say, "I just needed a little snack."

I'm not sure what Dwayne said to his friends as he delivered thawed turkeys to their house early the next morning for them to cook, but we never heard a bad word from him about Sadie or his brother, Larry. The rest of us chose not to bring up the subject, especially in front of Dwayne, but not a Thanksgiving goes by when we don't think about Sadie and her late-evening snack.

— Rita Durrett —

Natural Therapists

63

Christmas Blues

*Christmas is the spirit of giving without a thought of
getting. It is happiness because we see joy in people.
It is forgetting self and finding time for others.*
~Thomas S. Monson

If you have married children you most likely watch them juggle
parents at Christmas. I call it the "Every Other Holiday Syndrome."
Wife's parents on odd years and husband's family on even years.
Simple — except when unforeseen circumstances found this
unsuspecting mom and pop facing a lonely Christmas for the first
time. We were not looking forward to the holidays.

Okay, we can handle it, we're grown-ups and we understand, we
kept reminding ourselves. Okay, that is, until our Golden Retriever
collapsed under a massive seizure that forced us to say goodbye to
our beloved lady. We were heartsick over the loss of our Nikki. Oh,
dear God, I lamented, what a bummer just before Christmas. I cried
buckets while my husband, Ken, labored to keep his macho image
intact. Finally he let go and it was a dreadful scene.

Just a week later, severe arthritis and profound loneliness for Nikki
rendered our fifteen-year-old Border Collie withdrawn, incontinent,
and unable to walk. The excruciating trip to the veterinarian was
nearly more than we old souls could handle. Ginger had been what
we mountain folks call a "dump-off," and we had gladly adopted this
sweet and loyal herder. Celebration of our Lord's birth took a backseat
to the loss of adored family.

Christmas Eve morning, Ken popped out of bed full of vim and vigor. I, on the other hand, was still caught up in gloom and despair over the loss of our beloved dogs, and slightly miffed at his seemingly hard-nosed attitude. "I'll be back in a while, dear," he shouted on his way out the door, leaving me thinking he probably needed solitude in his grief. The house was deathly still as the rising sun's pink radiance surfaced the top of our mountain. I stood at the window pulling myself together and yearning for the holiday-charged din of impatient grandchildren around me.

At noon Ken returned through our front gate, opened the truck door, and out flew one great tri-colored mass of fur. What on earth! The ten-month-old Keeshond (Dutch barge dog) from the shelter raced through the snow into my outstretched arms. As if we had been bosom buddies forever, we fell over in a joyous heap of emotion, this medium-sized, wiggle-tailed bundle of yips and slurps and I. She had been the sorriest looking pup in the place, her brown eyes pleading, "Please Mister, take me home with you?" Ken was smitten.

Her curly tail dancing a jig atop her back, Keesha snuffled out all the interesting scents about our ranch. The sweet pup rolled and played in the snow, acquainting herself with the kitties, donkeys, ducks and geese. Gratefully, she had no desire to chase, bite, or torment. She was a keeper.

We old fools took our dog to town for a lovely Christmas Eve dinner (Keesha's was in the form of a doggy box), and then to the pet shop for all the right toys and perfect collar. She readily stuck her nose up over silly toys, her passion only to be talked to often, to sit close, to work hard, and to be loved unconditionally. Now that reminds me of just about everyone I know. The thoroughly content tousle-haired pup held down our big feather bed as we watched yuletide services between our toes. Twelve years later she still spends precious time in her place precisely between 10:00 and 11:00 PM, whether we're there or not.

Christmas morning arrived with the children's phone calls, our voices heralding joyful anticipations of the day, and sounds of excited grandchildren ringing across the miles. Instead of hanging around pretending we weren't sadly devoid of human companionship, we grabbed our new pup and headed for our Salvation Army Church headquarters. Captain Miss B welcomed all three of us as I began setting out table decorations and Ken knuckled down peeling spuds. Keesha was so frightened she might be abandoned again, she sat quiet as a mouse in the vestibule eyeing us with trepidation while Miss B's Schnauzer jumped in circles.

More volunteers arrived to help serve ham and turkey dinners to an overflowing dining room, a place where humble families and destitute homeless dined in the shadow of Jesus' house. A place where both Ken and I rose above our Christmas blues in rebirth of our faith, savoring the meaning of the day as never before. That evening we three wearily returned through our front gate to the echoes of waterfowl and heehaws lamenting their belated holiday fare. But it was such a good tired, the kind that firmly commits to memory that sharing and giving is the way of God, our most blessed Christmas ever.

— Kathe Campbell —

When I'm Sixty-Four

Love one another and you will be happy.
It's as simple and as difficult as that.
~Michael Leunig

I am sixty-four, just like in the old Beatles song. And I am in love! It is written that ladies don't find love at this age. Do you realize that the odds for a woman of sixty-four to find a match are about 100 to 1? Is it any wonder that I am giddy as a schoolgirl? I feel as giddy as I did over my first boyfriend, Doug McCoy, when I was fourteen.

Widows my age are doomed to life with a cat. Being allergic to cats, I was doomed to a life alone. But it was not meant to be.

I gave up on men. I'd been married twice. One I ran out and one I wore out. I was widowed for nearly twenty years and quite content. At least that's what I thought. But my friend Norma from square dancing insisted she knew my perfect "mate." When I finally gave in and consented to meet, it was absolutely love at first sight.

I'd always downplayed love at first sight. Even though Dad declared that Mom would be the woman he would marry the first time he laid eyes on her. Did it run in the family? Was I doomed before the first meeting? And why did this happen at sixty-four?

I'm supposed to be an old woman. Yet I feel like I've taken a Fountain of Youth pill. I'm suddenly dressing to kill, or at least to walk out of the house. Exercising! Eating more carrots than chocolate and sharing them with my love. And I am on a high! No drugs are needed! No alcohol, no cigarettes. I'm going to live forever and take care of my new love.

I look across the room at the hairy chest peeking out from the argyle sweater I just bought. Not a word of complaint. I vowed I would never fall for another hairy chest again. God must have laughed at all those times I said "never." He sure did have other plans.

And unlike the Beatles song, "When I'm Sixty-Four," my soul mate has plenty of head hair. No bad comb-over. How could I get this lucky?

And manners. I receive hand kisses that make my knees weak. Who knew the palm of the hand was an erogenous zone? Why wasn't I told? I thought I knew everything I needed to know about life.

Our romantic walks reveal new sights and smells I experience now that I am in love again. It truly doesn't matter where we go. Everything is more exciting when you experience it through the eyes of a lover. We even went to the hardware store to check out a new doorbell and had a fabulous time.

Stingy? No. In fact, the Baptist Church in my neighborhood would be the recipient of several anonymous donations left out front if I hadn't stepped in. After all the Beth Yeshua Messianic is directly across the street, and we do not play favorites.

My family has even come to accept us as a couple. They do, of course, recognize the good breeding and aristocratic demeanor. Our studio portrait is my favorite photo of all.

I believe that men in my age category are looking for Barbie Dolls and eye candy. I'm certainly not qualified in either of those areas. And I admit that sometimes when we are out and about I feel a pang of jealousy when my companion shows interest in someone else. But then, those big brown eyes turn to me with the look of adoration I know so well. That brown mustache can't hide the smile I feel in my heart.

How could I have been so foolish as to think love had died with my late husband? I never knew there was a Yorkie named Lucy that was ready to show me what love at sixty-four was all about.

— Linda Burks Lohman —

65

Mollie and Me

Scratch a dog and you'll find a permanent job.
~Franklin P. Jones

heard the garage door open and knew it wouldn't be long before my husband Paul would come through the door. I dreaded his arrival. Don't get me wrong—I love him dearly, but recently he had started to ask too many questions. He was really getting on my nerves.

"Hi babe, I'm home," came his booming voice. "Where are you?"

"In here," I replied. I was lying on our bed watching the five o'clock news in my pajamas.

"You're still in your pajamas, again? You would feel better if you got dressed."

"Why? I'm not going any place," I replied testily.

He just sighed and started changing his clothes.

"I suppose there isn't any dinner again tonight, either."

"No, it's 'make-your-own' night," I said.

"I thought you said when you retired you were going to make me dinner every night and do all the other things you were dying to do."

"Well, I lied," I said and popped the volume on the television up a notch.

Paul just walked out of the room shaking his head. We weren't fighting but we weren't exactly getting along famously either.

My early retirement had come unexpectedly and although it was due to health issues, they weren't severe enough to warrant staying in pajamas all day. I could still do a lot of things on my "good" days and rest on the "bad" ones.

If this was what people looked forward to their entire lives, they could have it. I was bored out of my skull My father had instilled in me a strong work ethic. Time was to be spent in useful endeavors, not frivolous ways, and I loved being a career woman. All my life I had worked at challenging jobs… for a city councilwoman, CEOs and presidents of Fortune 500 companies. Now I was reduced to a depressed zombie who couldn't even get dressed by dinnertime.

Not that I hadn't tried to pull myself out of this blue funk. I tried shopping as a diversion, but without my discretionary income this was a bad idea. My best friend asked me why I was hiding from her, but truthfully, getting dressed up and doing lunch was just too tiring. I tried reading… I had an entire bookshelf of goodies just waiting to be devoured, but how much can one read? Working in my craft room also took up part of my day. Somehow these activities didn't hold my interest for very long and I would find myself wanting to sleep. I missed the challenge of deadlines, meeting new people, and a sense of accomplishment. Some days I would be as tired when I woke up as when I fell asleep. This wasn't working out the way I planned.

Everyone kept telling me it took time to adjust, that I would be very busy if I gave myself a chance. I didn't want to be just busy; I wanted a purpose. I just hoped it involved something I could do in my pajamas.

Meanwhile, as I searched for meaning in my life again, my husband stepped in and suggested we get a dog. Ever since my beloved dog had died the previous year, I wasn't sure I wanted to experience that heartache again. But Paul was relentless.

The next Wednesday morning he said "Hey, get dressed. Today we're going to the shelter."

"Oh, no… I can't."

"Why not? You going somewhere?" he asked.

"Well, um, I'm not ready for that commitment," I replied.

"Sallie, we're getting a dog, not adopting a baby!" Little did he know. We went to the shelter and returned with a cuddly Beagle-Doxie mix. I named her Mollie, spelled with an "ie" just like my name.

I bounded out of bed the next morning, eager to see what Mollie was up to. I was greeted by doggie kisses and unconditional love. Mollie didn't care that I didn't have a career or that I have health issues. She just needed me.

I began her regime of training. I fed her, bathed her, and started our daily routine of walks. I taught her to catch the ball and bring it to me. Mollie and I were two needy souls who had found each other.

A funny thing happened: my energy returned. The pile of laundry disappeared; my house got cleaned and I tried cooking a couple of homemade meals. I found cooking wasn't really my thing and since my hubby loves to cook, I let that one go.

Instead, I decided to return to my writing and artwork. With Mollie at my feet, I sat at my worktable recently and began to once again design my own greeting cards. Friends came over to meet Mollie and soon we were making lunch plans. My life became meaningful and busy but Mollie and I don't miss a day walking or playing ball. Paul doesn't come home and find me in my pajamas.

I have experienced some losses in the past year — my health, my career, my own income — but I am determined not to look back, only forward.

One recent winter evening Mollie and I took our usual walk. As we crunched the crisp leaves on the sidewalk with each step, I marveled at how my life had turned around since retirement. My heart was full and the stars twinkled as bright as my future. I thought this is how life goes; you just keep putting one foot in front of the other until you reach your destination. Sometimes you need a little help along the way.

I looked down and whispered, "Thank you, Mollie, for coming into my life."

Just then Paul drove by on his way home from work.

"Hi girls! How're you two doing tonight?" he yelled.

I realized who really knew just what I needed. I couldn't wait to get home and thank him.

— Sallie A. Rodman —

66

December Morn

Concentrate on counting your blessings, and you'll
have little time to count anything else.
~Woodrow Kroll

A fresh white blanket of snow draped my favorite pine tree in our front yard. A smattering of snowflakes lingered in the air as daylight began. In the back yard, our Golden Retriever romped in the crisp snow and stopped briefly to let a couple of the flakes tickle her nose.

It was morning, just three weeks before Christmas Day.

I couldn't sleep so I got up early with the dog and took in the serene beauty of the first snowfall of the holiday season.

I stretched the kinks out of my fifty-year-old body, and then I turned on the lights of our two Christmas trees. I admired the beauty of the decorations and the memories they represented. These were memories that my wife, daughter and I had created. On one tree, we had ornaments from our various travels and favorite places. The other tree had a variety of ornaments made by our daughter. The scent of fresh pine lingered on each tree.

Below our neatly decorated fireplace mantel sat a red poinsettia plant. I laughed to myself as I thought that it was already a Christmas miracle that this plant had survived since Thanksgiving. My wife and I have a reputation for killing plants in record time.

I started a pot of coffee and took in the aroma of fresh hazelnut. I peeked out at the dog to see how she was doing. As I glanced outside,

I saw a bright red cardinal land on a pinecone birdfeeder. A streak of sunshine grazed the cardinal and made its red feathers seem even more brilliant. It was a simple snapshot of nature's beauty, and I felt lucky to see it.

I sat waiting for the dog and began thinking of the upcoming weeks and sighed. No gifts had been wrapped; half of them still needed to be purchased. The cookies had not been baked or iced. Christmas cards still needed to be filled out and mailed. Final decorations and planning had to be finished. Work projects would need to be completed before the end of the year. It was all a bit overwhelming.

Thankfully, the dog barked at the back door and helped me erase those thoughts of the upcoming tasks. I let her in, and she sat obediently so I could dry off her paws.

I petted her, and she wagged her tail as if to say thanks. She was ready for her favorite moment of the day. After she was released, she rumbled back to our bedroom to greet my wife and daughter who had snuck into bed with us. The dog jumped onto the bed and licked them both as if to say, "Good morning," and "I love you." From my spot in our bedroom doorway, I watched the proceedings and smiled. It may have been cold outside, but I had a warm feeling on the inside.

The three things I loved most in life were all in one spot. My wife, daughter and dog all seemed content on this early December morning.

In three weeks, it would be a morning of chaos. Wrapping paper would be strewn everywhere. We would be unwrapping and examining gifts, running around trying to decide what to wear to the afternoon gatherings, cooking last-minute dishes and who knows what else. It would be yet another hectic Christmas Day.

As for me, my Christmas gift had come early. Money can't buy gifts like a fresh white blanket of snow, a bright red cardinal or an unexpected quiet moment when I could cherish the memories that our Christmas trees represent. The gifts of unconditional love from my dog and the security of knowing my wife and daughter had slept warmly in their bed and woke up happy on a crisp and beautiful December morning were far better than anything one could find at a store.

Maybe I'm becoming a sentimental fool, but I know what I want for Christmas every year. I don't need the songs or the gifts or the cookies. Well, maybe a couple of cookies… What I really need is a quiet and beautiful December morning — the time when everything is just right and those who are closest to me are there to share my moment. That can always be my Christmas gift — a gift that costs nothing but means everything in the world to me.

— David Warren —

67

Believe in Miracles

Love is the great miracle cure.
~Louise Hay

I know he has arrived before I ever see him. Heads turn in his direction, and if he stops for just a minute, he draws a crowd. He walks through the halls with a swagger that is saved for the truly confident.

His name is Augie. He is a six-year-old Goldendoodle with a strawberry-blond coat that is made for petting, and his manners are impeccable. He is a trained therapy dog who visits patients in the hospital where I work as a dialysis nurse in Fredericksburg, Virginia. I have seen Augie come through the hospital, stopping for anyone who wants to pet him, and I have seen him go into patients' rooms. But I had never witnessed Augie providing the therapy that he was trained to give until I saw him with Mr. M.

Mr. M had been in ICU for many weeks and endured many medical complications. His wife rarely left his side. Family and former colleagues visited, and I quickly learned that, in his younger years, Mr. M had been a force to be reckoned with — if you were intent on breaking the law, that is. Prior to his retirement, Mr. M had worked as a canine police officer and developed strong bonds with his four-legged partners. It was a natural transition when, upon retiring from the police force, he became a trainer for the next generation of fearless police dogs. Sadly, Mr. M had been attending a training program for police dogs when he fell ill.

Although he was awake, and his beautiful green eyes were open, there was little indication that he was aware of his surroundings. Mrs. M was undeterred by the lack of response and kept talking to him while she exercised his arms, hoping he would make some effort to move them himself. I watched Mrs. M work with her husband's hands, opening and closing them. She told him gently that he needed to move his hands so he would not lose the use of them, but he did not seem to be able to do it. He moved his eyes to look at her when she spoke to him, but he didn't, or couldn't, move his head toward her voice. His bright green eyes seemed to shout, *I'm in here! I'm trying!*

Cue Augie. When the handler brought him to the door, it was as though Augie knew he had to make this visit. He sat at the doorway, his eyes fixed on Mr. M until he was invited in. Then he walked over to the bed and plopped down his big head, gently nudging Mr. M's hand. I took Mr. M's hand and placed it on Augie's head as I introduced them. The miracle started unfolding as the connection was made. As Mr. M felt the soft, curly fur under his hand, I could see him straining to move. And then, with fierce determination, he moved his hand ever so slightly. He moved his head, too, to try to look at Augie. It was incredible!

There was no doubt in that moment that Mr. M was not only aware of what was happening, but he was making a huge effort to participate in it. Augie's handler and I looked at each other and spoke the same word: "Powerful!" With tears in my eyes, I looked over at Mrs. M. She didn't look astonished; instead, she looked like she knew all along that this miracle would occur. In that moment, I knew two things: Mr. M was going to recover, and I had been forever changed. To see miracles, I only need to believe in the possibility that they will happen.

—Jacqueline Gray Carrico—

Puppy Therapy

*There is no psychiatrist in the world
like a puppy licking your face.*
~Bernard Williams

loved teaching fourth grade and I loved acting like a kid with the students. I used humor to reach them. Our class mascot was a rubber chicken in pajamas that went everywhere with us. Our days ended out on the playground doing the chicken dance together. Learning was accomplished through participation and teamwork, emphasizing much-needed social skills along the way. The kids loved our unique classroom style, and it worked—they were motivated and enthusiastic.

Then, one year, I was assigned a particularly unreachable student. Jeremy had been born with fetal alcohol syndrome, which probably accounted for his severe learning disabilities. He was impulsive and had no attention span. He also had few social skills and always seemed ready for a fight.

Jeremy didn't smile and he clearly didn't want to be in the classroom. Getting him to lighten up became my goal that year. Oh, sure, I wanted him to read, write and know his math facts. But more than that, I wanted him to experience happiness and excitement about learning.

I modified all his fourth grade work to make it easier for him. I let him take many of the tests orally. He needed encouragement or he would stop trying. I needed to boost his self-confidence.

I tried so many of my usual methods but I wasn't reaching him.

So I set up a conference with his mother. When I told Jeremy, he just shrugged. Then, without making eye contact, he said, "My mom won't come. She never comes to conferences."

"Yes, she will," I said, more confidently than I felt.

"No, she won't," said Jeremy. "Wait and see."

Now this woman *had* to come, if only to show Jeremy that people could change. I added a little note to my conference request. "If you are unable to come, I will be glad to drive over to your house to meet with you there. Just let me know what day and time is good for you."

Lo and behold, I got my conference! In the first five minutes, I understood a lot about Jeremy. His mother turned her back on him while we were talking. She never once looked at him. She did not speak any words of encouragement. She expected the worst.

At other conferences, teachers had told her everything that was wrong with Jeremy. Instead, I told her about the effort he was making and that he was trying. His mother had never had a good conference before. She did not believe in her son.

I realized that Jeremy was on his own as far as his education. He had no homework help. No one checked his planner. So Jeremy's homework became morning work. Each morning, he rode his bike to school early and worked in my class before school.

Yes, he still got in trouble in the cafeteria and in the halls. But while he was in my class, he knew the rules and followed them.

I continued to work with Jeremy on his academics. He had a long road ahead of him and always would. But I had more pressing matters: I still needed to make him smile.

How I tried! I walked beside him in line and told him funny stories, acted pretty silly for a teacher, and even put him in charge of R.C., our rubber chicken. No smile. A permanent scowl wrinkled his brow.

My husband heard about Jeremy every night. We discussed how to get him to lighten up. He needed so much more than I could provide. And I only had until June.

After the winter holiday break, my husband brought our brand-new miniature Dachshund puppy, Maggie, to school to show my students. I talked about her all the time, and the kids were looking forward to meeting her. At the end of the day, George, my husband, was waiting outside our classroom door with Maggie in his arms. The kids could pet her, but not hold her, just in case she wiggled her way out of their arms.

George and Maggie were immediately engulfed in a sea of fourth grade students all wanting to pet her. Maggie was a kisser, so each child was repaid with very wet doggy love. Jeremy stood near the back of the group watching. I took a chance.

I offered to let him hold my beloved puppy. He agreed. I had him sit down, and we placed Maggie in his lap. Of course, within three seconds, she was all over his face and licking it from forehead to chin with her own brand of puppy love.

Jeremy exploded with giggles. The whole class stood and watched, knowing that something out of the ordinary had just happened. Jeremy lay back on the ground and allowed her to lick him all over his face until we took pity on him and pulled her off. No one else asked to hold her; everyone knew it was Jeremy's time. My husband and I were both in tears watching Jeremy get his puppy-love therapy.

Jeremy would be about thirty years old now. I hope he remembers that day as vividly as I do. I don't recall his reading score or his math progress from that year, but I remember the sound of his laughter. I still see the crooked little grin that appeared more frequently with each passing day after Maggie the puppy's visit.

I don't know if I affected Jeremy, but he most definitely affected me. The memories I have of Jeremy embody what teaching is truly about. Teaching is not about test scores and mastery of tons of information. Teaching is all about heart.

— Jeanne Kraus —

69

Silly Me

I think dogs are the most amazing creatures;
they give unconditional love. For me they
are the role model for being alive.
~Gilda Radner

It started with a phone call from my son, Nate. "Mom, there's a
dog here. She needs help. She's lost, hungry and afraid of people.
Nobody can catch her. We tried, but she runs. I bet you can catch
her. Please?" My teenage son's dramatic plea came from a visitor
center where he volunteered.

"Not, now," I objected. I love dogs, but at that moment I did not
want to take on another project.

"Can you please just take a look at her when you come pick me
up?" He had confidence in my abilities.

I agreed, and soon I was looking at a scraggly, mud-covered
mongrel that was resting in the shade of a hundred-year-old oak tree.
Scratching from hordes of fleas, ticks and mange, the dog watched
intently as people came and went from the visitor center. If a person
approached her, she wagged her tail, then tucked it and ran. She was
medium-sized, gold and white, with warm, pleading, caramel-colored
eyes. She wanted to connect but she was afraid.

Many years of working with all kinds of distressed animals had
hardened my heart. I thought of a thousand reasons I could not take
a mangy dog home. I already had three dogs and when one of those
finally trotted over the rainbow bridge, I wanted to get a dog that I

could use as a therapy dog. I could see that this sad dog was not therapy dog material. Therapy dogs connect to people in ways that transcend human understanding. I turned and walked away.

I convinced Nate to wait a few days to see if the dog's owner would magically appear. Secretly, I was expecting the dog would disappear. She didn't.

A friend with a small animal rescue shelter took her for quarantine and treatment. I knew she was safe but the dog's eyes haunted me. That longing look kept returning to my mind, pleading for connection. After a couple of weeks, I succumbed and brought the dog home with me. She was quickly accepted by my "pack." Cleaned up and fed, she resembled a stocky gold and white Border Collie. I named her Leala.

A project she was. For six months, Leala avoided human contact. She was not at all aggressive, but she was terribly afraid to be touched by people. Then suddenly, one day, Nate engaged her in play. It did not take long before she actually wanted to be petted by all the house-humans.

A month or so later, at a routine checkup, the vet said, "This is a really good dog. You do not see many like this." His words opened my eyes to a new possibility.

Leala was kind to everyone, even the vet who stuck her with needles. Leala had quickly become the most well-behaved, sweetest dog I had ever owned. It was a stretch, but I wondered if she could be the therapy dog I had hoped for.

Within another month, Leala and I were in a therapy dog training class. She passed with flying colors. When we started making visits to nursing homes and mental hospitals, it was obvious Leala was one of those dogs that could relate to the internal pain so many people harbor. I do not know how it works but dogs can inspire hope in ways people cannot. I saw Leala do it.

On a visit to a children's group physical therapy session, a non-verbal ten-year-old girl suffering from a degenerative physiological condition had become depressed and refused to use her walker anymore. She insisted on being pushed in a wheelchair. When we first arrived, I avoided the girl as she indicated adamantly that she did not want Leala anywhere near her.

But the girl closely watched Leala as other children in the group took turns "walking the dog." I stood in the middle of the room with one long leash, while the kids held a second shorter leash and walked Leala in circles around me. Everyone, including Leala was having loads of fun.

Finally, the non-walking girl could not resist. She wanted a turn. She took hold of her walker, took the short leash, and away we went. She laughed and did not want to stop. Then she indicated she wanted to walk Leala without using her walker. Walking alone was a physical impossibility for this girl but a compassionate physical therapist walked behind the girl, supporting her under the arms.

Amazingly, the girl got even more adventurous. She indicated she wanted to leave the therapy room. So all four of us set off on a mini-adventure: the supporting therapist, the girl with the short leash, Leala and me with the long leash. We walked through the entire first floor of the hospital, through the lobby and down the halls. We all had a blast. When the girl left that day she was smiling. So was I.

I had my therapy dog. When I first looked into the warm caramel-colored eyes of that fearful, gold and white, flea-bitten dog resting under the tree, I did not dare to hope for an instant that she could be an outstanding therapy dog. Silly me.

—Jane Marie Allen Farmer—

70

Chicken Soup
for the Soul

Tails of a Therapy Dog

Those who loved you and were helped by you will
remember you when forget-me-nots have withered.
Carve your name on hearts, not on marble.
~Charles H. Spurgeon

"Touching Lives, Warming Hearts." That's the motto of the pet therapy group we are privileged to volunteer with, and these words perfectly describe Chester, my lovable, goofy, fluffy, and tenderhearted Golden Retriever.

Countless tales spring to mind when I think of our many pet therapy visits throughout the years — the many people, young and old, who have touched our hearts so deeply. We have visited hospitals, retirement communities, memory loss homes, domestic violence shelters, classrooms and cancer survivor camps, just to name a few. Wherever a caring canine can bring joy and hope, that is where we go. And my heart is forever changed.

This particular story takes place on an ordinary day in an elementary school gymnasium filled with children and teachers. I remember walking into the auditorium with Chester by my side in his bright yellow vest, and feeling the excitement that rocked the room. I delighted hearing the loud whispers — "LOOK, IT'S A DOG!" — as I soaked in the view. A sea of children sat cross-legged on the floor in their classroom groups, circled like wagons, waiting with wiggles of anticipation to meet the star of the day, Chester!

Chester and I were invited by the principal to speak at a school assembly about pet therapy and what makes Chester so dog-gone special that he gets to visit cool places like schools and hospitals and airports! While Chester worked the crowd with his smiles, wags and doggie tricks, I told the students about my furry friend and pet therapy. The students loved hearing our stories, but no doubt about it, the highlight of our time together was the meet and greet with Chester. And as often happens, an ordinary day became extraordinary.

After the talk, Chester and I made our way to each circle of students. We strolled past every single child who wanted a chance to pet the fluffy Golden Retriever. My buddy pranced with a silly grin, tail wagging, ears flopping. He gave out endless love and received a gazillion pats, ear rubs and back scratches. He was in doggie heaven. So were the children.

After a very full morning, Chester and I were in our final assembly of the day with our last group of children. As we moved around the circle, Chester paused. Then he stopped. I gave a little tug on his leash, urging him to move forward. My buddy was not moving. His big old paws were firmly planted on the shiny gymnasium floor in front of a little girl with long brown hair and downcast eyes. Her curls partially covered her face, and her tiny hand gently rested on Chester's head.

"Looks like Chester doesn't want to move," I said, winking at the little girl. I have learned that if Chester speaks, I should pay attention. And so I paused. While waiting for these two brown-eyed sweethearts to have their moment, I noticed a woman standing near. Tears filled her eyes. She looked directly at me, then silently mouthed the words, "Her dog died yesterday."

Sigh.

I leaned in closer to the tenderhearted teacher. She pointed toward Chester, then whispered in my ear, "It's like he knows."

Tears leaked out. "He knows. I don't know how he knows, but he knows." I gently squeezed her hand.

After a bit of time, we continued to move around the circle so the rest of the class could reach out to my four-legged buddy. "Touching Lives and Warming Hearts." It is Chester's specialty.

Because there is always time for one more hug, we strolled around the classroom circle one more time. As we approached Chester's friend again he stopped. This time he gave her a gentle slobbery kiss right on her little cheek. She smiled.

I knelt down, "Looks like Chester has found a friend," I said. "Would you like to give him a hug?"

She nodded, then gently wrapped her slender arms around Chester's fluffy tummy, nestling her head into the soft golden fur of his neck.

With tears, I waited.

—Diane Rima—

71

From Nuisance to Blessing

*A dog is one of the remaining reasons why some people
can be persuaded to go for a walk.*
~O.A. Battista

From the first, I thought of him privately as Natty the Nuisance. My husband had picked up the puppy as a freebie from the Flour Mill, a local feed and hardware store where people bring unwanted litters. He'd been advertised as a Great Pyrenees mix, but he looked more like a Heinz 57 to me.

"Look, isn't he a lively one?"

Ken set the black ball of fur on the floor and our usually aloof adult female Akita bounded over to nuzzle him. She immediately flopped on the floor and rolled over on her back so that he could pounce on her belly and gnaw on her ankle.

"I just know this mutt will be a great companion for her," Ken said. "She's been lonely."

I just stared at the rollicking seven-week-old pup. That's just what I needed… another creature to pick up after and a shaggy one, too. What a nuisance!

Besides the dogs, three cats also shared our house. I liked animals in theory, but Ken had been ailing for years, so feeding, grooming, walking and cleaning up after all of them fell on me.

I muttered through the weeks of mopping up messes until Natty was housebroken. I grumbled until he finally learned to lap water out of a bowl without tipping it over. He sensed I was not his fondest fan, and spent most of his time curled up in Ken's lap. When he got too big for that, he settled for resting his nose on Ken's knee as my ailing husband idled away his days watching reruns of *Gunsmoke* and *Cheyenne*. Whenever I walked into the living room, Natty would cast me a mournful glance, and then bound over to Ken's recliner to snag some petting.

The only time Natty ever came near me was when I ran a comb through our Akita's coat or cuddled a cat. Then he'd scamper over and nose my hand away from the other pet. If I ignored him and continued to groom or caress, he'd whine and whimper, and then poke my hand again, harder. A total nuisance, I'd say to myself, the world's biggest pest.

"I've never seen an animal that craved so much attention," I'd complain.

"Oh, he's just a puppy," Ken would say. "He'll outgrow it."

But he never did. Then last spring my husband died. In the days that followed, Natty's neediness quadrupled. He'd avoided me before, but now he wouldn't let me out of his sight. He'd track me from room to room, and if I settled down to read or to work on the computer, he'd immediately sidle up and start nudging my arm.

I felt sorry for him. Ken had been his constant companion. I know dogs mourn loss just as we humans do. Nonetheless, I didn't appreciate the annoying interruptions. I wondered vaguely if I should find another home for him, one where he could get all the attention he hungered for… maybe a family with children to play with. I had my Akita as a guard dog, so I couldn't figure out what purpose Natty really served.

Nearing his sixth birthday, which should be middle age for a dog of his size, Natty suddenly seemed to be sliding into an early senescence. I noticed that he spent most of his time in the backyard just lazing on the grass, watching the birds and occasionally barking as a truck passed the house. Where he used to shoot back and forth from the patio to the apple tree, now, if he even bothered to get up, he'd plod slowly across the lawn.

Kind of like me, I thought. But I'm well into my seventies and this dog was far too young to have severe arthritis as I do.

When I took Natty in for his annual checkup and shots, the vet didn't pull punches.

"No arthritis. He's pretty healthy. But he's overweight, and should lose around twenty-five pounds. I know it's hard, but see if you can walk him more."

I sighed. I needed to lose twenty-five pounds, too. I'd packed on weight during my husband's decline. In grief, I'd comforted myself with creamy casseroles and carrot cake. And though I lived on a country loop frequented by walkers, joggers and bikers, I found endless excuses to avoid walking that mile-long course myself. It was too hot. It was too cold. I was too tired. I was too old.

Twice daily I'd been taking the leashed Akita for a brief stroll up and down in front of my property, with Natty trotting along beside us. But I hadn't walked the mutt around the loop since his puppyhood.

The next morning I dragged out Natty's old leash. While I snapped it onto his collar he thudded his tail against the front door. At least one of us was excited. I put on my jacket and mittens and the two of us set out.

To my surprise, Natty confidently lead the way, keeping a steady pace, not stopping to sniff at every twig the way his Akita sister does. He marched ahead, tugging me in his wake, not even pausing when neighbor dogs scrambled to the front of their owner's property to growl their territorial rights.

To my surprise, I enjoyed breathing in the scent of lilacs on the fresh spring air, feeling my heart beat a little faster from the mild exercise, even running my fingers through Natty's coarse fur when I reached down to pat him in approval when he heeled rather than strained to chase a passing car.

The next day we did it again. Then again. Soon we settled into a routine. If I grow too engrossed in catching up on my e-mail correspondence, around 10 AM Natty will be at my side, shoving his snout under my arm. Or if I become too distracted by household chores, he'll plant himself by the front door and rumble until I remember it's time for our walk.

Nowadays I see Natty as a blessing rather than a nuisance. Though the Akita remains my bodyguard, my elegant and diligent protector, scruffy Natty has become my personal untrained therapy dog. Together we're striding into shape.

He's nudged me into a new lease on life.

— Terri Elders —

72

Pet Connections

I love these little people, and it is nct a slight thing
when they, who are so fresh from God, love us.
~Charles Dickens

My son Dmitry was six years old when we adopted him, after he'd spent his entire life in a children's home in Russia. It was love at first sight for us. But the first few months here were difficult and stressful for Dmitry, who had to adjust to an entirely new life and a new language. The predictable tantrums and the phrases, "No, I won't and you can't make me!" or, "I didn't did it!" punctuated his initial time here. To complicate matters further, just as life was settling down and Dmitry was beginning to understand that he was truly loved and appreciated, my nine-year-old stepson, Frank, suddenly and unexpectedly came to live with us. Dmitry became distraught at this turn of events. It was only later that we discovered, to our horror, that his immediate worry had been that there was, perhaps, a plan to exchange an unruly child for a better-behaved one.

It was in the midst of all this change and confusion that we decided to add a puppy to the mix. We talked with the boys about how the new puppy would become part of our family and how we should treat and take care of it. My husband and I had always had dogs in our lives and never even remotely considered the possibility that this would present any problems we couldn't easily transcend.

When the big day came, all four of us went to Save-a-Stray. We chose an adorable eight-week-old wriggly black and tan puppy that had just been brought in with its littermates.

The woman at the shelter gave the dog a bath, wrapped her in a towel, and handed her to Dmitry. She sat between the boys in the car on the way home. Our first clue that this dog was not going to be easy came when she shredded the towel by the time we got her home.

The boys named her Maverick, and the name turned out to be appropriate. Maverick had a wild streak and a mind of her own, but she was ours, for better or worse. Unfortunately, in that early time, it turned out mostly to be for worse.

Past experience told me that it was within the normal range of puppy behavior to chew socks and shoes. But when I put the dog in the bedroom for ten minutes so I could talk to someone at the door, I returned to discover she'd chewed my down blanket and had begun stripping the wallpaper off the walls and gnawing at the edges of the carpet! Maverick wasn't malicious, just anxious and high-strung beyond words. She was also affectionate and would, unbidden, sit on your lap and lick your ear all evening. She was, as Dmitry put it, a good dog with bad behavior.

There came a point in time, I shudder to admit, when in desperation, I considered, momentarily, trying to find her a new home. She seemed unmanageable. She jumped on elderly visitors; she ran wildly around the house; she destroyed anything that could be chewed. We tried crate training, but despite our best efforts, she was claustrophobic and shook uncontrollably and howled. We tried doggie obedience school, private training sessions, and discussions with the vet, who prescribed anti-anxiety meds short-term (for her, not me).

But Maverick remained a terror. I was at wit's end. I was trying to manage the needs of two displaced kids, and the dog was receiving the lion's share of my time.

"You can't give her away," my husband said flatly. "The kids will think they're next. They think of her as a member of the family. They have to know we keep members of our family, even when they don't behave." He had a point. In my heart I believed he was right, but I was totally exhausted.

I hung in there, though. I kept my patience, threw away the

destroyed items, and reassured the dog every chance I got. Gradually, her behavior calmed down.

One day, after things had settled down, when Dmitry and I were folding laundry together, Dmitry said, "Well, I guess no matter what Maverick does, she will always stay with us."

"Yes, she will. After all, she's ours."

Then he furrowed his brow. "So you mean there's nothing Maverick could do that would make us send her somewhere else?"

I thought about this for a minute. "Well, if she bit people we would have to do something different. We couldn't allow her to hurt anyone," I said, cautiously.

He nodded in agreement. "Oh, she would never do that. She has a good heart. She doesn't want to hurt us."

"That's true," I said.

A short time after that conversation a friend came to visit Dmitry. As he was showing the other child how to pat Maverick, the dog began running wildly around, grabbing things, and generally misbehaving.

Before I could intervene, Dmitry looked at the other child and said, "You know, you don't have to be perfect to be in our family. You just have to not bite."

— Ellie Porte Parker, Ph.D. —

Feline Friends

The Instigator

The belly rules the mind.
~Spanish Proverb

It started innocently enough when I decided to rescue a cat from our local animal shelter. Even my husband had agreed to the plan. With the kids grown and out of the house, things were a little too quiet. A cat would be a great companion for all of us, including our elderly Schnauzer, Indy, who slept too much and played too little.

As I wandered past rows of cages in the shelter's cat room, I felt a tap on my shoulder. A gray tiger-striped tabby had stretched out a paw from between steel bars to get my attention. I looked at the card attached to his cage. Apparently he'd been in a foster home with dogs. The note went on to say that the animals played together and appeared to get along well. Intrigued, I opened his cage door and the cat leaped into my arms, purring like a motorboat as I stroked his soft fur. Who could say no to that? So I filled out adoption papers and took Bogey home.

The first hurdle we conquered easily. When Bogey met Indy, neither of them raised a hair. They sniffed and eyed each other for about five minutes. With introductions complete, they became as comfortable as two best friends reunited after a long separation. I breathed a sigh of relief.

I knew cats were agile, but soon discovered Bogey combined the energy of a lightning bolt with the dexterity of Houdini. He climbed the drapes to become King of the Curtains, conquered the curio cabinet, and maneuvered himself to the top of the foyer closet. It seemed the cat could do anything. Indy couldn't follow all the places Bogey led, but it soon became clear that years had rolled off my aging dog's life. He bounced around the house as though he were a puppy again, while Bogey sprinted circles around him. It seemed a perfect arrangement until a few strange things began to happen.

I found a chewed water bottle lid on the floor. I must have dropped it, and with Indy's newly rediscovered puppy energy, he'd done the rest. My fault, though it surely seemed that I last saw it sitting on the counter top.

The next day I found a plastic clamp chewed to pieces — then a pencil. How in the world did Indy get hold of all these things? He hadn't been so destructive in years. Then I caught Bogey pawing a rubber eraser from the table to the floor where Indy waited. Apparently the two had become colleagues in crime. As a result, I no longer left things on tables or countertops.

Bogey had other talents. Cabinet doors were a favorite. I watched him stand tall on his hind legs and grab the top of the door with his front paws to pull it open. This activity apparently provided endless amusement. Whenever I'd return home, there would be half a dozen cabinets standing in perfect imitation of open-mouthed amazement.

Not long after Bogey's first birthday, I started a backyard project that required running in and out of the house. After several trips back and forth, I found the sliding glass door open. Both Bogey and Indy were gone. Horrified, I scoured the area until I found the two of them hanging out under the neighbors' deck two doors up the street. I brought the runaways home and shut the door firmly. Bogey scampered straight for it and pawed with the talent of a true cat burglar. Indy watched him with ears pricked forward and tail at stiff attention. In no time at all, Bogey had worked the door open. I now keep it locked.

But soon another issue came along that overshadowed Bogey's behavior. I complained to my husband.

"Our refrigerator is getting too old. The magnet doesn't hold the door tight enough anymore. Please be sure to close it completely. I don't know how many times I've come home lately to find the thing standing wide open."

He looked bewildered.

"I could have sworn I closed it before I left for work today." But like any smart husband he quickly amended the comment. "Yes, dear. I'll be sure to shut it next time."

Only a few days later I found the door open again. This time my blood pressure achieved never-before-seen heights. I touched the top shelf. It felt practically room temperature with the motor chugging loud as a freight train. Worse yet, when I examined the contents for spoilage, I noticed my beautifully prepared salmon dip had been plundered.

I tapped my foot in aggravation. My husband had not only left the door open again, but he had also sneaked a sample of something he shouldn't have. He knew I'd made that dip for a party. When he got home, he'd certainly get an earful from me.

I fumed silently for a while, but soon noticed the house seemed eerily quiet. I crept toward the kitchen and saw Bogey stroll to the refrigerator. Then he nonchalantly flopped on his back and pushed his paws against the refrigerator door's rubber tubing. Only a minute later, it swung open. Indy joined his pal as two noses sniffed the shelf at muzzle height. Bogey went for the salmon dip while Indy lapped leftover ham salad. My eyebrows shot up and I hurried to stop them. Indy backed away, but Bogey didn't budge, emitting a few loud and proud meows. Better than a dead field mouse, this box of delights had evidently become the catch of the day, his crowning achievement. I could only shut the door and shake my head.

Perhaps every Baby Boomer needs excitement, even if it comes in the form of a four-footed juvenile delinquent. Things have certainly changed since Bogey came to live with us. Indy got a friend and regained his youth. I became much more nimble trying to outguess a cat who thankfully does not have opposable thumbs. My husband has someone else to blame for unfortunate household incidents. He describes Bogey quite accurately.

"That cat is like a two-year-old with four-wheel drive."

Meanwhile, until the refrigerator is finally replaced, we keep a chair propped in front of the door. Lucky for us, Bogey hasn't yet learned to move furniture.

—Pat Wahler—

Mandrake

Cats are kindly masters, just so long
as you remember your place.
~Paul Gray

Mandrake was a never a "here kitty, kitty" kind of cat. Black as midnight, it was clear from kittenhood that this cat had channeled more of the wild, dominant genes than those of his more domestic ancestors. He tolerated us as a family. We were, after all, his main source of food. But he made it clear from Day One who was King.

My parents brought Mandrake and a black Lab puppy, Sugar, into our home the day I turned one. We were a formidable trio, but Mandrake established the pecking order early. The wiry, black kitten ruled. Sugar and I gave him a wide berth. This "live and let live" philosophy pretty much governed the rest of Mandrake's existence. A few years later, when my sister and then my brother arrived, Mandrake still ruled. Even my dad held no sway when Mandrake was around.

The first time we realized how fearsome our black cat was, our family had run out to the front yard in response to strange sounds. The neighborhood terror, a large aggressive German Shepherd, was a biter of children and pets. Now he was whining and running out of our yard at a full sprint. We stared in astonishment at the bully's uncharacteristic behavior. Soon we saw the cause.

Mandrake sat crouched on all fours on the Shepherd's back, riding the dog out of our yard. Seeing Mandrake repeat this performance became a monthly ritual. He perched on the fence leading between the front yard and back. When unsuspecting large neighborhood dogs passed by on our property, Mandrake, self-appointed defender of our land, jumped on their backs, dug in his claws and rode them off our land.

Through the years this pattern continued. Mandrake defended our property, purposely walking widely around Sugar and the rest of us, and ignoring us as if we didn't exist. That changed one night. Twelve-year-old Sugar disappeared. She had not been looking her normal spry self. Gray whiskers mingled with the black. Her walking had become labored.

We set off around the neighborhood calling for her. When we looked back, Mandrake was following, twenty feet behind. We walked a good mile before we located Sugar, belly down in a ditch. Her sad eyes looked up as we carried her home. Mandrake followed us, still twenty feet behind. We set up a comfortable bed for Sugar and wrapped her in blankets.

As soon as we closed the door, Mandrake went wild. He scratched. He yowled. He climbed the screen. When we opened the door, Mandrake, the cat that loved no one, climbed in the bed with Sugar. No amount of moving him would make him leave. We put him outside. He yowled and waited until the door opened. Then he headed back to Sugar's bed. For two days, Mandrake refused to leave Sugar's side. He wouldn't leave for food. He didn't leave for water.

The time came when Dad said the end was near. We gathered around our sweet dog. Mandrake left his recent home curled up by Sugar's belly. He walked over to Sugar, lay down by her head, and placed his nose on hers. Mandrake gently rubbed his nose on Sugar's as she closed her eyes for the last time.

Mandrake was old and fierce and independent. After Sugar died, we got a new dog, Rocky. Mandrake went back to his old ways, riding neighborhood dogs out of our yard, ignoring us and our new dog. Anyone watching him would have said he didn't care.

We all knew better.

— Julie Reece-DeMarco —

Cats Are Excellent Dog Trainers

The family is one of nature's masterpieces.
~George Santayana

My three children, ages two, three and five, had just finished breakfast and made a run for outside when I heard them exclaiming over something on the front porch. When I went to investigate I was greeted with cries of, "Can we keep him? Please, please!" The "him" was a small, brown puppy about the size of a croquet ball that was shivering and crying in the corner of the porch.

Before I could make a judgment call, our mama cat Mits and her five kittens arrived on the scene. Mits examined the pup from one end to the other, looked back at me, and took the pup away with her kittens, who were approximately the same age. From then on Norton was part of her family.

We operated a bird-dog training kennel at that time and Norton was the only dog that was allowed to run loose in the yard. His constant companions were Mits and her kittens. One of the males, Oscar, became his particular buddy.

Mits took her maternal duties very seriously and decided Norton needed a lot of training to meet the standard she had set for her kittens. At that time she had the litter Norton's age and four almost grown kittens from a previous litter. When Norton was about three months old I noticed Mits and the kittens had formed a circle in the yard with Norton in the center. When I went to investigate I discovered he wasn't alone. There was a field rat in the circle also. As the rat would try to escape the cats would turn it back towards Norton. When he got the message and killed the rat, all of the cats got up and went on about their business. Lesson learned.

As they got older, Norton and Oscar spent more and more time together. We had a row of multiflora roses, a vine used to stop erosion in open fields, running across part of the pasture. Norton was sleeping on the porch when Oscar began to summon him loudly. I followed Norton as he headed for the barn. Oscar was waiting at the end of that row. As soon as Norton arrived they stood facing each other, noses just inches apart and apparently decided on their method of attack. They then got on opposite sides of the line of bushes and began systematically working the cover, hunting rats.

On cold days, a pile of cats would appear on the porch. If you looked closely, Norton would be at the bottom of the pile keeping their feet warm while they provided a warm place for him to sleep.

Over the eighteen years he lived, he never developed a friendship with another dog, but every cat we had considered him a very close relative. Over and over, especially when he was still a pup, I would see a cat correct him if he didn't follow correct cat procedure in a situation. Mits oversaw his training for the first three years, and as cats came and went, others imparted their knowledge.

I'm sure you've heard the old adage, "You can't train a cat," but Mits and her descendants proved a cat can do a very good job of training a pup.

— Charlotte Blood Smith —

Mother's Helper

*Fun fact: Polydactyl cats, most commonly found in
eastern North America and the UK, have up to
eight toes on each paw versus five on front
paws and four on hind paws.*

Kiki the cat only had to yowl once for me to know the kittens must be on their way. Missy, my Border Collie-Greyhound mix, followed us into the tiny, downstairs bathroom where I'd prepared a box for the blessed event. Being Kiki's first litter, I expected her to be nervous. What I didn't expect was Missy's furious whining and tail wagging.

When the kittens finally started coming, the dog calmed down. Missy and I just sat there marveling at the miracle of birth. The dog appeared mesmerized by the six tiny fur balls. And her fascination didn't end there.

The following morning I awoke to something warm and sticky on my neck. Missy had brought the kittens upstairs to me. Kiki hovered nearby, but didn't seem to object. That wasn't the last time Missy transferred the kittens to my bed. She wouldn't leave those babies alone! And, of course, she always snatched them up when I wasn't looking. "Bad dog!" I kept saying. But she didn't care.

When the kittens were a little older, all six of them, Kiki, Missy, my husband and I sloshed around on our waterbed every night. During the day, Missy continued carrying the kittens around by the nape of the neck, often hiding them behind the couch. Sometimes she'd deposit them near the sliding doors in the sun so they'd be warm and cozy. And, of course, she kept placing them on the bed for the afternoon nap she took with them.

Then Missy did the unthinkable. She stretched out on the living room carpet more than once, and then nosed the kittens into her belly. She made believe they were nursing! She did this time and again, always panting as if nursing was hard work. Apparently, Missy felt the kittens belonged to her. And they might as well have! She continuously snatched them from their bewildered mom. We sometimes feared she might hurt them, but she never did.

Missy was a loving dog in other ways too. She was a real nurturer, tuned in emotionally to anyone around her. A grief group convened at my home regularly and Missy got to know the women well. Once, when one of them burst into tears, Missy quickly reached her side, and licked her tears away. She then put her head in the woman's lap.

Eventually, we found homes for all but one kitten, Missy's favorite, whose name was Paws. He was a polydactyl like his mother. Missy continued to carry Paws around in her mouth even as he grew larger.

When Paws disappeared, we looked everywhere. During the first few days of his absence, Missy whined and spent her time in the tiny, downstairs bathroom where she'd watched Paws come into the world. But when he didn't turn up, she eventually dealt with her grief and re-directed her efforts toward terrorizing Kiki.

We never had more kittens, but sometimes I asked my husband, "Do you think we should let Missy have her own litter?"

"No. I think this was her first and last mothering experience!" was his response.

And so it was. But it endeared her that much more to me.

— Jill Davis —

77

A Special Independence Day

Who would believe such pleasure
from a wee ball o' fur?
~Irish Saying

My kids cheered as soon as they woke up on the Fourth of July. "It's Fireworks Day! How soon can we go downtown to watch them?"

"Guys, it's 7:00 a.m.," I said. "It has to be dark to watch fireworks."

"We have to wait all day?" They groaned. "This is going to be the slowest day in history."

"No, it won't. We'll have fun, and it will be time to go before you know it. Let's start by eating breakfast."

I made the kids' favorite breakfast: chocolate-chip pancakes. After we ate, I told each of the kids to pick four things they wanted to do to help pass the time until we could leave to watch the fireworks.

Jordan decided that he wanted to watch his favorite movie, play Battleship, and build with his Legos. "And for my fourth thing, I want to play with the dogs and Tigger," he said.

Julia also chose to watch a movie, play a game, and hang out with our pets. "And I want to bake cookies," she said.

Our day was filling up with fun activities that would pass the time until dark.

We settled in to watch the kids' movie choices, each with a pet on our laps. Then we had lunch and played some games.

"Can we bake the cookies now?" Julia asked.

I gathered the ingredients and showed Julia which ones to mix into the bowl. Tigger, our black cat, jumped onto the counter to watch.

"Sorry, Tig," Julia told him. "Cats can't eat chocolate-chip cookies." She looked down at the dogs — a Beagle and a Poodle mix — on the floor. "Dogs can't either."

Soon, the batter was mixed, spooned onto cookie sheets, and put into the oven.

"I can't wait to eat a million cookies," Jordan said.

"You can have two cookies," I told him.

"Two?" he whined and folded his arms.

"Two for now, Bud," I said firmly. "You can eat another one after we have dinner."

When the timer went off, I pulled the cookies from the oven and set them on the cooling racks.

"Let's play *Candy Land* while we're waiting for the cookies to be cool enough to eat," I suggested to Julia.

She nodded, and we headed upstairs to play.

An hour later, Jordan came upstairs, holding his stomach. "My tummy hurts," he groaned.

I sighed, already suspecting the cause. "Did you eat more than two cookies?"

He nodded.

"How many more?"

"A few."

But when I looked at the cooling racks, I estimated that he'd eaten half a dozen cookies. No wonder his stomach hurt.

Hours went by, and things only got worse. The stomachache turned to vomiting.

"Are we still going to go watch the fireworks?" Julia asked.

Sadly, I shook my head. "We can't go. Your brother is too sick."

"It's his fault he's sick. It's not fair that I have to miss the fireworks because he didn't follow the rules."

I rubbed her back. "You're right, honey. It's not fair. But your dad is out of town, so there's nothing I can do about it."

I got Jordan settled in his room with a blanket and a bucket, just in case.

Later, Julia and I ate her favorite dinner, but the yummy food didn't soften the sting of missing the fireworks.

When it got dark, we began to hear the loud booms of our town's fireworks display. Immediately, both of our dogs ran under the desk and huddled together. I could see them trembling.

"I'm sorry, boys," I said to them. "I know the Fourth of July isn't your favorite night."

"How come?" Julia asked. "Don't they like fireworks?"

I shook my head. "Beamer and Mugsy are afraid of fireworks. The noise scares them."

Julia's attention moved from the dogs hiding under the desk to the cat lying calmly on top of it. "Do cats like fireworks?"

"I don't know about all cats, but Tigger doesn't mind them."

Julia stroked the cat's head. "You're braver than the dogs," she told him.

We heard another boom from the fireworks. Tigger stretched his back legs and glanced at his canine friends under the desk. He was definitely enjoying being the brave one.

Julia and I sat on the couch. I rubbed her back and apologized again for her missing the fireworks.

She shrugged. "It's okay. Dad said we were going to a baseball game this weekend. There's always fireworks at the games."

"Thank you for understanding," I said, still rubbing her back.

Tigger jumped down off the desk and went underneath it where the dogs were.

"Oh, no! Tigger is afraid now, too," Julia said. "He's going to hide under the desk with Beamer and Mugsy."

Tigger snuggled down between the dogs. Slowly, he smoothed his paw down Mugsy's back. Then he did the same thing to Beamer.

"He's petting them, Mom!" Julia said. "He knows they're scared, and he's making them feel better."

"I think Tigger saw me rubbing your back, and we always rub his back, so he must've realized that would comfort the dogs."

Julia and I sat on the couch, listening to the fireworks, and watching our cat pet our dogs.

"This is way better than fireworks," Julia said. "Everyone has seen those. But how many people have seen a cat rub a dog's back?"

I smiled. "How many people have seen a cat rub two dogs' backs?"

As we watched, I noticed the dogs' trembling had lessened. Tigger's back rubs were visibly calming them.

When the loud noises ended, Tigger and the dogs came out from under the desk as though nothing unique or special had happened.

But Julia and I knew we'd never forget it.

That Independence Day, Tigger was not only brave, but he was kind when he didn't have to be.

And kindness is always worth remembering.

— Diane Stark —

78

Hide and Seek

I have studied many philosophers and many cats.
The wisdom of cats is infinitely superior.
~Hippolyte Taine

He had been found wandering, weak and hungry, when he was rescued. Given his penchant for drinking from the water faucet, I suspect that's how he managed to survive. The vet estimated that this beautiful, mink-colored Siamese was just shy of a year old.

The staff of the Humane Society that took him in named him DC, short for "Darn Cat." I met DC when I took my two Cockapoos to be groomed at the Humane Society, an event they always dreaded, as evidenced by their trembling and crying. When I picked them up that afternoon, the groomer pointed to DC and told me how the cat had jumped onto the groomer's table and sat calmly with each dog as it was groomed, easing its fears and forming a heartwarming bond. Since DC was about to be put up for adoption, I jumped at the chance. My dogs obviously loved him, and his personality stole my heart. He quickly bonded with me and my husband acting as though he had known us all his life.

Often we would find him hiding under a throw rug or cuddled into the back of a recliner. If not playing hide-and-seek, he and the dogs would take turns chasing each other through the house, up and down the stairs, and in a circle from the kitchen to the living room, to the dining room and back to the kitchen. They loved to cuddle together for naps and they became inseparable friends.

One day became forever etched in my memory. It was especially hectic as I tried to get the house straightened up, furniture dusted, supper planned, dishes put away, and laundry done. I transferred the first load of wash into the dryer and placed a second load in the washer. The family room was in need of a good vacuuming, so I lugged the vacuum out of the hall closet and down to the family room, plugged it in and moved some items out of the way. Just as I was about to turn it on, I heard a strange soft thump, then several more muted thumps, evenly spaced, several seconds apart. I knew I hadn't put any sneakers in the dryer, so what might it be?

Suddenly, I knew. I raced to the dryer and frantically started pulling out wet towels. As I had feared, there was DC, buried in towels. He was hot, dizzy, and smelled of wet fur. Apparently, he thought the dryer would be a great hiding place, and he had jumped in unnoticed.

I carried him to the next room and carefully placed him on the floor. He rested on his side, panting heavily. The dogs rushed to his side, licking him and whining softly. He seemed to feel the love and responded meekly with a little meow. No doubt he was sore from the tumbling he had endured, but apparently the towels had cushioned him, protecting him against broken bones and internal injuries.

The dogs and I sat next to him, gently soothing him with soft touches and encouraging words. After about ten minutes, his breathing slowed, and he sat up cautiously. He tried to take a few staggering steps, but vertigo got the better of him. He lay back down and willingly drank some water from a syringe.

As he relaxed, I folded some laundry and carried it up to my bedroom. I debated with myself about taking him to the vet or giving him a while longer to recuperate. After a few minutes, DC climbed the stairs, joined me in the bedroom, and jumped up on the bed as though nothing had happened. With a sigh of relief, I knew he was going to be okay. The dogs followed behind him and settled down on the floor next to the bed as though vowing never to let him out of their sight.

Thankfully, DC never used the dryer as a hiding place again, but I never turned it on after that without checking first to be sure he was safe.

We enjoyed twelve more years with DC until he passed quietly in his sleep. Our lives were made much richer for the love and antics of this little character. That adorable "Darn Cat" will live forever in our hearts.

— Marti Robards —

79

War and Peace

Meow means "woof" in cat.
~George Carlin

A tough, tiger-striped tabby, Bogey isn't the sort of cat who takes to strangers. He never runs away or hides like most cats do when alarmed. Bogey's behavior is far more dog-like. He heads straight to the front door, determined to sniff out the facts on whether the person who rang the bell is friend or foe.

Given his personality, I worried about what would happen when I brought home a rescue pup named Winston. Would Bogey hiss and swipe at his new housemate? Determined to make the situation work, I introduced them slowly. Bogey eyed Winston with a wary gaze, his tail straight up and his hair puffed out so far that he looked enormous. Winston's tail wagged to a blur, and he dropped into play bow position, clearly showing he wanted to be friends. But Bogey glared at him with disdain and stalked away, not a bit interested in a canine companion.

This went on for days, with the addition of deep feline growls whenever Winston got too close. I sighed. Not only were my cat and dog apparently not destined to be chums, but Bogey had declared war. The best I could hope for would be tolerance. Even when feeding them, I kept their bowls a room's length apart. It wouldn't help matters to have either animal treading near the other's food.

A few weeks after Winston's arrival, I was preparing their dinners when the doorbell rang. I plopped the bowls on the floor and scurried to answer the door. Neither of them followed me. When it came to a choice between food or checking out a stranger, they agreed on one thing: Food came first.

After I signed for the package, I realized I hadn't separated the food bowls! I raced for the kitchen. There I found them finishing up their meal while giving each other the side-eye. Fearing a potential conflict was brewing, I stepped to the area where both bowls sat empty on the floor. My cat stayed still as a statue while Winston inched toward him… and then slurped his face. I held my breath, prepared to intervene, but nothing happened. No puffball of fur. No hissing. No swipe of the paw.

From that day forward, things changed. I caught Bogey and Winston lying side by side on the sofa. Some days they'd chase each other — for all the world like a couple of dogs playing tag. They delighted in wrestling their way across the carpet, obviously having a wonderful time. I'd never seen anything like it between a cat and a dog.

The kicker came on the day my son stopped by. He played with Winston by holding a toy just out of reach while Winston jumped for it, barking loudly. Soon, Bogey came on the run. He hissed at my son, apparently thinking Winston was getting a raw deal. Amused, my son let Winston have his toy. This settled Bogey down, who then leaped to a tabletop where he kept a watchful eye on the proceedings.

My cat had transformed from enemy to protector in a swift détente. I never would have guessed at such an outcome.

"You two are a pair," I told them after I stopped laughing.

Who knows? Maybe world peace is possible after all.

— Pat Wahler —

80

Perfect Love

*Some people say man is the most dangerous animal
on the planet. Obviously those people
have never met an angry cat.*
~Lillian Johnson

I was sitting in my veterinarian's office when a young family rushed in. The father held a bundle of blood-soaked towels in his arms. He was followed by a young boy carrying the largest, fattest, yellow-striped tomcat I'd ever seen draped across his shoulder and crying as if his little heart was completely broken. The mother held the door and followed up the rear, comforting the sobbing boy. The cat simply viewed everyone with disinterest and remained as calm as a rag doll, lying across the boy's shoulder.

A medical team hustled the man and his precious bundle into the examining rooms. As the mother, boy and cat settled in on the seats in the waiting room, I couldn't help but ask what this was all about. I assumed that the pet in the bloody towels, a dog or another cat, must have been hit by a car. What unfolded was one of the most bizarre and yet heartwarming stories I had ever heard.

The cat, named Tom, was the first family pet, now an old codger of twelve years. They had rescued him as an abandoned kitten. He was a typical tomcat, aloof, self-centered, and quite independent, but very gentle. He had grudgingly acknowledged the birth of their son and finally accepted the little boy's pokings and proddings as the child grew. Although he accepted everyone in the family—on his own terms, of course — Tom was not overly affectionate, and definitely not a "lap cat." He wanted a good meal and a pat now and then, but preferred to be left alone to bask in the sun on his favorite windowsill.

Then, a year before this incident, a pup came into the picture. A gift from the maternal grandparents, Scotty was a West Highland White Terrier of noble bloodlines. The family was at first fearful about how Tom would accept the newcomer, but a strange thing happened. The old cat took to the pup as if he were a long lost little brother. He absolutely adored the little guy. He allowed the pup to chew his tail. He played for hours with him as if the dog were his own personal pet. When the boy was playing with Scotty, and Tom felt he was getting too rough, he would slip his huge yellow body between them and gently swat at the boy as if to say, "Okay. Enough is enough."

The family told everyone, took videos of the pair together, and marveled at the way the old cat and young dog bonded.

The family lived in a new housing tract in an upscale area near the hills in the west San Fernando Valley. We had experienced a fairly wet winter in Southern California that year, which meant that both the fauna and flora was overabundant that summer. We get used to the opossums and raccoons turning trash cans, and make sure to bring in all pet food and clean up fruit dropped from trees to slow down the critters a bit. The biggest problem is coyotes who stalk the populated areas at night, searching for cats and other small pets that make easy meals.

Tom and Scotty were kept in at night and even though their yard had a six-foot brick wall around it, the family often heard the predators scrabbling at the trash cans on the outside of the fence. Nobody ever thought there would be a problem in the daylight, however.

That Sunday afternoon, the family had returned from church and let Scotty out into the yard to romp. Suddenly, the air was filled with barking, then snarls and finally screams of pain. The family rushed to the sliding glass doors in time to see a coyote with Scotty in his jaws. The small white dog was fighting bravely but the coyote had the definite advantage.

The father grabbed a nearby chair and rushed out the door just in time to see a blazing flash of yellow fly past his head. Tom, seeing "his" pet in the jaws of the coyote, had leaped from the upper bedroom balcony and onto the coyote's head. Screaming and spitting, with claws flying like a buzz saw, the old tom lit into the beast, shocking him enough so that he dropped the little dog.

The father followed suit, swinging the chair at the coyote, who immediately decided that the meal wasn't worth losing an eye to an insane cat or getting thrashed by a wild man, and leapt back over the six-foot wall as if it weren't even there.

Scotty lay in a bloody heap, with Tom meowing and licking him gently. The little dog was still breathing. The mother ran out and wrapped him in a towel and they rushed to the vet's office.

Now we waited for news. The cat watched all of us as if he knew there was nothing to worry about, and he was right. Soon the father came out and told us that Scotty was going to be fine. He had been chewed up, but had no broken bones or internal damage. After some stitches, antibiotics, and one night in the hospital just for observation, he would be fine and could go home.

When the family started to leave, the cat squirmed from the boy's arms and ran back to the door that led to the inner examination room area. He meowed loudly and rubbed back and forth against the door. The family and an orderly tried several times to get the cat into a box to carry him out, but he hissed and spat at them.

Finally, one of the doctors came out and said that Tom could stay with Scotty in a divided cage overnight. They could not let him in the same cage as the dog for sanitation reasons, but they could put them in side by side recovery cages where they could see each other. When the door was opened the cat literally dashed into the back kennels.

I went out to my car, my heart feeling lighter than it had in a long time. I never saw the family, Scotty, or Tom again, but I will never forget their story and the most dramatic example I had ever heard of "perfect love casting out fear."

— Joyce Laird —

Calvin's Best Friend

When a cat chooses to be friendly, it's a big deal
because a cat is picky.
~Mike Deupree

Calvin walked into the family room and stopped, lifted up his nose and sniffed. His tail twitched. Something smelled different.

On the couch lay my dog Tucker, his head encircled by a plastic veterinary cone large enough to pick up signals from space. He had just come home from the vet, where he had been treated for a split toenail. The sensitive quick was exposed — a very painful condition, particularly in the middle of winter when below-freezing temperatures exacerbated his discomfort. Tucker would lick his wound incessantly and thus had to wear the dreaded Cone of Shame.

Calvin must have noticed the unfamiliar scent of the dog's injury and perhaps the aroma of vet that clung to his scruffy fur. He approached Tucker slowly, his body stretched and low to the ground. The dog opened his eyes and barely seemed to register the kitty's approach. Emboldened, Calvin crept closer and then leapt up onto the couch. He padded softly over to Tucker and cautiously sniffed the edge of the cone.

Tucker sighed, repositioned himself, and closed his eyes, which was a bit unusual considering his shaky relationship with our four cats. Tucker loved to snuggle real close with my other two dogs, as well as the humans who inhabit our home, but he was a bit wary of the kitties. If any of his feline housemates walked into our bedroom, the dog would purposefully get up from his preferred spot on our bed, jump to the floor and army-crawl his way underneath, squeezing himself into the darkness and away from the cats.

If I were to guess, this precaution was related to the Ambush the Dog game our Tortie cat Athena played when the mood struck her. Positioning herself on the corner of the family-room coffee table, she would wait for Tucker to walk by on his way to drop a slobbery ball in one of the humans' laps; the dog was a bit ball obsessed. If he got close enough, the cat would deliver a formidable hiss/swat combination, teaching Tucker to be wary of the resident cats.

The cats also learned to give Tucker a wide berth. He was an effervescent presence in our house, always in motion: nosy, loud and bouncy. When he ran after his ball inside the house, he didn't stop to see if there was a cat in the way, which sometimes resulted in near collisions and puffed-up, indignant kitties muttering about the rudeness of Terriers.

So, for the most part, while cats and dogs lived together in our home, they left each other alone.

But a coned Tucker was a chastened Tucker. A sad Tucker. A quiet Tucker.

Up on the couch, Calvin stretched out his neck further, curving his head around the cone's edge. The movement was so subtle that the dog didn't seem to notice. Calvin leaned in and gently inspected the dog's eyebrows, nose and mouth.

I stood close by, just a tad concerned that Tucker might be a little unnerved at a cat in his space — about as in his space as one can get. Being restricted by a cone was bad enough, but to have someone — in particular, a feline someone — stick his face in there with him? Even a calm, accepting dog might have had an issue with that, let alone a pup who looked at cats and saw the sharp and pointy bits instead of the warm and furry ones.

But Calvin moved slowly, deliberately, ever so gentle. Then he slid out his bubblegum-pink tongue and gave Tucker's head a lick. Tucker opened his eyes again — and then closed them with a sigh. This was the permission Calvin was looking for, and he began grooming Tucker's head — inside the cone — in earnest.

It was a sweet moment between two individuals — of different species — who had mostly avoided each other until then.

And that moment changed things between Calvin and Tucker. The dog recovered, and within a week or so, the cone came off. While the other cats maintained their distance, Calvin would seek out Tucker. At first, Tucker was a bit suspicious, not quite sure whether to trust this particular cat. But Calvin worked his charms on the dog. He'd lie next to him, then inch a little closer, and then lay his head on Tucker's paw. The dog's eyes would widen at first and then soften as Calvin's purrs of contentment breached the language barrier between canine and feline.

When I opened the door to our bedroom in the mornings, Calvin would march in, meowing his greeting and looking for Tucker. Sometimes, Tucker would leap up onto the bed, and Calvin would read his body language and intention so fast that he'd jump up, too, with both dog and cat landing at the same time.

Now Tucker stayed on the bed instead of hiding underneath. And Calvin would parade around him, purring and rubbing him, and eventually snuggling up next to him. He was respectful of the dog, understanding intuitively that there were certain lines he shouldn't cross — like climbing on Tucker's back. But often I'd see Calvin put his small paw on top of the dog's foot or sometimes lay his head on Tucker's leg.

Being a ball-chasing, squirrel/chipmunk/groundhog-hunting, non-stop Terrier, Tucker wound up getting injured and had to wear a cone multiple times during his life. We all learned to give him a wide berth when he was coned since it didn't always prevent him from being his bouncy, in-your-face self. He was not quite aware of the width of the cone, which meant we humans would often get startled by a jab in our calves. Calvin's sibling, Elsa Clair, would skitter out of his way when she saw a coned Tucker coming, possibly afraid she'd be scooped up by the huge plastic collar.

But Calvin loved his friend, no matter what he was wearing. And every time Tucker was sentenced to the cone, Calvin would find a way to show he cared. He'd seek out Tucker to lie next to him, keeping him company. He'd purr at him and groom him.

The two had a special relationship that grew throughout Tucker's life. Calvin stood by him as the dog battled an aggressive cancer and offered comfort to his companion right up until the end. After Tucker died, Calvin found ways to connect with my other two dogs, and they now let him rub them, but it's not quite the same. I know my cat still misses his buddy and holds a special place in his heart for the Terrier who became his friend.

— Susan C. Willett —

82

Big Bang Bailey

Most of us rather like our cats to have a streak
of wickedness. I should not feel quite easy
in the company of any cat that walked
about the house with a saintly expression.
~Beverly Nichols

Little did my fiancé, Rich, know that when he agreed to take home a cute little abused and abandoned kitten that he was really getting a lot more than he bargained for. Our running, jumping, climbing trees cat, Bailey, had a personality the size of a Great Dane and the attitude to match.

There were no problems at first, other than the typical antics of living with a kitten. He liked to climb, and therefore was on the counters, tables, couches, the CD tower, etc. Once he knocked over the CD tower while attempting to jump from it onto the top of the wall unit. Down crashed five hundred of Rich's over-a-thousand-strong music collection, waking us up from a dead sleep on Saturday morning. I thought Bailey was history. Luckily for him, no CDs were harmed in the execution of this feat. He had character and no trick was too great for him. He was a blast, and he made our first house a home.

Remember when I said he had the personality of a Great Dane? He had the voice of one, too. On our first Halloween as a family, the neighborhood kids started to arrive and ring the doorbell as is customary. On the first chime of the doorbell, Bailey ran for the door and began barking. Rich looked at me, and I looked at him, and in unison we asked: "Did Bailey just bark?" Yes, it seemed that our lovable little man didn't want to run and hide like most cats; he wanted to greet the costumed kids as much as we did.

His voice was never too far away. Bailey would have a running commentary as he walked around the house, as if informing us of the current situation. If we were in another room and he wanted us to come out, he would cry out in a tone of voice that sounded as if he were saying "Helloooo?" and wondering where we were.

However, as Bailey grew into adulthood, he began having crazy tirades where his pupils would dilate, his hair would stand up, and he would run spastically around the house crying and talking more than usual. I thought they were normal occurrences, and we knew that during these episodes we couldn't touch him and just had to let him be. But out of these spells came an increased aggressiveness towards Rich. At first I didn't see it. Since I was the one who found him, we bonded instantly. Rich, on the other hand, was the "other man," or so Bailey thought.

One morning, as Rich was getting ready for work and I was in the kitchen preparing breakfast, I heard a loud crash, boom, and a very loud scream. Wondering if Rich was okay, I called out and ran into the bedroom to see what happened. There was my fiancé, fresh out of the shower and looking rather perturbed. He informed me that "my" cat had tripped him.

"Don't be ridiculous," I told him. "Bailey can't trip you."

"Yes," he assured me, "he did." He was coming around the corner of the bed and Bailey stuck out his little beige-and-white paw and tripped him. He fell into the nightstand on the way to his final destination, the wall. Trying not to laugh, I suggested Bailey was probably trying to crawl out from under the bed at the same time Rich was walking by. Rich thought otherwise.

A while later, Rich told me that Bailey also tried to scare him by jumping out from behind walls, furniture, and other hiding places. I thought the game was cute and told Rich that Bailey was just trying to bond. Again, Rich felt otherwise. Several days later, Rich called me into the family room. Having spotted Bailey coyly hiding around the corner of the recliner, he decided this would be an opportune time to demonstrate Bailey's evil ways. Sure enough, as Rich approached the end of the chair, Bailey jumped out, standing on his hind legs, and began boxing like a kangaroo. It was adorable, but, I had to admit Rich was right; Bailey was acting overly aggressive toward him. It wasn't that Bailey completely despised Rich — he would knead Rich, and he slept on Rich's side of the bed. However, when Bailey got annoyed or agitated, Rich bore the brunt of it.

Bailey's episodes became more regular and I began experiencing some of his aggression as well. I began to wonder if something was really wrong. I dreaded the thought of having to give him up. I decided that was not an option. He was a family member and we would work through this. The vet suggested behavior modification classes, but that seemed ridiculous and it was out of our price range. I sought a second opinion. It turns out that Bailey's behavior was common and occurs in cats that are weaned too early or abandoned. Anti-anxiety drugs usually help. Relieved I went home and told Rich the good news.

"Great!" he replied. "Now we have to pay for drugs for the cat too."

The drugs worked, and although it was a bit tedious to give Bailey the liquid cocktail each morning, it was worth it since we got our lovable character-filled cat back.

When our lives began to settle down, we adopted Jazmine, a white German Shepherd/Yellow Lab mix. Usually when you add a large dog to the family, you worry about how the dog will treat the cat. Well, not us. We were more fearful of how Bailey would treat Jazmine. Could Jazmine handle him? Bailey really didn't think he was small and his bravado rivaled that of a Doberman when prompted. Thankfully, Jazmine was just what the doctor ordered... literally. Jazmine and Bailey became best friends. Within a month of Jazmine's arrival, Bailey was completely off the medication and he hasn't needed it since.

Bailey has brought life into our home. His lively personality, crazy antics, abandonment issues, and unceasing zest for life have kept us rolling in laughter and sometimes crying. But most of all, Bailey has taught us what family is truly about. Family can drive you crazy, make you laugh till you cry, and push the limits. But, in the end, regardless of all its foibles and flaws, headaches and heartaches, we never give up on them—they are family. We fight till the end to keep our loved ones no matter how much of a bang they make.

—Francesca Lang—

Chapter

9

A Dog's Purpose

83

Tailor-Made

Never lose hope. Just when you think it's over...
God sends you a miracle.
~Author Unknown

I n the still quiet of the early morning mist, the sound of the garage door opening was unsettlingly familiar. Another transient had sheltered in our garage for the night.

As the sound of man's coughing filled the air, I looked over at one of my brothers sleeping soundly beside me. Outside the window, I heard heavy footfalls passing by, and then a shadow paused by the window.

Suddenly, I was up on my feet, running and screaming to my mother's bedroom, waking her and my three brothers. Our mother was raising us alone in a house on a lonely street that ran close beside railroad tracks. Our house was the only one on the little, dirt road.

It was the late 1960s, and we lived in the part of Southern California that never caught the glamour that shimmered from Hollywood. Ours was the backward part, the blue-collar, never-mentioned, vast swath of semi-desert known sarcastically as the "Inland Empire."

Populated by working-class families made up almost exclusively of "Okies" and "Arkies" who poured into California during the Great Depression, it possessed at the time a sort of homogeneity of transplanted southernness. We were proud of being people of faith and tradition. We were self-sufficient. We made do.

But, mostly, we were alone.

Our mother hadn't planned on this. Like most women of her generation, she had planned on marriage and family. But our father had other ideas. Although they remained married for many years, he was pretty much out of the picture by the time I was born. My mother made the best of it, but raising four young sons alone was hard.

Settling in this little home by the railroad tracks was not anyone's ideal situation, but it was available and affordable, so we moved in. But the isolated location coupled with the proximity of the railroad tracks made for an insecure situation. We found that homeless men, "hobos" who rode the rails and stopped wherever their whims chose, visited us frequently.

Our garage became their frequent lodgings for the night, or perhaps it had long been so even before we lived there. Many of them seemed harmless enough, sometimes knocking on the door and asking politely for a handout, but a few of them were threatening.

More than once, I huddled in fear with the brother I shared a bed with as an inebriated stranger fumbled with our front door. We had no phone or neighbors, only our young mother for protection. One night as a man tried to force his way inside, our mother crept up to the door with the old shotgun given to her by our grandfather. Shaking with nerves, she pulled the trigger.

The blast blew out a chunk of the wooden floor. The man at the door ran off, calling behind him to please not shoot him. Mother took to staying awake all night, trying to catch some sleep during the day. Something had to change.

Gathering us all together, mother led our little family in asking for help in the only way available to us: prayer. We prayed for protection, asking God to keep his hand upon us and keep us safe. Faith was our foundation, and our mother, the daughter of ministers, prayed for divine intervention. With this assurance, we went to bed for the night.

The next morning, the sound of barking woke us. A dog was on the front porch.

For four young boys, a dog was certainly welcome. We crowded around, petting her. It was plain to see that she was a "mutt," a Collie-mix, perfect for a family. She was friendly, with a wagging tail and one of those cheerful doggie smiles. There couldn't have been a better addition to our family if she had been tailor-made specifically for us.

And so, "Angel" as our mother christened her, became part of the family — the only daughter among four sons. My mother was very clear that she was our answered prayer. And she was indeed everything we prayed for, proving herself a fine guard dog, chasing away our nightly visitors with a ferocity that she never displayed toward us.

The front porch became her home and guard tower. She refused to come inside the house, obviously used to being outdoors and preferring it. All night long, we rested secure, knowing we were safe. As a young boy, I accepted my mother's explanation: Angel was a demonstration of the power of simple faith.

And so she remained our faithful protector, friend and sister, until one morning when she disappeared as mysteriously as she had shown up. It was the morning that we were moving from the lonely house by the railroad tracks.

The night before, I had hugged her, chattering about our new house, which my mother had found on a street full of families, busy with children. I was sure Angel would love it there. My mother had already made friends with our new next-door neighbor, another young mother with two children our age. Angel would have so many new friends to play with!

With her tongue hanging from her open mouth and her tail wagging, Angel assured me in her own way that she would always be with me, protecting us. She gave me a slobbery "kiss," and I went to bed excited and happy. With our guardian keeping watch on the front porch, we all slept soundly that last night in the lonely, little house at the end of the dirt road.

But in the morning, Angel was nowhere to be found.

We searched for her, calling her name as we packed up our old car. My older brothers scampered up and down the road with me during breaks, looking for her. Later, as we drove away, I looked out the car's back window through the clouds of dust stirred up by the tires, gazing at the humble, little house partly hidden by the tall laurel trees that towered high. I couldn't keep from crying, thinking of our dog.

My mother, who knew Angel's origin with assurance, also knew with the same assurance where she had gone. "She is back in Heaven. We don't need her now. The Bible says that we entertain angels unaware, you know. She was our angel and kept us safe, like we asked for when we prayed."

My mother was right. Angel's job with us was done. But I learned that angels do not always have wings. They do not always carry harps. Sometimes, they look like mutts with wagging tails and big smiles, perfect for a single mother raising four young boys alone.

She was tailor-made for us, of course.

—Jack Byron—

A Desperate Situation

The golden moments in the stream of life rush past us
and we see nothing but sand; the angels come to visit
us and we only know them when they are gone.
~George Eliot

t was nearly midnight in a small town in New Mexico and I was terrified. I cowered in my car, on a deserted side street, while five angry young men milled around my car, shouting obscenities. My hound dog Sheba was barking furiously, doing her best to keep between the menacing men and me.

One of the men, his face twisted with rage, glared through the windshield and yelled, "I could kill that dog with my bare hands." Several replies came to my mind, but I said nothing, because I didn't want to antagonize him and make matters worse. But things did get worse anyway.

The frustrated men began pounding their fists on the roof of my car and kicking their boots against its doors. Sheba jumped from window to window, snapping in vain at the men through the glass.

I couldn't believe the predicament I was in. It had all started because I had gone out of my way to give a friend a lift home from work. After I had dropped my friend off, a clean cut young man walked up to my car and asked if I could please help him get his car started. All he needed was someone to jumpstart his battery.

Even though it was night, and I was alone with my dog, I didn't feel threatened at that point. And so I agreed to help this polite stranger get his car started. After all, I had grown up in the West, where it was traditional to lend a helping hand. Never had I refused to help another motorist and never had anyone ever refused to help me when I had car trouble. So helping this stranger simply seemed like the ordinary thing to do.

I had slowly driven my car around the corner from my friend's house, following the young man as he walked along on the sidewalk. When I saw the older model car with its hood up, I pulled my car parallel to it. Then the man opened the hood of my car and connected jumper cables from his battery to mine. Four other men suddenly came from behind a row of bushes and surrounded my car. That was when the polite young man turned vicious and ugly.

So there I sat, with my hood up and my battery attached to the other car's battery by jumper cables. Even though I still had the motor running, I was effectively trapped, because I couldn't see to drive with the hood up and I didn't dare get out of the car to close it.

I was helpless and I knew it. For the time being, Sheba was keeping the men from breaking the windows to get at me. But how long could she keep it up? She wasn't a young dog anymore — would she finally drop from exhaustion? I had raised her from the day she was born, and for nearly ten years Sheba had been my constant companion. And so I feared for her as well as for myself.

Even though I was terrified, I tried not to think about the "what ifs" — what if they broke the windows, what if they got one of the car doors open, what if they got their hands on Sheba and me.

I was on the verge of becoming hysterical and although it took every ounce of my self-control, I wouldn't let myself scream or even cry. First of all, I wasn't about to give those men the satisfaction of seeing me fall to pieces. But even more importantly, I knew that if I gave in to my emotions, I'd really be lost. I had to keep thinking clearly or I would have no chance of saving myself if an opportunity to escape did present itself.

As scared as I was, I was even angrier, and I think that helped me regain control of my emotions. I was indignant — I had gone out of my way to help that "polite" young man start his car. And this was how he repaid me?

I glanced at the gas gauge. It was nearly full, so at least I didn't have to worry about running out of gas anytime soon.

I hadn't realized that the window on the driver's side was down about three inches until I heard a low, soft voice close to my ear. Glancing at the side window, I saw the outline of a figure, but I couldn't make out the words he was saying. "What?" I asked.

"Get ready," he whispered. "I'm going to pull the cables loose and slam the hood. Then you get out of here — quick!"

I slid the gearshift into low and waited. My hands were trembling so hard I could scarcely grasp the steering wheel.

The instant the hood slammed shut I jammed the gas pedal completely to the floor and the car shot forward. My surprised attackers, in danger of being run over, leaped away from the car.

I never looked back and I didn't dare stop until I was downtown. The local movie theater had just closed and the sidewalks were full of people walking to their cars. Then, and only then, did I park my car and give in to my emotions. I leaned my head against the steering wheel and waited until my pulse slowed down to normal and my hands weren't shaking anymore. Then I drove the rest of the way home, grateful that I had escaped a dangerous situation unscathed.

I've often thought about that man who saved me and I wish I had been able to thank him, but there hadn't been time. I never even got a glimpse of his face, and to this day, I wonder what he looked like.

But I was left with a lot of other unanswered questions about that night. This quiet man, who saved Sheba and me, where did he come from? He appeared from out of nowhere; one minute he wasn't there and the very next instant there he was, standing by my window. Why was it that the other men, who were threatening me, didn't even seem to notice him? How was he able to unhook the cable and slam the hood shut right under their very noses, without them stopping him? After all, there were five of them and he was alone.

Only later did I realize that my dog never barked at the man who saved us, not even when he leaned close to whisper into my ear. This during a time when Sheba was excited, ready to fight, and trying to protect me from everyone out there. Why was it that she didn't feel the need to protect me from the man who was trying to save us? She acted as if she hadn't even seen him.

I know that each of us is supposed to have a guardian angel, and I believe mine came to my rescue that night. For me, it's the only conclusion that makes any sense.

— Connie Kutac —

Life Lessons from the Lab

*Be content with what you have, rejoice in the way
things are. When you realize there is nothing
lacking, the whole world belongs to you.*
~Lao Tzu

everal years ago in Oregon, three climbers on Mount Hood slipped off a ledge and slid more than five hundred feet in the ice and snow. After spending the night on the mountainside in whiteout conditions, with winds swirling at up to seventy miles per hour, the signals they beamed with a live transmitter were picked up by rescuers down below.

Despite the nifty technology that helped to pinpoint the climbers' location, one of the rescuers gave credit to Velvet, the black Labrador Retriever that had accompanied the climbers and huddled with them throughout the bitter night. "The dog probably saved their lives," he said.

What I love about this story — besides the fact that they were all rescued safe and sound — is that Velvet became a hero by virtue of just being a dog. There was no mention of the Labrador's extraordinary valor or intelligence or training. Apparently, Velvet's big life-saving technique was The Huddle. There she was, along for the climb, and when the going got rough, Velvet the Life-Saving Dog just lay there in a heap with the climbers, sharing warmth on a cold night.

Although my own black Lab has never rescued me from an 11,239-foot mountain, she has saved the day more than once when I've felt a frown coming on. And just like Velvet, what Lizzie does comes as naturally and instinctively to her as licking the dirt off her paws or rolling around on her back spastically when she has an itch to scratch.

When life gets too complicated, when the demands on my time are more numerous than there are hours in a day, Lizzie will rush up to me with her suggestion, tail wagging, leash in mouth. Somehow she knows there's nothing like a walk for slowing down your day, for taking in a breath of fresh air, and, as they say, for stopping to smell the roses — although I don't think that's quite what Lizzie stops to smell along the way.

Every day, she reminds me that when someone comes through the door, returning home from work or from school or just stopping by for a visit, there's only one way to respond. Put on a happy face. No matter what kind of day she's had, whether she's been out for hours or cooped up in the house all day, she never fails to run to the door and shower whoever enters with all the drooly affection of her canine heart.

In Lizzie's world, there's no time to waste on fussy little details that could eat up time when there are so many more satisfying things to, well, eat. Just throw some of those nuggets from that giant bag of food in one bowl, pour a little water in the other and watch it disappear. Same food, same bowls, same enthusiastic response night after night. Why not be happy with what you've got?

She pulls out her best mood-altering tactic when I'm sitting at the little round table in the alcove in our kitchen. There I am, helping with homework or sewing ribbons onto ballet shoes, paying bills or just kicking back with a book. The next thing you know, this warm mound of fur plunks herself down at my feet, wrapping her front paws tightly around one of my ankles, as if to say: "It's about time you're sitting down. Why don't you stay a while?" I like to think of it as a hug.

In fact, if all else fails, Lizzie's solution is as simple as it is effective. Wherever you are, in the middle of the morning, in the middle of a movie, in the middle of anything — except, of course, dinner — it doesn't matter. Just nod off. Take a nap. And when you come back to join the rest of the world, surely you will have regained your stride.

There's nothing like a dog to remind me that in this complex world we really need to stay in touch with a simpler existence. As

Velvet showed us, just being who you are is enough to make you a hero. And as long as you've got food in your bowl, a warm bed to curl up in and someone to wag your tail for, I mean, come on. Life is good.

— Rita Lussier —

Cleansing the Soul

*Everyone who has run knows that its most important
value is in removing tension and allowing a release
from whatever other cares the day may bring.*
~Jimmy Carter

The crisp air stings my face. While I lace my shoe, she circles me with anticipation. The sun winks a sleepy greeting and I stretch my arms to the clouds above me. I breathe in the fragrant morning and exhale with intent. It's time to begin. I move forward and she responds, taking the first steps in this well-practiced routine that never ends the way it begins. My footfalls are heavy next to hers. We struggle to find rhythm in this dance we've done a hundred times. Our warm breath escapes in front of us.

The smell of licorice tickles my nose while dawn creeps up on the still and silent Earth. The hillside glistens with dew; the skyline, freshly painted, meets the mountain's outline. The colors are more vibrant than at any other time of the day. I'm breathing deeply, and I slow our pace. She is always too anxious in the beginning. I hear my shoes on the pavement and the clinking of her collar.

It isn't long before we find our stride and move in unison. I feel my body lighten as the worry and stress of life falls from my shoulders and is carried away by the breeze. My faithful partner runs silently beside me, often glancing in my direction. Is she happy? Is this process as healing for her as it is for me?

Now moving as one, I loosen my hold on her leash. I relax and extend my limbs. Momentum carries us up and down the country hills effortlessly. I feel like I am floating and my mind is flooded with thoughts and ideas. I notice the sounds of birds now echoing in the trees. The sun has fully risen and beams down. Deer stand statuesque in the distance, watching us. I'm thankful for their quiet stance; she doesn't notice them.

We follow our well-worn path and sometimes find a place of euphoria, unexplainable and intoxicating. Our pace quickens and the air no longer feels cold against my skin. We are lost in time. Time is not always my own, but in this moment, it is. Only I will say how far I go and how long I run. There are no interruptions. No demands on my time. When I run, I am not Mrs. or Mom. I am a writer, a runner. Limits only exist if I've set them for myself. She is content just being with me.

This moment carries me deeper into a sense of self. I feel I could run forever. However, life awaits my presence. We slow our pace and begin our journey back. Now, free of all burdens, I am inspired by the day; I am ready to take on all that life might throw in my direction. Slowing to a walk, I take a deep breath and release her. She hesitates to leave my side.

I whisper "go home." She, so obedient, turns and runs up the drive.

As I take my final steps through this ritual, I reflect. I feel strong and energized. Renewed. Running, my addiction, has worked its cleansing magic on my soul once again. I am now ready to enjoy what I love most — being a wife and mother.

— Machille Legoullon —

87

Our Own Incredible Journey

The language of friendship is not words but meanings.
~Henry David Thoreau

Soon after we moved to a remote parcel of land in the Sierra foothills that hadn't been built on for miles around, we brought in two feral cats, Nosey and Quincy, to keep down the critter population. We had never been cat owners before, and I feared it would be a challenge for our aging Terrier, Lacy, but she became their best friend right from the start. She let them drink from her water bowl, sleep on her dog bed, and I even watched her licking cat food from their fur a time or two. The three amigos formed quite a bond.

As Lacy continued to age, her cat friends stayed close. When we drove up our long driveway coming home from work, Lacy would hobble to greet us, trailed by the cats, even when her arthritis made it hard for her to get off the porch. As her condition worsened, we spent a lot of time at the vet's office trying to find the right medication to ease her pain.

On one of those visits, I questioned the doc. "There are times now when our dog seems disoriented. I know she has suffered some hearing loss, but there seems to be more to her behavior than just that. Am I imagining things?"

"No, you're not." Her reply was unexpected. "Dogs can get a form of dementia," she continued. "It's hard to know if that's happening, but I would suggest that you keep her in for the most part. She could wander off and forget how to come home, especially on all that land around your house, Linda."

I recruited the help of my three teenagers to keep an eye on Lacy. With a house full of teenagers, things tended to get pretty chaotic, but I encouraged them. "We can't let the dog go outside unless somebody goes with her."

They all agreed to keep watch, and they did until one bustling Thursday night. The house was full of their friends, who were hanging out until Youth Group started at church later that night. There were kids coming and going from every door. Just as the last kid left I realized that Lacy was nowhere in the house to be found. By then it was dark, so my husband and I grabbed flashlights and looked all over the hillside. We called for her for hours even though I doubted that she could hear us. We didn't see the cats either, but we figured they were on their nightly prowl around the property. At midnight we gave up our search and decided to we would have better odds during the light of day.

The next morning the entire family joined in the search. We combed the countryside until the kids had to be at school and we had to be at work. That night was a usual busy Friday night, but I kept checking the porch, hoping to see Lacy resting there on her doggie bed, curled up with her cat buddies.

Saturday brought more busyness. My oldest had to be dropped off at work while my son was heading for music practice, and my youngest needed me to pick up a friend who was spending the day with her. As I went out to start the car, I couldn't believe my eyes. Walking up the long driveway was Lacy, alive and well, with Nosey on one side and Quincy guarding the other! The two cats nudged and rubbed against her, guiding her up the driveway.

"Kids come quickly. You have to see this!" I needed witnesses. I wasn't sure I believed what I was seeing!

One by one my children lined up behind me wide-eyed and slack-jawed. We stood there silently until the three animals had made their way onto the porch and were fiercely lapping up water. "They had their own personal *Incredible Journey*," my son commented, remembering an old Disney movie we watched over and over when he was younger.

"I needed you to see this because I knew you wouldn't believe me if I told you what I saw," I agreed.

— Linda Newton —

88

Finding Dexter

Dogs have owners; cats have staff.
~Author Unknown

Dexter never missed a meal, which was followed by a nap on the sofa. During his non-nap hours, he played at being wild on our three acres. But when it came to comfort, he knew that *inside* was the place to be. Dexter was an elegant cat who liked his outdoor adventures in small doses.

One day, Dexter did not show up for breakfast. That was okay, but given his preference for staying indoors, I got really worried when he did not return by the evening. In rural Mississippi, there were all kinds of terrifying possibilities, so I spent hours calling for him outside.

Before I went to bed I had to try one more thing. I leashed up Timber, our brilliant Jack Russell Terrier. Timber loved to play the "find him" game with our son. Maybe he could find the cat. They had been buddies for six years, ever since we brought Dexter home as a kitten.

"Outside"

Miraculously, Timber sniffed the air and headed off. "Good boy, Tim. Find Dexter!" I had no idea what the dog was smelling, but he was definitely following a scent. I hoped it was not a raccoon, or worse… a skunk.

Timber stopped at the corner of our property where the fence was supported by a thick, round fence post, perfect for a cat to scale. "Did he go up here, Tim? Find Dexter!"

The dog turned and looked at me like I was nuts. There was no way he could scale the post, but placating me, he walked back and forth along the fence, each time stopping and sniffing at the corner post.

It was not a good idea to wander through my neighbors' pastures in the dark, so I planned to go out first thing in the morning. I prayed that Dexter would be okay for the night.

I barely slept at all that night, and I got up several times to see if Dexter was back. He was not. I forced myself to wait until good light at seven o'clock in the morning, and then I grabbed Timber, hopped in the car, and drove to the closest outside access to that corner post.

"Find Dexter!" Timber took off with his nose to the ground. A couple of hundred feet later, we were stopped by another fence.

My only hope was that Timber was truly onto Dexter's scent. The dog was intent on a cat-sized hole in the fence. If he really was following Dexter, the cat was headed into the hayfield directly behind our property. Three abandoned silos stood there in the field, beckoning to all forms of small, wild animals and enticing an energetic explorer like Dexter. Timber kept air-scenting toward the silos.

Across the fence, I bellowed loudly enough to wake any still-sleeping neighbors. "DEXTER!"

"MEEEEOOOOOWWW" came the almost equally loud yowl echoing from inside one of the old silos.

"Timber! You are wonderful!" I exclaimed. "Good dog! You found Dex. Good, good dog!"

The next task was to remove the cat from the twelve-foot-high cross-beam inside the silo. He had gotten up there but, in classic cat fashion, could not get down. I retrieved a six-foot ladder and my six-foot-four-inch son. It would be a stretch, but a rescue was initiated.

Successfully extricated and back in the house, Dexter chowed down and napped stretched out, taking up the major part of our sofa. As he snoozed, I wished I could read his kitty mind. Was he dreaming about his night on the silo beam? Was he planning a new adventure for us? Was he grateful or humiliated that he was rescued by a dog? Did he even care?

Most likely, he simply felt that his rescue crew barely met his expectations, and that they were awfully slow in doing so.

— Gretchen Allen —

The Calico Puppy

Fun fact: Kittens enter their primary socialization period at two–three weeks of age. This is when the brain is primed for attachment to other beings.

We have no idea when Poppy, our Golden Retriever, had her rendezvous but by mid-summer it was quite evident that she had been naughty. When our vet confirmed that Poppy would soon present us with a litter of grand-puppies we were at first stunned but that soon gave way to excitement. Since we had no idea whom our naughty girl had seduced we were eager to see what her pups would look like.

On the Fourth of July the local fireworks were forgotten when Poppy went into labor. Leave it to Poppy to upstage the annual celebration. The sound of distant fireworks heralded in the birth of her three pups. Their parental lineage still escaped us. One short-haired male was brown and white, his brother had a long silky coat like Poppy but was black, and their sister looked a lot like Poppy, right down to her golden fur. Tired but exhausted, Poppy beamed first at her babies at then at us, clearly delighted in the fuss we were making over her and her pups.

My husband, Joe, came in from feeding the horses one morning, scowling as he cradled something against his chest. "Some people," he muttered, as he showed me a tiny, frightened calico kitten that was small enough to nestle in one of his big hands. We live in the country and it isn't unusual to find abandoned pets, but we never get used to the callousness it takes to leave an animal on its own to slowly starve or become wild. The most heartbreaking of all is to find babies who either were tossed out to die or whose mother was killed.

"I couldn't find any more," Joe said. "The mother and any other kittens that there may have been are most likely dead. This one wouldn't have made it much longer." He put the kitten in my hands. "I'll go into town and get a dropper and some formula. She might make it if we can get some food into her soon."

While Joe was gone I found a shoebox and an old soft receiving blanket and made a bed for the kitten. In a few days she was putting on weight and mewling happily when I took her out of her bed to be fed and cuddled for a while.

Poppy's puppies were getting fat and beginning to frolic, though never venturing far from her watchful eye. One morning, out of curiosity, I placed the kitten next to the pups to see how they would react to each other. The pups looked curiously at the funny little thing that made such odd sounds. They examined her for a few moments, then lost interest and wandered back to Poppy for some milk. To my surprise the kitten followed the pups timidly, mewling all the while.

When Poppy saw her brood approaching she dutifully lay down so they could nurse. She eyed the kitten and decided the tiny thing posed no threat to her pups, so she relaxed and turned her attention to her babies as they nuzzled around for a spot to nurse. To my surprise, the kitten started pushing forward between two of the pups, instinctively knowing what her reward would be if she could snag a teat.

I jumped up, ready to snatch her away. I didn't know how Poppy would react to this intrusion. Poppy looked alarmed for few seconds as if she didn't know how to react either. She looked up at me for guidance. I patted her head and talked softly to her. "It's okay, girl. She's just another hungry baby."

I never had to feed the kitten after that. Poppy totally accepted her into her family. As time went on Poppy became very protective of her special baby. And the kitten followed the pups everywhere they went and seemed to think that she was a puppy too. We began to call her Rover because she clearly identified with the dogs.

When Poppy watched her babies play she kept a close eye on Rover, who was diminutive next to her large puppies, who turned out to be part Husky. Often, if one of the pups got too rough with Rover, Poppy would run over to inspect her smallest baby to make sure she was all right. Then she would give the offending sibling a warning look.

Initially we had planned on finding a home for Rover when she was weaned. But Poppy got so attached to her little calico "puppy" that we didn't have the heart to separate them. To this day the two of them are inseparable. And Rover still thinks she is a dog.

— Elizabeth Atwater —

Ring to the Rescue

No animal I know can consistently be more
of a friend and companion than a dog.
~Stanley Leinwoll

In the early 1940s my father, Alvin Eklund, lived in the Twin Butte district of Southern Alberta. He was a rancher, and a farmer. When it came to animals, he was known as one of the kindest men around.

In summer he and his friend Owen Leavitt moved their sheep into the mountains. In winter, my dad brought his herd down into the farming districts of Hill Spring and Glenwood where he rented grain fields to run his sheep. It was almost impossible to handle sheep without dogs to help, so both my father and Owen had very good dogs.

Ring was my dad's dog. Ring was a dog you could send out around the sheep in the brush, and if he found one that was caught or unable to return to the herd he would bark until someone came to his aid. Ring would go up the mountain and bring sheep down that were so high they could scarcely be seen. He could be sent ahead to turn the flock either way at a signal, or he could be left to drive from the rear of the flock while the herder drove a small bunch in the lead. Ring would bunch the flock in a tight circle and hold them until you relieved him of the chore.

One winter my father stayed with Owen while his sheep grazed in fields two miles away. It was January, and of course very cold at night. Dad began complaining of not feeling well. Owen tried to get him to stay indoors, but my father would not stand for pampering. After a few days had passed he was still sick, but he really wanted to go home to his ranch in Twin Butte.

Owen tried to dissuade him, as at that point he had no family and lived alone. His nearest neighbors were about two miles away. But he said that if Owen would take care of his sheep, he would be back well and able in a few days. So he left for home with Ring at his side.

About a week went by and Owen had received no word from Alvin. Then one morning — early, about seven o'clock, Ring came scratching and whining at the door. When Owen went to see what he wanted, he barked a few times and started back out to the road. When Owen didn't follow Ring came back, and whined and barked again.

Quickly realizing what he wanted, Owen said, "I understand Ring, I'm coming."

Owen later said, "There was about fourteen inches of snow on the ground, and it was twenty-five miles back to Alvin's ranch. I thought I'd better get some help to go with me, so in a short time Ted Green and I hopped in my car with Ring, and set out for Alvin's ranch. We brought a big snow shovel along to dig the snow away. We couldn't make very good time as the snow was pretty deep for a car, but at last we were on the hill above Alvin's ranch. I'll never forget looking down on the scene of that little ranch all covered with white, not a single track anywhere except those Ring had made coming out. When I saw smoke coming out of the chimney, I said to Ted, "Well he's still alive."

"When we got down to the house and found Alvin, he was scarcely able to stand. He just stood and looked at us with tears running down his cheeks. He wasn't able to say a word."

Owen and Ted tucked their friend in the car and brought him back home with them. It turned out he had smallpox, and was sick for a very long time. Alvin later told them that when he got too sick to go to the door, Ring would scratch on the wall under his window several times a day and he would talk to him.

"I must have lost track of time," Alvin told Owen, "because when I finally realized Ring was gone, I hoped and prayed he would go to you. My neighbours wouldn't have understood him — they didn't know I had come home."

Ring had braved the deep and treacherous snow, travelling twenty-five miles to go for help without hesitation. And he knew exactly where to go. He was a hero to all of us from then on. My dad, of course, recovered, and none of us will ever forget Ring's incredible heroic act of love.

—David A. Eklund—

Our Amazing Christmas Gift

*It is amazing how much love and laughter they bring
into our lives and even how much closer we become
with each other because of them.*
~John Grogan, Marley & Me

t was a bitterly cold Yuletide drive from Regina to Saskatoon, my
birthplace, but it was truly beautiful, with its stands of snow-
covered trees and arched bridges along the South Saskatchewan
River. We'd loaded up our trusty Jeep on December 21st with
suitcases, survival gear, boxes of wrapped presents, and our ten-year-
old Shih Tzu named Keiko. We'd adopted him six years earlier, and
he seemed to love road trips as much as we did.

We enjoyed sumptuous dinners and quality time with family
for a couple of leisurely days in Saskatoon. Then we headed to Ivan's
brother's farm outside Yorkton, which was Ivan's first home, to celebrate
Christmas with his parents, brother and sister-in-law, and nephew.
Smoky, their five-year-old Siberian Husky, was there, too, lying on
a mat recovering from emergency surgery after being hit by a truck.

We opened gifts and were having a relaxing Christmas Eve dinner
when it happened. We were all so preoccupied with the delicious food,
conversation and each other's company that we didn't notice — until
we finished eating, pushed back our chairs and stood up. It was then
that we saw the neat little piles of kibble under the table where our
feet had been. Keiko had placed them there — deliberately making
many trips from his supper dish nearby, carefully taking one or two

at a time in his lips and depositing them at our feet — back and forth, back and forth. There was also a small pile beside the stainless-steel feeding dish — undoubtedly for Smoky.

Gentle and affectionate Keiko had shared the most special thing he had — the only thing he had — the food in his dish. Our little rescue dog was saying thank you. We were awestruck by this rare display of generosity.

— Kathie Leier —

Over the Rainbow

92

Stewie to the Rescue

To err is human, to forgive, canine.
~Author Unknown

The funny thing was, I didn't even want the dog. I didn't have one growing up, and I didn't see any reason to become a pet owner in my thirties. I tried to convince my girlfriend that it wasn't a good idea. We both worked full-time, and I wasn't missing something that I'd never had or wanted.

"Please?" she beseeched.

I stood my ground.

She batted her baby blues.

I held firm.

Sometime during the second month of her pleading, while not thinking clearly, I made a tactical mistake

I asked, "If we were to get a dog, what kind of dog would you want?"

And that was that. We bought a dog and named him Stewie.

For story arc purposes, I should say how at first I didn't take too kindly to Stewie's intrusion in my life, how my normal day-to-day schedule was turned upside down, how I viewed Stewie's very existence as an inconvenience, until slowly but surely, I came to love him and how the very things about Stewie that irritated me were now enchanting. But that's not what happened.

Stewie owned me from Day One. I didn't mind when he peed on the carpet. I didn't mind when he used my socks as chew toys.

I didn't mind when he ate a twenty-dollar bill that had fallen to the floor. (Okay, I did mind that a little.)

Things went incredibly well for the next two years. I even stopped going away as I used up all my vacation time (and sick days — shhh!) to stay home and play with Stewie. We'd go to the park, where he would play with the other dogs or fetch his favorite ball for hours. And then we'd go home where he'd bring me his indoor (i.e. non-squeaky) ball, and we would play fetch. For hours.

Though my girlfriend loved him too, she didn't have the time to spend with Stewie that I did. While my accounting job was strictly nine to five weekdays (and sometimes I'd even sneak out earlier), she worked as a hairstylist, which meant long days and some weekends as well. That's probably why Stewie followed me, and not her, from room to room like a two-foot stalker.

Unfortunately, things started to change. What was cute and lovable at the beginning grew tiresome. Though I had loved making sacrifices, I became less apt to compromise. Our relationship was strained, to the point where I didn't see any point in continuing. So my girlfriend and I broke up. (You didn't think I was talking about Stewie and me, did you?)

There wasn't even a discussion about who was going to take Stewie. He was my dog.

Eventually, I met my wife, Josie, and we became a family of three. On the morning of November 26th, a month after our wedding and one day after my birthday, I was walking Stewie off-leash in Riverside Park, as I had mostly done, whether it was legal or not. But on this day, he was straying a little far from me….

"Stewie!" I called out, and he froze, staring at me but not moving at all. It was almost as if he heard his name but couldn't see me. I took off the black knit hat I was wearing.

"Stewie, get over here!"

This time, instead of staring or coming to me, he took off, running south towards the entrance to the park. I took off as well, following, but soon lost sight of him. Someone near the entrance saw me running and asked if I was chasing a small dog.

"Yes!"

"He ran out that way," she said, pointing to the entrance.

"Shoot!" I thought, and climbed the stone stairs.

When I reached the street, I immediately spotted him, lying on Riverside Drive, lifeless, with blood everywhere. Stewie was four years old. The car that hit him didn't even stop.

For the next six months, I walked around like a zombie, not caring about anything. I agreed to go to therapy but it wasn't really doing anything for my grief or me. Eventually, I decided that for my own wellbeing I had to do something. Stewie's death couldn't be for nothing.

We decided to adopt a homeless dog. We were looking for a senior dog, as we couldn't afford a dog walker and with a day gig and a comedy career, I didn't have the time to give a younger dog the attention it'd need. I also knew that it was tougher to find homes for seniors. Online, I found a post by a woman advocating for a nine-year-old great-on-the-leash Pit Bull mix named Kilo who was scheduled to be euthanized in the morning.

I decided right then and there… this dog was not going to die. I wrote to her immediately.

We met outside the animal shelter, known as (NYC) Animal Care & Control. From the outside, it is a depressing building, located on a depressing block in East Harlem. Walking in was no better. I felt like I was entering a prison (which, in one respect, I was), and a smelly prison at that.

We walked back to where the dogs were kept. The barking was loud and constant.

When she took Kilo out of his cage, Josie and I looked at each other, as if to say, "Are you sure this is the same dog described in the ad?"

He was a maniac. We thought he might be a little hyper from being in the cage, so we took him for a walk. After twenty minutes of him literally dragging me around Harlem, we asked, "Are you sure this is Kilo?"

Yes, he was insane, but like I said, this dog was not going to die. I owed it to Stewie. We took Kilo home and loved him, in spite of his high energy (or maybe because of it).

But that wasn't enough to ease my pain. Thankfully, Josie came up with an idea....

"Why don't you start your own rescue, and name it after Stewie?"

That sounded great! Not only would I be memorializing Stewie in a more public manner, but, being the founder and president, I could focus on what I felt was important, and direct my energy where it was needed the most.

In July of 2010, Stewie to the Rescue was founded.

In the two years we've been around, Stewie has helped save the lives of more than 100 animals. We have raised over $100,000 for our rescue and others by producing comedy fundraisers (I am a also stand-up comedian). We have partnered with more than thirty other animal rescues to lend our time and fundraising talents to their efforts. Personally, I have become a leading animal advocate in New York, and I no longer eat meat or chicken, and was even recently named cable channel NY1's "New Yorker of the Week" for my work in animal rescue.

And to think, I didn't even want a dog.

— Harris Bloom —

93

Password

May the wings of the butterfly kiss the sun
And find your shoulder to light on,
To bring you luck, happiness and riches
Today, tomorrow and beyond.
~Irish Blessing

I was nothing less than devastated by the news that my beloved black Labrador, Lady, had a cancerous tumor in her lung, and was so enlarged it had literally pushed her heart to the other side of her chest. Fortunately, Lady didn't even look ill, and certainly failed to exhibit any outward signs of pain. The veterinarian explained that surgery was an option, we decided surgery was pointless and cruel and would not extend her life.

So, Lady was expected to live another three or four weeks.

It was decided that putting Lady on a high-protein diet of "people food" was the best choice under the circumstances. She loved scrambled eggs, baked turkey and chicken breasts, cheeses, and her favorite — prime rib cooked just to her liking. I snuck her a few pieces of pizza too.

I spent many long hours talking with my brother about Lady and the great joy she brought me over a decade. A month passed, then two, then three and four. Lady was holding her own and I treasured every single day she lived.

The veterinarian came to the house regularly to check on Lady. She was amazed at how well she appeared, and the remarkable fact she was clearly not declining.

Nevertheless, I continued to break down and my brother continued to comfort me. Another couple of months passed and soon we reached an unbelievable marker of ten months! Lady continued to feast on her high-protein foods and although her weight stayed the same, she exhibited absolutely no signs of discomfort. By Christmas, I wondered if the diagnosis had been a horrible mistake.

That was not to be the case. After the holidays, Lady suddenly lost weight at an accelerated rate, and I could no longer postpone a very important decision about euthanasia. I knew the day would come when I would be forced to call the veterinarian and ask her to come to the house to see Lady one final time. I agonized over that decision, and even worse was choosing "when" that exact day would be. I started losing my courage to make that final decision, and I discussed this at length with my dear brother. He suggested that I "talk" to Lady about the issue. I took his advice.

I sat on the floor with Lady, looked into those incredibly loving brown eyes, hugged her closely to me, and cried myself to sleep at her side — for two days and two nights. Yes, Lady gave me a sign that she was ready, an unmistakable body language message distinctly hers, and I made the dreaded call to the vet.

The inevitable day of Lady's passing was a serene moment in my life and one of a true blessing. I was so privileged to have had her love, and I held her as she took her last breath. The impression of her soul leaving her body and soaring to lofty heights nearly overtook me. I told her, "Run like the wind, my precious Lady, run like the wind!"

Strangely, I cried no more tears that day and again my brother offered words of comfort, acknowledging and honoring the profound love we share with our pets. He reassured me that one day I would have another dog. He reiterated this on many occasions.

Several years came and went, and there was no talk of getting another dog.

Another inevitable day presented itself; my dear brother was gravely ill and not expected to live. I was devastated. Nevertheless, my brother was upbeat and in total acceptance. He reassured me that once he had passed, he would somehow relay a message to me from the other side, or wherever he was destined to be. We decided on a password and he vowed to contact me.

Several weeks later, I asked my brother if he remembered what his message or password was; he laughed loudly and answered that he'd forgotten it too! He then suggested a new password, evidently a word chosen at random, and one that I felt had no significance for either of us. The password was "butterfly." I agreed to this and promised my brother I would remember his password and he vowed to do the same.

Although my brother passed away very soon after this conversation, I felt so blessed to have had the opportunity to say goodbye, and to thank him for his genuine sweetness, his love and all his words of comfort throughout my dark days. He winked at me and said, "Don't forget the password, Sis."

Several months later, my husband brought home an unexpected early birthday present for me, and something totally out of character. After parking his truck, I watched my husband walk along our sidewalk as he approached the house, and trailing behind him was a bouncing white and brown puppy with a long snout and impossibly large floppy ears. He was the cutest puppy in the world!

"Whatever possessed you to bring a puppy home?"

My husband smiled. "Just waiting for the right time, I guess."

"That's so... unlike you."

"True enough. I just felt a strong compulsion, and well, who could resist that face?"

I kissed and cuddled and played with my new puppy; my heart overjoyed. That evening I called a few friends to tell them of our new puppy. On one such call, I looked at my calendar as I spoke. I suddenly realized it would have been my brother's birthday and mentioned this to my friend on the phone.

"My brother would have been so happy for me to get this new puppy. I only wish he could have lived long enough to see him," I said.

"Have you picked out a name? What breed of dog is the new puppy?"

"Well, his name is Pappy, and he's a Toy Spaniel, a Papillon."

I stopped speaking, and I think I stopped breathing for a long moment as my mind raced back to the promise my brother had made before he died.

"Oh!" I said, as the realization hit. "Yes, he's a Papillon, which is the French word for butterfly!"

The long anticipated message from my brother finally came through loud and clear. Tears of joy covered my face and the small puppy licked them away. Butterfly… butterfly… butterfly!

This was a miraculous confirmation sent with love from my brother, and I do believe perhaps my precious Lady too.

— Louetta Jensen —

94

Angels Slobber Too

Some pursue happiness, others create it.
~Author Unknown

One morning I had been married to my best friend, Mart, for 20 years, and the next I was a 43-year-old widow. I felt lost and wondered how I was supposed to continue living, and then an angel in disguise appeared to help me.

I don't remember where I had been on the day that I discovered the path to my own personal angel. But I do recall realizing on my way home that I had not eaten in a long time. I stopped at a burger joint and bought a newspaper on my way in so I would have something to do while I ate alone. I still don't know why I was looking through the classifieds. I never read them before. Mart would peruse them almost every day for a good deal on something we really didn't need. I normally just read the front page and the entertainment section. But on this fateful day, I ate food I had no taste for and idly flipped through the classifieds. In just a few minutes my eyes filled with tears. There, in big bold letters, was the answer to a prayer that I had not yet uttered: "Rare — Clumber Spaniel for Sale."

For over ten years Mart and I had haphazardly looked for a Clumber Spaniel. But we could never find one, or we couldn't afford the price, or it just wasn't a good time for a new puppy. But now, here was my Clumber Spaniel, right in front of me. I immediately called the listed number. I learned that the puppy was seven months old, approximately 60 pounds, and had to be sold because the family had just adopted a baby who was allergic to him. I agreed to meet the owner the next day in a bookstore parking lot on the other side of town. And in that parking lot, I caught sight of the first angel I had ever seen!

From the back of an SUV, peering out of a dog kennel, he looked into my eyes as slobber hung from his huge jowls. Hmmmm... definitely not most people's idea of a first angel sighting. However, in my mind's eye, I could almost see his beautiful angel wings hidden under the thick and shedding white fur on his muscular back. As the two of us looked into one another's eyes, I somehow knew, deep in my soul, that this dog and I were meant to be together. I paid the previous owner and loaded my new angel into the back of my Jeep and we headed home.

However, just a couple of miles down the road I had to wonder if I might have been mistaken. A stench unlike any I had ever smelled filled the interior of the Jeep. With outside temperatures in the low 30s it didn't take long for the Jeep to completely fog up with his musk! A few more miles and I found myself driving down the interstate with the heater on high and all the windows open, desperately trying to clear my nose. Even my eyes were watering from the smell! I kept thinking that perhaps this wasn't the angel I had envisioned, because surely nothing from heaven could smell this bad.

Twenty windy and cold miles later we paid a surprise visit to the vet. She quickly diagnosed infected glands and said I would have to help her clear them since she had no vet tech on Saturdays. I'll tell you right now, angel or not, I don't think I would ever agree to do that again. I don't know what she did, but as I firmly held his sturdy body, a stench was unleashed that rivaled that of a stockyard auction! Whatever she did fixed the problem because on the rest of the way home, my angel no longer emitted his foul smell. What a relief! But there was still another challenge ahead of me.

At home, there were two very spoiled girls who I doubted would view this new addition as the angel I believed him to be. Abbey, a 14-year-old English Cocker Spaniel and Casey, a 12-year-old West Highland Whitey ruled the house. I feared that they might be too set in their ways to accept a new member of the family. But I had to make it work because deep in my heart I knew that Mart had sent this dog to me. So with a hopeful heart and sweaty palms, I introduced him to my two old spoiled girls through the backyard fence.

Typical excited dog sniffing took place and then some barking from the old girls ensued. My angel calmly took it all in, his tail wagging in a funny little circular way. Strange, I never knew angels could wag their entire behinds. Things appeared to be going well, so I opened the gate and let him join the girls.

Within a few hours it was like he had always been there with us. Known as King Solomon in his first life, he quickly adopted his new name, Sully. He brought life back into the house. In the evening, when other families were settling in to eat dinner or watch television, I would curl up on the couch, feeling the loss of Mart as strongly as I did on that first day. But Sully would come put a slobbery face on my lap and look up at me with those two beautiful light brown eyes and I couldn't stop myself from smiling. Other times he would be so intent on scratching an itch he would literally fall over in the middle of the floor. It's impossible not to laugh at a 70-pound dog when he just falls over!

His sheer joy at seeing me come home from work every day and the way his tail wagged in a complete circle added joy to my life. Not known for being very outspoken, it is pure joy to hear the occasional WOO-WOO bark Clumbers are known for. And "Clumber" describes the movements of this breed perfectly. Watching him clumber across the yard and tumble head over heels trying to not overrun the toy I've thrown for him makes me laugh so hard I worry the neighbors will think I have lost my mind.

On the other hand, there have been days when I thought I could just shoot him. For example, there was the day I came home to discover that he had eaten part of the linoleum in the laundry room. Then there was the phase of pulling all the toilet paper off the roll and shredding it throughout the house. And apparently, television remote controls can be mistaken for rawhide bones. That's all in addition to the daily antics that many of my friends find repulsive, but that I have learned to accept as just another part of living with a Clumber angel.

He sleeps at my bedroom door and snores so loudly that he

sometimes wakes me up and I have to get up and roll him over! He snorts like a pig when he's excited. White fur covers my furniture, carpet, basically everything in the house, including me. But hey, lint brushes aren't that expensive and I should vacuum more often anyway. Worse than the fur, my angel feels an instinctive need to share his slobber with everyone who enters the house. And it doesn't matter how he shares it. Pant legs, shoes, and sleeves are apparently great places to deposit a little Clumber love, but hands and faces are the best! Most people just don't seem to understand his need to share with them, but they can't see his angel wings like I can. And every single day he makes me laugh and brings joy to my broken heart.

Almost a year later, I still have bad days along with the good. Marty is in my every thought every second of every day. But through it all, I have a 70-pound Clumber Spaniel angel, sent to me from my beloved husband, who helps me realize that life is short and that some slobber in your life is okay, as long as it comes from a funny, furry angel.

—Kelly Van Etten—

95

Kisses from Lady

If there is a heaven, it's certain our animals
are to be there. Their lives become so
interwoven with our own, it would take
more than an archangel to detangle them.
~Pam Brown

I was diagnosed with the first of my three cancers almost twenty years ago — a cancer which I was deemed "too young" to have. It was a cancer for which I was completely unprepared as I never knew it ran in my family — a colon cancer that required surgery, chemotherapy, radiation and years of recovery.

Of course, I had wonderful doctors. I had dedicated technicians and advisors. I had great friends and family members cheering me on. I had the best care in one of the best medical facilities in the world. But, most of all, I had Lady.

Lady was my love — a big, strong, yellow Labrador Retriever. And, although my family always had dogs when I was a kid growing up, Lady was my first dog as an adult. My charge. My constant companion.

Throughout my cancer experience, she never left my side. Through the long days of pain, trips to the hospital, and continuous IVs of cancer-fighting drugs. Through the never-ending nights of nausea and diarrhea. We slept in the bathroom together, with me on her doggie bed placed next to the toilet. She lay on the tile floor next to me, with her head on my chest, kissing my chin with her tongue whenever I moaned or cried. I would sometimes wake up and see her watching me — listening to my breathing and making sure I was all right.

Months went by. And months turned into years. Suffering mostly from radiation poisoning, I slowly began to regain my health. I got stronger. I began to eat. I began to walk. And Lady was by my side, encouraging me, wagging her tail for me and kissing my chin at every opportunity.

Yet as I grew stronger, I began to notice she was growing weaker. As I began to eat more, she began to eat less. As I began to walk faster, she began to walk slower. Then she was diagnosed with cancer.

I took her in for surgery one cloudy Saturday in January. I told her everything was going to be okay, and I said goodbye. With her nose next to mine, she kissed my chin with her wet tongue, turned and walked away with the technician. That was the last time I saw her. I lost her on the operating table that day — one week before she was to turn thirteen.

Death was no stranger to me. I'd lost loved ones before, but it's different when we lose an animal. Perhaps it's because there is no ego involved. There is no history of disagreement or anger. There are no unresolved issues that often remain stuck between human beings. There are no feelings of betrayal or guilt or remorse. An animal — a beloved pet — is only there to love us. Unconditionally. Without question. No matter what. That is what we receive, and that is what we remember. There's nothing more to it.

When I lost Lady, I wasn't sure I could continue with my recovery. My support system unraveled. My strength disappeared. I felt alone. Lost. Inconsolable. For heartbreak is real. The physical tissue or muscle or nerve endings of the heart are damaged. They're broken. They hurt. And the pain can be excruciating. I became unsure of my ability to recover my health, and I began to slide into doubt and despair.

Then two events occurred that changed my life.

The first occurred on a rainy night in May. Having returned to my bed, I cried myself to sleep, due to the physical pain I still experienced and the heartbreak that consumed me. Yet, this night a peace began to envelop me. An embracing comfort.

As I surrendered to it, I became aware of a person — or, rather, a

Being. Male, I think. I could not distinguish the face as it was obscured by a cape or coat or garment of some kind. This Being was holding a small cloth bundle in his hands.

He approached and held it out to me. I could see there was a tiny creature wrapped in the cloth. It wasn't human nor was it any animal with which I was familiar. Not a dog or cat. It was clearly an infant of some kind — a baby. Small and fragile.

I received the small creature and held it to my chest. To my heart. And in doing so, I could feel the tiny creature's life force enter my body. A soothing warmth encompassed me and permeated my chest. Penetrating deeper and deeper, it burrowed into my heart. And we remained in that state for hours — the tiny creature and me — until I became aware of a growing light around me, the light of sunrise. And with that awareness, the Being returned, holding out his arms to indicate it was time to give the baby back. So, I did.

That morning, I opened my eyes to a new world. I was completely aware that something extraordinary had happened. For the first time in a long time, my heart didn't hurt. I could breathe again. The crushing pain was gone. The enormous burden had been lifted. I went through my day and into the night with relief, renewed hope and gratitude. Then the second event occurred.

Falling asleep that night, I became aware of another light. As I watched, the light began to move toward me. It clearly was another Being — vibrating with energy. As it got closer, it took shape. It was a shape with which I was all too familiar — four legs, thick beaver tail, floppy ears, and deep, soulful eyes. It was Lady.

She was shimmering. Shining. Surrounded with light. Indeed, she was the light. My gorgeous girl glowed with health and vitality. And as she glided toward me, I knelt to greet her. Her beautiful face met mine. Her eyes shone into mine. And she lifted her head and kissed me on the chin — in her familiar way. I smelled her thick fur coat. I felt her breath on my face. And in that instant — with that gesture — she told me everything would be okay. She was okay. And I, too, would be okay. And then she retreated into the light and faded away — leaving me with love, hope and all good things that life and the universe have to offer.

I don't pretend for a second to understand the inner workings of our physical world, our spiritual world, or any other world that makes up the vast reality of which we are a part. Were these events dreams? Premonitions? Fantasies? Figments of my imagination? The result of loose neural wiring brought on by grief and illness? I don't know. I'm an academic. An attorney. I believe in evidence, hard facts and things I can see and touch. Yet, something happened to me that I cannot deny. And these two events changed me forever. The first healed my heart. The second healed my soul.

I know that Lady orchestrated both events. Love in all its forms is a powerful thing. I see no reason why it can't punch a hole between the worlds of life and death. Or any world in between. And with her love — her kiss — she imparted to me the knowledge that I would recover and go on without her.

Love is the force that unites us all — of that, I'm sure. I know in my heart she will always be with me — and there will always be kisses from Lady.

— Susan Wilking Horan —

96

A License to Love

*Our perfect companions never
have fewer than four feet.*
~Colette

t was love at first sight. The first time I held him in my arms, I knew I had to have him. No, it wasn't a man who won my affections! It was a Peek-a-Poo dubbed Micado by the boyfriend who bought him for me. "Cado" was small in size, but big on attitude. He resembled a gremlin and had an under-bite that made you quietly giggle every time you looked at him. His vocabulary was impressive. He understood words like ride, walk, kids, potty, bed, eat, bath, and especially ice cream! But it was more than that. He intently studied my face when I talked to him, trying to understand what I was saying. Even if he couldn't understand my words, he always seemed to know what I was feeling. We had a deep connection, an unbreakable bond.

Cado seemed to think it was his God-given right to be pampered and I certainly did my best to oblige! After fifteen Christmases, he learned to open gifts and came to expect his own when everyone got theirs. In fact, one year I didn't buy or wrap any presents for him. Not a problem, he just opened mine! Needless to say, he never had another gift-less Christmas!

As he started to age and developed typical senior maladies, I tried to prepare for the eventuality of life without my loyal companion. I told myself that as long as he was happy and not in pain, I would not let him go. I also made a silent promise that I would never let him suffer, but would do the right thing if it got to that point. In spite of arthritis, he continued to play. We took shorter walks. When he lost his appetite, I changed his diet from dry dog food to canned dog food, then to people food like soups, rice and broth.

When he couldn't keep any food down for several days straight, we made the emergency trip to the vet's office. It was a Friday. X-rays and ultrasound showed what appeared to be a large tumor on his stomach. I had three choices — surgery, an agonizing death when the tumor burst (as it was sure to do within days) or euthanasia. Surgery offered no guarantees and I couldn't put him through such an ordeal. There was really only one option. I wanted his last moments on earth to be peaceful. I would be with him to the end. I wanted the last face he saw to be mine and his last memories to be the overwhelming love I had for him. The shot was administered and the vet left the room. Cado's eyes were fixed on me while I softly told him how glad I was to have had him in my life, how much I would miss him and how we would someday meet again. His eyes slowly closed and he was gone.

I can't even begin to describe the sadness and loneliness I felt at the loss of my Micado. For many nights, I lay in bed clutching his favorite sweater and crying myself to sleep. Eventually I started visiting local animal shelters and the pet refuge looking for a dog to fill the huge empty place in my heart. But every visit resulted in the same outcome. None of the dogs, no matter how sweet, how playful, how deserving, were Micado. No dog measured up to him. I just couldn't disrespect his memory by allowing another dog to take his place in my home or in my heart.

I continued to grieve for about a year. Then one night, Micado came to me in a dream. In this dream, I looked out my living room window to see my front yard filled with hundreds of dogs, all sizes, colors and breeds! As I stood there in awe, a voice said, "They are here for you. I want another dog to know the kind of love you gave to me. Pick me up so I can see them too!" It was Micado. I picked him up, and as I held him in my arms, I could truly feel the weight and warmth of his body against mine. I could feel the love he had for me.

As he and I surveyed the dogs outside, I reluctantly awakened from the comforting moments I had spent with him. As I thought about the strange and powerful dream, a deep understanding washed over me. The bond between us had transcended death. Micado had come back to ease my pain. He had come back to let me know that he knew how much I loved him and that his special place in my heart would never be threatened, even by another dog. He was there to let me know he didn't want me to be lonely or sad any longer.

A few weeks after the dream, a message went out to all users on our corporate e-mail system advertising a Shih Tzu free to a good home. I was the first of fifteen callers and told the young doctor's wife about Micado, my loss, and finally being ready to get another dog. I made arrangements to meet Xander that very night. Although they had many responses to the e-mail, they told me they had no plans to interview other people. If I was interested, Xander was mine. In spite of Xander's complete disinterest in me (in fact he growled, barked and would not let me near him), I knew he was the one. I knew I would take him home with me and win him over. That was four years ago. Xander is not Micado, but he doesn't need to be. Xander is very special in his own right and I pamper him shamelessly! He has found a permanent home and a lasting place in my heart. He can thank Micado for that.

— Luann Warner —

97

Jake's Last Gift

I have found that when you are deeply troubled,
there are things you get from the silent,
devoted companionship of a dog that
you can get from no other source.
~Doris Day

When I was a young woman, my best friend by far was my Border Collie, Jake. He joined my family when I was fourteen years old and he was fourteen weeks, so the two of us grew up side by side. We hit our awkward adolescent phase at the same time, and while Jake naturally grew out of his much faster than I did, he never held it against me. The two of us were inseparable until he passed away from cancer at the ripe old age of thirteen.

The day we had to say goodbye was a very difficult one for me. On the one hand, I was grateful that Jake had lived such a good long life, and I didn't want to sully that gratitude with too much sorrow. But at the same time, my house suddenly felt very empty, my kitchen too quiet, and my back yard much, much too big. I managed to stand the silence for several hours. Then I got in my car and drove to Smith Rock State Park in Terrebonne, Oregon.

Smith Rock State Park is one of those stunning natural places that is hard to describe with mere words. Although the beautiful stone cliffs there are beloved by competitive rock climbers worldwide, one doesn't have to be a rock climber to enjoy them. The park also has several wonderful pet-friendly hiking trails for those of us whose athletic abilities are more, shall we say, down-to-earth. Jake and I had spent many happy hours exploring them together, and walking beneath the ancient rocks had never failed to fill me with a deep sense of peace.

That day was no exception. I spent maybe half an hour hiking up one of the easier trails, and while I missed my beautiful dog fiercely with every step, just being alone in nature helped to ease my heart. I was just wondering if it was time to turn back and head home when a little ball of black-and-white fur suddenly came streaking up the trail. It was dragging a nylon leash behind it.

The blur was moving so quickly that I didn't really get a look at it, but some dog-person instincts never fade. I knew instantly that the blur was a dog that had somehow tugged its leash out of its owner's hand, and I quickly moved to intervene. I stepped on the leash, halting the little runaway in mid-flight. And when I looked down to see what I'd caught, I couldn't believe my eyes.

It was a little black-and-white Border Collie puppy — one that could have been the twin of my Jake when we first met.

I didn't have much time to stare. A few seconds later, the puppy's human mom, red-faced and sweating, came sprinting around the bend in the trail. "Oh, thank you so much!" she said when she saw that I had caught her furry fugitive. "I don't know why Jake took off like that except that he's been cooped up in the car all day. I guess he just decided he really needed a good run."

"Jake?" I repeated. "This puppy is named Jake?" And then I burst into tears.

Looking back on it, I'm a little amazed that the woman didn't snatch up her puppy and run. Having a total stranger suddenly fall apart on you in the middle of a wilderness trail is hardly likely to inspire much confidence. But true dog people are a rare breed. The woman took one look at me, then gently took Jake's leash from my hand and guided me to a nearby picnic table. She urged me to sit down. Then she lifted the puppy onto the table and asked me to tell her what was wrong.

By the time I'd finished stuttering out my story, she was looking very thoughtful. "You know," she said, "my husband and I are driving home to Seattle — we've been visiting our daughter down in California. Normally, we wouldn't have stopped for a break until we reached Madras. But when I saw the sign for Smith Rock, something told me we needed to stop." She smiled at Jake and me, who had crossed the table and put his tiny paws on my shoulders, trying frantically to lick my face. "I think I know why now. I think your Jake is using our Jake to say goodbye."

My hands froze in Jake's soft baby fur. It couldn't be possible. Or could it? But before I could voice my doubts, the woman smiled again, laughing a little as Jake's still insistently licking tongue went up my nose. "Are you going to get another dog?" she asked.

I shook my head. "I could never," I said. "My Jake was far too special for me to ever want to replace him."

"Not replace, no," the woman said. "That would be impossible. But I still think you'll have another dog in your life one day, when the time is right." She cocked her head thoughtfully to one side. "I think perhaps your Jake will see to it that you find the right one."

"I could never," I repeated — and at that moment, I honestly believed it was true. To her credit, the woman didn't try to push. She just walked me back to the parking lot, where we spent a few minutes talking about inconsequential things with her husband before they all got back in their truck and resumed their trip home to Seattle. I never even learned her name.

But her words stuck with me anyway, as did the incredible coincidence of running into Jake at Smith Rock that day. What, after all, were the odds of meeting a puppy of the same breed, the same coloring, and even the same name as my Jake only a few hours after he passed away? In many ways, the chance encounter really did feel like my dog's final gift to me, his way of assuring me that he'd never leave me entirely. And that thought comforted me greatly during all the days and weeks ahead.

But the story doesn't end there. About a year later, I received a surprise phone call from my vet. "I don't know if you're interested," she said. "But one of my other clients just had a litter of Border Collie pups, and they're all lovely young dogs. The second that Brittney said she was looking for good homes for them, I thought of you. You might want to drive out and have a look."

"Well..." I said hesitantly. "I suppose it wouldn't hurt to visit. Where does Brittney live?"

"She has a small ranch in Terrebonne, right next to Smith Rock State Park," my vet said. "The pups were born right in the shadow of the cliffs."

— Kerrie R. Barney —

Gone On to a Better Place

When people are laughing, they're generally
not killing each other.
~Alan Alda

My husband's family members all live within an hour's drive of each other, and one summer they decided to take a big, multi-generational vacation to the beach — despite the fact that getting together for even a quick coffee can often result in what I like to call "an unfortunate incident." But in theory, this trip would be a blissful assemblage of aunts, uncles, grandparents, cousins, siblings, parents and kids spending a week together in one big, laughter-filled house by the shore. And though any such venture will doubtless include a few bumps in the road, no one could have anticipated the bizarre occurrence that would form everyone's lasting memory of this familial voyage.

The morning my mother-in-law, Caroline, and father-in-law, Daniel, were about to hit the road for this trek, Daniel made a grim discovery in the back yard. Boogie, their elderly German Shepherd, had quietly passed away in the shade of his favorite weeping willow. Worried that this news would start the vacation off on the worst possible note, Daniel decided to keep Boogie's untimely demise to himself, ship Caroline off to the beach with their daughter Ellen, and then bury the dog by himself once everyone was out of town.

"I called Ellen to come pick you up and take you with her," he announced rather gruffly, preoccupied by the dark task ahead. "I've got some things I need to do today. I'll head down tomorrow and meet up with you at the rental house."

"What are you talking about?" Caroline asked, dismayed by this last-minute upheaval. "That's ridiculous!"

By now, Daniel, who could be a bit short-tempered, was starting to feel overwhelmed by the heat of the August day, melancholy over Boogie's death and general anxiety over the impending family get-together. The volatile combination caused Daniel to erupt, rather loudly, at his wife.

"For heaven's sake, Caroline, just DO WHAT I ASK!" he yelled. "Why can't you just GO and not make a big deal of it?"

Caroline snapped back at him, returning his elevated and angry tone. The spat continued for a few moments before Daniel caught himself and apologized.

"Please," he said quietly, placing a hand on her shoulder. "I really need you to do this, but I promise I'll be there tomorrow, and everything will be fine."

Ellen pulled up just then, so Caroline shrugged an "okay," got her luggage and left for the beach with her daughter.

As soon as they were gone, Daniel got to work on making Boogie's final arrangements. He gathered up a few of the dog's favorite toys, the old green blanket Boogie always slept on, and a half-chewed rawhide bone. Finding the shovel and pickax in the garage took a while, and by the time Daniel had everything he needed, it was mid-afternoon. Concerned about the oppressive heat and humidity, he decided to wait until after sundown to begin excavating Boogie's grave, and settled into his easy chair for a quick nap.

It was after 10:00 p.m. when the sound of pouring rain woke my father-in-law, who was stiff from his unexpectedly long sleep in the recliner. He felt groggy and disoriented, but the thought of poor Boogie alone in the storm compelled him to action. Daniel went outside, lovingly wrapped Boogie and his playthings in the blanket, and began digging the dog's final resting place. He chose a spot close to where the canine had died, but Daniel soon hit a large root and had to adjust his plan, shifting the perimeter of the hole away from the willow's trunk. It wasn't long before he came upon another unyielding patch, and then another. Both times, he had to realign the grave's border to circumvent the obstacles.

The heavy rain made it difficult for him to proceed in the darkness, so Daniel got an old camping lantern and set it atop a nearby fencepost. When he turned it on, the splash of yellow light revealed a jagged, sprawling pit beneath the willow's sheltering branches. Aided by the lantern, Daniel continued to dig, straightening and deepening the trench as he went. At last, he placed the green-wrapped bundle in the hole, said a few parting words, and then began re-filling the cavity with muddy earth.

Meanwhile, at the beach, the adults had finally gotten the children settled in and were enjoying a late-night comedy show. We were right in the middle of planning the next day's activities when Caroline's phone rang.

"Hello? Yes, this is Caroline," we heard her say, and then there was a lengthy pause while she listened to the caller.

"I'm sorry," Caroline said at last. "I have to put this on speaker so everybody can hear that." She hit the button, and then asked the person on the other end, "Would you mind repeating what you just said?"

"Sure, ma'am," a man's voice replied. "This is Officer Green of the Prince William County Police. I just got a call from one of your neighbors saying he heard shouting at your house earlier today. And then about an hour ago, his wife saw your husband outside in the rain digging a pretty big hole. Neither of them had seen you since the shouting earlier, and they say your husband was definitely burying something in the back yard. And, well…" the policeman hesitated a moment before continuing, "well, ma'am, we just wanted to make sure that 'something' wasn't you."

— Miriam Van Scott —

99

Merlin's Miracle

The gift which I am sending you is called a dog,
and is in fact the most precious and
valuable possession of mankind.
~Theodorus Gaza

etey guards our storm door. His silky ears pop up, and his bright eyes shine as I approach the house. His tail wags furiously when I bend down to accept his kisses.

He has lived with us for only two weeks, yet he already rules the house. The couches and the bed we swore were off limits are already among Petey's favorite spots.

Chewed twigs and paper-towel rolls litter the family room, but we're not in any hurry to clean them up. And I've learned to fall asleep faster after taking him out for his middle-of-the-night potty breaks.

My husband and teenage daughters had wanted a puppy, but I hadn't. I found house-training our first dog a real headache, and I didn't want to deal with a pup's incessant chewing. I wanted an older dog so those problems would be behind us.

I'd grown accustomed to living with our thirteen-year-old Wirehaired Dachshund, Merlin. He slept a lot and rarely got into things he shouldn't.

But poor Merlin was diagnosed with a baseball-sized tumor on his spleen and was gone six months later. I couldn't imagine life without his sweet spirit in our home. I wrote journal entries to him every couple of days as immense grief colored my daily life.

We visited animal shelters several times that fall, but we never found a dog that interested us. The holidays and cold weather temporarily halted our efforts.

I still thought of Merlin daily, but my journal entries became more sporadic, and my memories held less pain. I began to ask Merlin's spirit to help us find just the right dog. I didn't understand why we were having such a hard time finding a new dog. After all, our hearts were open and we loved dogs.

As the days grew longer and spring flowers bloomed, we renewed our hunt. A Basset Hound stared mournfully at us, but my husband, Mark, said she would drool too much. I could barely control a male mutt as I walked him around the shelter yard. I played briefly with a female Chow at another shelter, but she wasn't our answer either.

Mark and I decided to visit two more locations the following weekend. We never reached the second one. The Humane Society had assembled a dozen dogs of different sizes, shapes and colors at a local pet adoption event. They yapped, barked, whined and climbed all over each other as they frantically jockeyed for human contact.

Mark spotted the pup first. White and gray, gangly and seemingly overwhelmed by his more aggressive sister, he rested happily in Mark's arms. When the pup snuggled into the crook of my elbow, all my arguments for an older dog melted away instantly.

We had never seen such a mellow puppy. We couldn't tell his breed, but we knew we wanted him.

A volunteer asked questions about our yard, our house and other family members. We signed the appropriate papers and headed home. We would pick up the pup several days later, after he was neutered.

Our daughters came with us. They took turns carrying Petey as we chose a collar and a new water bowl, and then they giggled while entertaining him in the back seat.

When we got home, we all played with and held Petey. He bounced after toys, dove into our laps, kissed our faces enthusiastically and sniffed everywhere. Smiles and laughter filled the room. I had forgotten how much fun a puppy could be. Maybe we had been ready for a puppy after all!

As I placed Petey's paperwork on the table, I spotted the official name of his coloring—Blue Merle. Hairs stood up on my neck, and I silently thanked Merlin's spirit, which I was now convinced had indeed helped us find our wonderful new dog.

—Lisa Waterman Gray—

100

With Us Always

*If you have a dog, you will most likely outlive it; to
get a dog is to open yourself to profound joy and,
prospectively, to equally profound sadness.*
~Marjorie Garber

Our dog Johnathon was special. I purchased him for my husband as a Christmas gift, and we made the long trek over the snowy mountains to pick him up in Eastern Washington. A beautiful dark gray color, his eyes shone bright blue in the light, and his fur felt like velvet.

My husband decided to name him Johnathon since he had always liked that name. We called him Johnny for short. He was smart and learned tricks quickly. He always had a smile on his face and was infatuated with his tennis balls. He played with them for hours. When tired, he would hide his tennis balls under the couch so our other dog, Jasmyn, would not take them.

Water was Johnny's vice, and he would swim for hours, or open his mouth wide to be doused when we ran the hose. He was the king of making funny faces, and he loved nothing more than being fawned over and loved. He would even "dance" by chasing his tail when we played music. He especially loved the song by the Charlie Daniels Band, "The Devil Went Down to Georgia," because they sang his name in it.

One day, when he was about nineteen months old, he began having terrible seizures. Some would last five minutes; some would last more than forty-five minutes. It was terrifying to watch him have those episodes. We took him to see the veterinarian and they put him on an anti-seizure medication. This medication did not stop the seizures, so we took him to a veterinarian neurologist who diagnosed him with idiopathic epilepsy. They recommended that we start him on a custom compounded medication that we had to pick up from a special pharmacy. This combination of medications did nothing to help Johnny. They made him nauseous and he was unable to keep anything down, or in for that matter. He lost interest in his tennis balls and forgot his tricks. The doctors recommended that we restrict his activity, as they thought possibly too much stimulation was adding to his issue.

After being on the medications for close to three months, he still was having seizures, and even started to have more frequent tremors. We were unable to stop them, even with injectable anti-seizure medication. The specialist told us that Johnny most likely had a brain tumor, and he wanted to do a CT scan of his brain to make sure. Johnny was suffering and wasting away in front of our eyes, and it was unbearable. We made the heart-wrenching decision to euthanize him. We chose to do it on the Fourth of July because we felt that every year his life would be celebrated by the fireworks.

That morning, as we drove him to the veterinarian, he relished the wind on his handsome face. While spending our last moments with him, he kissed away our tears. It seemed like he was telling us not to be worried, that he would still be here for us. He loved us, and forgave us.

We were distraught for the next few weeks and our house seemed devoid of happiness. It seemed so unfair that Johnny had gotten sick so young and, worse, we had not been able to cure him. My husband was inconsolable.

One lonely evening, after sharing our favorite memories of Johnny once again, we headed upstairs to bed. Our other dog Jasmyn refused to climb the stairs behind us. As Christians, we believe wholeheartedly in life after death, so we asked aloud if Johnny was home. Suddenly, the phone rang! I looked at the caller ID, and it said it was my husband's cell phone calling. Confused, he pulled his phone out of his pocket and the screen showed that it was not actually calling. We let the call go to the answering machine. After our recorded greeting, four barks sounded from the speaker. The call hung up then, and it didn't save the message or the caller ID. Slow smiles crept across our faces as we realized Johnny had come back to let us know he was still around.

That night my husband had a dream that he visited Johnny in a large field with a pond, where Johnny was running around with other dogs, a huge smile on his face. We strongly feel that he is at the Rainbow Bridge waiting for us to join him. And because he was my husband's special friend, he was the privileged one to view him in that setting. Johnny now seems to come visit us when we miss him or need him the most. When my husband's knee was bothering him, he prayed to God to take away his pain. He woke up in the middle of that same night to find the bedroom bathed in bright light, and Johnny lying on that specific knee, licking it. He has never had discomfort in that knee again.

Though Johnny is no longer with us physically, we are grateful that he still visits us from time to time.

— Megan LeeAnn Waterman-Fouch —

Lady

A ladybug sighting has been linked with luck in love,
marriage, healing and newness in life.
~Author Unknown

My husband came home from work that day, frantic and totally in love with a stray dog he befriended while working outside on a bulldozer. The black Lab and Springer Spaniel mix came out of nowhere, licking his ear and nuzzling his hand. He gave her water, tied her to a nearby tree in the shade, and promised she would come home with him later that day.

Unfortunately, an office worker noticed the stray dog earlier that day and had called the animal control offices to send someone to retrieve it. When my husband came out at the end of his shift, he was brokenhearted to find the dog was gone. Someone told him the animal control van was there not an hour before, and the stray dog had been taken to the pound.

That evening my husband repeated the sad story to me. It was easy to see that this stray had completely won his heart and he was totally devastated. I'd never seen my husband so enamored of an animal and we'd had plenty in our years of marriage.

He looked to me with tears in his eyes. "This dog is very special. We have to find her!"

"Then find her, we will," I agreed.

Five minutes later, we were in our truck and headed to the first of several locations where the animal control officers could have taken the black Lab. The third stop proved to be the right one; we'd found her. Before they led us back to the compound where she was being held, we were advised the dog would be held for seventy-two hours to give the legal owners a chance to retrieve her.

"We understand there is a waiting period," my husband said. "We want to be her new family, and we'll do whatever is necessary."

We followed the animal control officer to the rear of the compound where dozens of dogs were barking and snarling, along with dozens of cats mewing and pacing back and forth in cages.

Around another corner and the officer paused, looking to my husband. "Is this the dog you found earlier today?"

"Yes, yes!" He looked over to the black Lab and smiled. "I came back for you, girl."

The officer opened the gated door and gestured for us to enter. The Lab was curled up on the floor; her head drooped, big brown eyes hopeful but shy. I knelt down and lifted her chin, patting her head at the same time.

"Hello there, sweet girl."

My husband beamed. "Isn't she beautiful? I told you she was special."

"She is; I can see it in her eyes."

Those impossibly big brown eyes were so transparent; it was almost like she was conveying to us a promise that she would look much better once she'd had a decent bath, and that she was apologizing for her condition. It was also clear that someone had abused her, perhaps even beaten her and then thrown her away like trash. My husband and I were both touched deeply.

The next day I went shopping for a dog bed, collar, cans of wet food and bags of dry dog food, a half dozen treats and at least that many toys.

"So, what shall we name her?" my husband questioned when he arrived home from work.

"Lady. She's the perfect little lady." I hadn't even thought this out, but the name had come to my mind quickly and easily.

My husband agreed. "That she is!"

The next few days felt like weeks, the time dragging until the day came we finally brought Lady home. She walked throughout the house, sniffing as she went, eventually settling onto her plush round bed situated in our family room. We both sat in our recliners and just stared at Lady as she slept peacefully. Our two cats sauntered through the room, trying their best to look casual as they stopped and stared at the dark creature softly snoring in the corner. They approached her cautiously, sniffed a bit at Lady's feet, and carried on with their business as if this were not a momentous occasion. Everyone knew it was, however, sensing that our lives would never be the same and Lady had everything to do with it.

We lived in a rural area off a dead-end street and down a graveled road. Our property was just under two acres, and Lady seemed to know just where her boundaries were and what was off limits. She made friends with the neighbor dogs, and was especially kind to Ace, the big German shepherd next door who was fast losing his eyesight. Lady would walk with him, nudging him right or left along the gravel road if a car would approach, and she led him home in the evenings at about the dinner hour. Friends came to know and love Lady, recognizing her gentle, loving spirit and ever smiling face. One friend joked repeatedly about having her cloned; he loved her too!

One afternoon my husband and I were picking weeds in the front yard when a neighbor's chicken strayed into our space. Directly before us, Lady instantly froze, her body held in a beautifully poised point, her brown eyes locked on the bird.

My husband grinned at me and called out to Lady. "Go get it, girl."

Two seconds later, we had a dead chicken on our hands. That night my husband fried up that chicken, along with mashed potatoes and corn, serving a plate of everything to Lady. "This is for you, Lady. Tomorrow, we're going to take you pheasant and quail hunting."

And that became Lady's glory; she was magic out among the sagebrush. Pure beauty, pure instinct, and doing what she loved best. I went on every hunt with my husband, just to watch Lady dance with grace among nature's own.

The years went by and we loved Lady every day, month, and

moment. She always had a bright smile and a spring in her step until the day came we learned she had cancer. We were devastated at the diagnosis and horrified at the prospect of losing our precious Lady, but that final day came and changed our lives forever.

We each had a chance to say goodbye to Lady, and friends, family members and neighbors all had private moments in which they shared with her. Then, exactly one week after Lady passed away, I was talking with a good friend on the phone. The friend was outside in her hammock, chattering away with me, when suddenly she stopped.

"That's strange," my friend said.

"What? What's strange?"

"A ladybug just landed on me."

"Nothing strange about that."

"Yes there is. This ladybug is gold in color."

Our conversation continued and later that same afternoon my son called, just to chat.

"So, how was your day?"

"Great," my son answered. "I went out on the lake today with a buddy and we water-skied. It was great, but guess what happened?"

"What happened?"

"A ladybug landed on me, a golden ladybug. I didn't even know there were golden ladybugs."

"I didn't know that, either."

That evening after my husband arrived home from work, he was eager to tell me what happened that day.

"I was outside working on a bulldozer." He grinned. "And this golden ladybug landed on me!"

I grinned back at my husband. "You and everybody else, it would seem."

I told him of the earlier calls where golden ladybugs had shown themselves.

"Wow, isn't that weird but kind of wonderful, all at the same time?"

"Yes," I agreed. "Our favorite nickname for Lady was Ladybug and I don't think this is just a coincidence."

We talked all evening of the special times we shared with our precious Lady. The next morning I was taking one of our cats into the veterinarian for his yearly immunizations. The doctor came in the waiting room and smiled warmly.

"I'm so glad to see you," the vet said to me. "Something happened to me yesterday and I wanted you to know."

I smiled. "Let me take a guess. A ladybug landed on you — a golden ladybug."

The vet grinned widely. "Yes indeed! Lady came to me for a visit. This is her way of letting everyone know that she's okay and she's sending love to all."

"They really do get a message through to us," I said. "Don't they?"

"Indeed they do," the vet answered. "I've seen this happen many times."

The tears that fell were happy tears. We love you, dear sweet Lady!

— Louetta Jensen —

Meet Our Contributors

We are pleased to introduce you to the writers whose stories were compiled from our past books to create this new collection. These bios were the ones that ran when the stories were originally published. They were current as of the publication dates of those books.

Gretchen Allen teaches people about the wonderful natural and cultural resources of our country. In her free time, she visits the elderly with her therapy dog, plays with her two non-therapy dogs and three cats, enjoys riding her horse, and paints and draws.

Elizabeth Atwater lives in a small Southern town with her husband Joe. She discovered the joy of reading in first grade and that naturally seemed to evolve into a joy of writing. Writing brings Elizabeth so much pleasure that she cannot imagine ever stopping. She sold her first story to a romance magazine when she was seventeen years old.

Kerrie R. Barney is currently a full-time graduate student studying accounting at the University of New Mexico — go Lobos! You can find her book *Life, the Universe, and Houseplants*, all about her humorous adventures growing indoor plants, on Amazon.

Carolyn Barrett has lived in New Jersey her entire life and enjoys her work as an ultrasound technologist. She has four children and will soon become an empty nester. Carolyn enjoys music, flower gardening, the beach, antiquing, reading and writing. She is working on an inspirational book and blogs at www.lifeisnteasy.com.

While **Harris Bloom** is a writer and stand-up comedian in New York City, he is most proud of founding and running Stewie to the Rescue, the subject of the essay included in this book. Well, he's also

REALLY proud of his daughter Zadie and his wife Josie (and his dog, River).

Alandra Blume is a West Virginian animal lover who adores reading, music, and rainstorms. She is a Christian, a freshman in college, and can be reached via e-mail at alblume@bluefield.edu. Bonnie is now a healthy ten-year-old and loves being with the family.

Tamra Anne Bolles received her Bachelor of Arts in Journalism from the University of Georgia in 1988, and Master of Education from Georgia State University in 2000. She teaches for the Cobb County School District and enjoys kayaking and exploring nature. She plans to retire from teaching soon and move to Blue Ridge, GA.

Michele Boy received her Bachelor of Arts in Communications at Queens College, NY. She is a transplanted New Yorker living in western Kansas where she helps her husband on their farm and raises their daughter. She writes a blog for Kansas Agland. E-mail her at Micheleaboy@gmail.com.

Cate Bronson is an accountant turned author of speculative fiction and nonfiction. She is also a *Writer's Digest* awarded writer in mainstream fiction, and contributor to magazines and anthologies. In her spare time, Cate lounges with her husband and Greyhounds in Florida, and helps retired racing dogs find loving homes.

Jack Byron received his degree in illustration and has published art criticism in addition to writing for the *Chicken Soup for the Soul* series. Always encouraging others to write, he believes that the best stories are written first in our daily lives before ever being committed to paper. Follow him on Twitter @JackByron13.

Christy A. Caballero lives a couple of deer trails off the beaten path in Northwest Oregon. She has earned four Maxwell Awards from the Dog Writers Association of America, along with national awards from the National Federation of Press Women. Her focus now is on more personal writing.

Kathe Campbell lives her dream on a Montana mountain with her mammoth donkeys, a Keeshond, and a few kitties. Three children, eleven grands and many greats round out her herd. She is a prolific writer on Alzheimer's, and her stories are found on many e-zines.

Deborah Cannon is a fiction writer. She recently won an honourable mention for her story, "Twilight Glyph," published in *Canadian Tales of the Fantastic* (2014). She is best known for her archaeological suspense novel series, *The Raven Chronicles*. She lives in Hamilton, Ontario with her archaeologist husband and two dogs.

Jacqueline Gray Carrico has contributed stories for two previous *Chicken Soup for the Soul* books. She is the mother of a grown son who will soon be married. Jacqueline is a dedicated nurse who often finds inspiration from her patients. She enjoys refinishing furniture in her spare time.

Jennifer Crites is a writer/photographer whose work has appeared in magazines and books worldwide, including *Islands*, *Fodor's*, and *Travel+Leisure* among many others. She loves to explore far-off places like Thailand, India, Dubai and Argentina. Her travel blog can be found at jennnifercrites.wordpress.com.

William Dameron is an award-winning blogger, essayist and the author of *The Lie: A Memoir of Two Marriages, Catfishing & Coming Out*. His work has appeared in *The New York Times*, *The Boston Globe*, *Salon*, *The Huffington Post*, and in the book, *Fashionably Late: Gay, Bi and Trans Men Who Came Out Later in Life*.

Joanne Darlington is a retired nurse-manager, married to her husband Steve for thirty-nine years, mother of four, grandmother of three, a life-long reader and writer, who lives in the country not far from Annie's Fish Pond.

Jill Davis lives with her husband Gary in Florida.

Nancy Lee Davis has been a writer since the times of the big black typewriters. She wrote her first play at age twelve, and later had a small column in a small town weekly newspaper Mother, grandmother and now, great-grandmother, Nancy draws on plenty of past experiences and hopes, bits of wisdom and humor to pass on.

Piper M. Dellums is an author, public and inspirational speaker, international victims advocate, member of the United Nations delegate commission on the status of women, film producer, mother of two, environmentalist, international human rights and dignities activist, and survivor. She received degrees from UC Berkeley and New York

University.

Marie Duffoo is a full-time writer and animal activist. When she is not writing she spends her time rescuing sick, abandoned and injured animals.

Rita Durrett lives in Elk City, OK. She is the mother of two sons and grandmother of six boys and one girl. When Rita isn't playing with grandchildren, she is writing, traveling, or crafting. She is also a reluctant blogger. Learn more at www.RitaDurrett.com.

Wendy Newell Dyer is a member of the Passamaquoddy tribe of Maine. She graduated from the University of Maine at Machias in 2003. She has three sons and three grandsons. Wendy enjoys writing, running, hiking and mountain climbing on the coast of Maine. Read her blog at wendynewelldyer.wordpress.com/.

Roberta Marie Easley likes adventure and stories that are well told.

Janice R. Edwards received her BAT degree in 1974. She taught English and Journalism before working at Texaco. She is a freelance writer for *Image Magazine* and has been published numerous times in the *Chicken Soup for the Soul* series.

David A. Eklund was born and has lived in Alberta all his life. The story of his father and his faithful dog Ring is well known in the Eklund family. They hope to share the story with animal lovers everywhere.

Terri Elders, LCSW, served with the Peace Corps in Belize, Dominican Republic and Seychelles, as well as in the USA following Hurricanes Rita and Katrina. Her stories appear in over a hundred anthologies, including two dozen *Chicken Soup for the Soul* books. She blogs at atouchoftarragon.blogspot.com.

Jane Marie Allen Farmer is employed teaching people how to understand and enjoy the wonderful natural and cultural resources of our country. In her free time, she makes visits with her two therapy dogs, plays with her two non-therapy dogs and three cats, and enjoys riding her horses. She also paints and draws.

Lisa Fowler lives in the Blue Ridge Mountains of Western North Carolina with her goofy American Bulldog, Hazel, and her loyal Pit Bull, Abby. Her writing interests are concentrated on middle-grade novels and early chapter books. When not penning stories, Lisa enjoys playing trumpet, reading, and flower gardening.

Halia Grace is a writer, hiker, psychotherapist, and crazy dog lady. She lives in a one-room shack in the Catskills with five rescued dogs and her long-suffering husband.

Longtime freelance writer, **Lisa Waterman Gray**, enjoys finding the mystery and magic in life — whether at home or while on the road. She has described great food and terrific travels through the U.S., Quebec, and Italy for publications from USAToday.com to *The Kansas City Star*.

Mary Guinane is a professional writer who has enjoyed helping raise money for nearly two decades for nonprofit organizations across the country by telling their powerful stories. She is the proud mom of two adult daughters, a bonus son-in-law and her constant shadow, Bella. And everyone knows the fur kid is the favorite.

Chelsea Hall is a world traveler, animal lover, tennis player and professional editor. She graduated from Oregon State University in 2010. She currently resides in Tucson, AZ with her baby girl and husband.

Pam Hawley also writes short fiction and is working on her first novel. Her work has appeared in *eFiction* magazine and *The Spirit of Poe* anthology. She lives in Baltimore, works in higher education, and enjoys reading, hiking, ferrets, and cheering for the Pittsburgh Steelers. E-mail her at sixweasels@comcast.net.

Helen Heavirland enjoys reading, international volunteering, hiking, observing wildlife, and watching the escapades of pets. A nurse, bookkeeper, and author, she especially enjoys writing stories and teaching others how to write theirs. Learn more at www.helenheavirland.com.

Gregg Heid was a Peace Corps volunteer in the seventies and worked for the U.S. Forest Service upon his return from Paraguay. He also taught high school mathematics in Denver for twenty-seven years. He enjoys skiing, hiking, biking, and traveling with his family.

Zach Hively writes poetry, nonfiction, alt-folk music, and the award-winning "Fools Gold" humor column. He plays guitar and harmonica in the duo Oxygen on Embers, and his poetry is proudly displayed at the Magdalena Lily McCarson gallery in Santa Fe, NM. He dances Argentine tango and lives near Abiquiu, NM with his dog.

Susan Wilking Horan is a three-time cancer survivor, wellness advocate, blogger, businesswoman and inspirational speaker. She has a Bachelor of Arts in Psychology, a Juris Doctor in Law and is an Amazon best-selling author of *The Single Source Cancer Course* and *Betty Boop's Guide to a Bold and Balanced Life*.

Alton Housworth was born on his family's farm in rural Georgia during the Depression. At the age of seventeen, he joined the United States Marine Corps and served during the Korean War era. He later became a successful real estate broker and land developer. He lives with his wife of sixty years in the metro Atlanta area.

Jeffree Wyn Itrich has been a professional writer for thirty years. Though writing nonfiction since the mid-80s, she's also written two novels and a children's book. When not writing she's a quilting maniac, a theme that carries through her blog, "The Goodness Principle."

Jennie Ivey lives in Tennessee. She is the author of several works of fiction and nonfiction, including stories in many *Chicken Soup for the Soul* books. Learn more at jennieivey.com.

JP Jackson observes and records the daily absurdities of life. Kids and dogs keep her humble, as well as providing poignant material. Part-time nursing helps to support her writing habit… soon to be a collection of humorous short stories! E-mail her at jpoi@live.com.

As a member of the International Women's Writing Guild, **Louetta Jensen** has authored four novels and three screenplays. Her novel, *Bittersweet Serenity*, was a winner in the North American Fiction Writer Awards, and also received a Certificate of Merit in the 9th Annual Writer's Digest National Book Awards.

Jill Kemerer writes inspirational romance novels. Coffee fuels her mornings; chocolate, her afternoons. After graduating *magna cum laude* and working as an electrical engineer, Jill became a stay-at-home mom. When not writing, she adores magazines, fluffy animals, and her hilarious family. Learn more at www.jillkemerer.com.

Lynn Kinnaman is a writing instructor at Montana State University and the author of several books and numerous articles. She's been publishing since college and loves to tell stories, teach people, and create connections. She's a creativity coach for writers and offers workshops and classes. E-mail her at Lynn@LynnKinnaman.com.

Jeanne Kraus is a retired elementary teacher with thirty-eight years of experience. She is a public speaker and author of children's books. Her three children's books deal with issues related to ADD in children. Currently, Jeanne is a private tutor and volunteer in a local elementary school.

Joyce Laird has made her living as a freelance writer/journalist since 1984. She has also published many human-interest essays and short fiction stories. Her artwork, photography and a house full of fur-babies round out her busy life, along with three great-grandsons.

Sharon Landeen, mother, grandma, great-grandma and retired elementary teacher, believes that working with children helps keep her young. She stays busy volunteering at schools, being a reading mentor and helping with the 4-H program. She enjoys traveling, reading and following the University of Arizona's basketball team.

Francesca Lang lives in Orlando with her husband Richard and son Aiden, along with Bailey the cat and Jazmine the dog. She holds a degree in Intercultural Communications and Sociology, however, her passion lies in health and wellness and she's working toward a license in exercise physiology and personal training.

Kathryn Lay is a full-time writer for children and adults in books, magazines, and anthologies. She enjoys speaking at schools and to writer's groups. She and her husband own Days Gone By Antiques/Vintage. The site can be found on Facebook and at Etsy at LaysDaysGoneBy. E-mail her at rlay15@aol.com.

A criminal court reporter by day, **Jody Lebel** writes romantic suspense novels and short stories, which have sold to *Woman's World* and dozens of other publications. She was raised in charming New England, was an only child who had an only child (claiming she didn't breed well in captivity) and lives with her two cats in South Florida.

Machille Legoullon is a children's book author, wife, and proud mother of four boys. She is currently working on her first middle grade novel and has completed a picture book manuscript she is hoping to publish soon. Machille is extremely involved with her sons' school and the family business. E-mail her at writerinside@comcast.net.

Kathie Leier, her husband Ivan, and Keiko, their beloved senior Shih Tzu, moved from Regina, SK in 2016 to retire to the beauty and solitude of Riding Mountain National Park, MB. In November 2017, after being a most loving companion for ten years, Keiko went to doggie heaven at the age of fourteen. He is dearly missed.

Jaye Lewis is an inspirational author who lives near Whitetop Mountain in Virginia. By her side is her service dog Dixie Mae Doxie, a ten-pound Dachshund, who has changed her life. Visit both of them at www.facebook.com/jaye.lewis.7 or www.facebook.com/DixieMaeDoxie?ref=hl.

A frequent contributor to the *Chicken Soup for the Soul* series, **Linda Burks Lohman** thanks her parole officer, Lucy, the four-footed Yorkie that encourages use of the exercise yard daily. Living in Sacramento, CA, she is retired and loving life as a Red Hat Society Ambassador. E-mail her at laborelations@yahoo.com.

Rita Lussier's column, "For the Moment," has been a popular weekly feature in *The Providence Journal* for twelve years. She was awarded First Place in the 2010 Erma Bombeck International Writing Competition, an honor she also won in 2006. Her writing has been featured in *The Boston Globe* and on NPR.

A graduate of Queen's University, **Gail MacMillan** is an award-winning author with thirty-four published books, and short stories and articles published across North America and Western Europe. Gail lives in New Brunswick, Canada with her husband and Little River Duck Dog named Fancy.

Margaret M. Marty is a retired wife, mother, grandmother, and professional secretary. Margaret enjoys flower gardening, yard work, and scrapbooking. She has pursued a memoir writing career in retirement, taking classes and establishing a personal historian business, Portraits in Prose. Please e-mail her at mmarty@northlc.com.

Nicole Ann Rook McAlister studied journalism and has pursued a self-study of world religion. She and her husband live with their seven-year-old daughter, nineteen-year-old son, and a plethora of fur, feather and finned babies in a log cabin in the Pine Barrens. When she isn't writing, she is painting, crafting, canning, gardening or reading.

Vickie McEntire has been published in several anthologies and magazines. In 2018, she won Georgia Author of the Year for her second children's book, *Little Bird & Myrtle Turtle*. Her passion is writing and promoting literacy. She lives in Northwest Georgia with her husband and cat and is currently working on her first novel.

Brook-Lynn Meijer lives in north-western Canada with her mom and dad, two younger sisters, two dogs and one cat. Brook-Lynn can often be found with her nose in a book, but the busy teenager's life also includes playing the piano, swimming and snowboarding.

Marya Morin is a freelance writer. Her stories and poems have appeared in publications such as *Woman's World* and Hallmark. Marya also penned a weekly humor column for an online newsletter and writes custom poetry on request. She lives in the country with her husband. E-mail her at Akushla514@hotmail.com.

Lisa Morris currently teaches fourth grade ELA in Niceville, FL. She has been teaching for twenty-three years and recently added adjunct professor of education to her résumé. Lisa has published five educational books to date and many memoirs and articles. E-mail her at lovealab@aol.com.

A recent, self-described escapee of the corporate world, Lauren Mosher now enjoys a career with a dog-walking company. She is devoted to her volunteer work with animal-rescue nonprofits and human-welfare organizations. She believes that living life in service to others is paramount. Her favorite color is pink.

Sandy Nadeau spent thirty years exploring the back country of Colorado. She loves writing stories connected to that time. She has published two inspirational fiction books: *Red Gold* and *Rescue Me*. She and her husband now live in Texas two miles from their grand-children, discovering even more adventures. E-mail her at sandy@sandynadeau.com.

Linda Newton is an Empowerment Educator, and the author of *12 Ways to Turn Your Pain into Praise*. She speaks all over the country, and currently hosts a popular blog with her husband, "Answers from Mom and Dad" on YouTube https://www.youtube.com/user/answersfrommomanddad.

Peggy Omarzu lives in a household comprised of four dogs, three cats, a guinea pig and an untold number of fish. She divides her time between working for a large non-profit agency, animal rescue and shelters, and veterinary medicine. Peggy writes stories about the animals and their people that have crossed her path while following these pursuits.

Julie Osborne is a contributor to the *Chicken Soup for the Soul* series and former editor and feature writer for Current Publishing. Her blog, "Tales of Oz", became "Tales of Oz with Julie Osborne (and Toto Too!)" after adopting a rescue — his name, of course, was Toto. Follow Oz and Toto's tales at www.OzandToto.com or e-mail them at info@OzandToto.com.

Ellie Porte Parker, Ph.D., is a licensed psychologist and a writer. She adopted her son, Dmitry, from Russia when he was six years old, and he and his brother, Franklin, as well as the dog, Maverick, are all grown up and doing well. The story "Pet Connections" appears in the author's memoir *Six When He Came to Us — A Memoir of International Adoption*, which is available in paperback and as an eBook. E-mail her at ellieparker@hotmail.com.

Connie K. Pombo is an inspirational author, speaker, and freelance writer. She is a frequent contributor to the *Chicken Soup for the Soul* series and other anthologies. When not speaking, writing, or traveling, Connie enjoys spending time with her three grandchildren. Contact her at www.conniepombo.com.

Robin Pressnall is Executive Director of Small Paws Rescue Inc., which has been featured on *Animal Planet*. She is a frequent guest on the Fox News Network's *Fox & Friends* in New York City. Robin has also appeared on *Inside Edition* with Deborah Norville and is a frequent contributor to *Chicken Soup for the Soul* books.

Julie Reece-DeMarco is an attorney, educator, and author. She is married with four daughters and enjoys being a mom, spending time outdoors in the great Northwest and playing sports. Approximately one million copies of her books are in print.

Sandy Alexander Reid has taught high school English in St. Louis for thirty-nine years. She is the mother of three sons and collects flamingos. She uses the story "My Heroes" to introduce herself to her students every year and asks them to write a story of their own, introducing themselves to her.

Diane Rima lives on the Central Coast of California with her husband and Chester, their lovable Golden Retriever. She is a wife, mom, Gigi, and teacher. Diane enjoys her family, the sea, writing, working with children, and bringing joy and tail wags to young and old through pet therapy.

Marti Robards resides in scenic Colorado. Her first published story, "The Loneliest Number" appears in *Chicken Soup for the Soul: Random Acts of Kindness*. Marti's passions include church, family, reading, writing, crafts, and gardening. She and her daughter, Mary, are co-owners of an Etsy Shop: ReverieCraftsLLC.

Sallie A. Rodman's stories appear in various *Chicken Soup for the Soul* anthologies. She loves writing about the foibles of her crazy pets. She enjoys reading, writing, and raising Monarch butterflies. Sallie also teaches writing at Cal State University, Long Beach's OLLI campus. E-mail her at writergal222@gmail.com.

Jeannie Rogers is the mother of three and grandmother of four. A retired writer for a nonprofit organization, she is currently working on her own 365-page devotional book. Jeannie also creates artwork in colored pencil, reads a lot, and plays golf (enjoying the challenge of occasionally shooting her age).

Sue-Ellen Sanders is community development manager for a nonprofit promoting early childhood education, a community activist, local journalist and host of a radio talk show. A 1981 University of Florida grad, she is married with two young adult children and loves running, reading, rescue puppies and adventures.

Charlotte Blood Smith has been a freelance writer for fifty years. She has written for over 115 publications. Charlotte has had cats since she was four and spent a lot of time watching them, especially their interaction with other animals.

Diane Stark is a wife, mother, and freelance writer. She is a frequent contributor to the *Chicken Soup for the Soul* series. She loves to write about the important things in life: her family and her faith.

Lynn Sunday is an artist, writer, and animal advocate living in Northern California with her husband and two senior rescue dogs. Her stories have appeared in several *Chicken Soup for the Soul* books, and numerous other publications. E-mail her at Sunday11@aol.com.

Marla H. Thurman lives in Signal Mountain, TN with her dogs Sophie and Jasper. The three of them try to write something of value every day, but some days really "are" better than others. Still, they strive for the best! E-mail her at sizoda1@yahoo.com.

Kelly Van Etten spent twenty-two years in the Air Force and now works in Air Force Emergency Management as a civilian. She is also a senior at The University of Oklahoma pursuing a bachelor's degree in administrative leadership. Kelly enjoys traveling, swimming, gardening, and her four dogs. E-mail her at kellyinok@yahoo.com.

Miriam Van Scott is an author and photographer whose credits include children's books, magazine articles, television productions, website content and reference books. Her latest titles include *Song of Old: An Advent Calendar for the Spirit* and the *Shakespeare Goes Pop* series. Learn more at miriamvanscott.com.

Sharon Van Zandt teaches fourth grade and loves reading and writing. She is currently working on her second middle grade novel. She is still jogging.

Pat Wahler is a Missouri native and proud contributor to twenty previous titles in the *Chicken Soup for the Soul* series. She is the author of five novels written under the supervision of one bossy cat and a lively Pekingese-mix. Connect with Pat at www.PatWahler.com.

Kelly Sullivan Walden is on a mission to awaken the world to the power of dreams. She is the author of ten books, including *Chicken Soup for the Soul: Dreams & Premonitions*, *I Had the Strangest Dream*, *It's All in Your Dreams*, and the *Dream Oracle Cards*. It is whispered she is the love child of Lucille Ball and Carl Jung.

With over thirty years experience in advertising and marketing, **Luann Warner** is a freelance writer. In addition to her contributions to *Chicken Soup for the Soul* books, she hopes to complete her first book in the near future. Luann enjoys photography and spending time with her family. E-mail her at lkwarner3@comcast.net.

David Warren resides in Kettering, OH with his wife Angela. They have a daughter named Marissa. He's a frequent contributor to the *Chicken Soup for the Soul* series and other publications. David is VP of Lutz Blades and enjoys travel, sports, and music.

Megan LeeAnn Waterman-Fouch enjoys sharing her stories with the world. She currently writes a monthly column called "Paws and Reflect" for a local newspaper, and continues to submit her inspirational children's book manuscripts to publishing houses for consideration. Her biggest joy is spending time with her family.

Susan C. Willett is a writer and blogger whose award-winning stories, poems, and humor appear in print and online, including on her website LifeWithDogsAndCats.com. She shares her home with three dogs and four cats—all rescues. Follow them all on Facebook, Twitter @WithDogsAndCats, and Instagram @LifeWithDogsAndCats.

A love of books set **Tammy Zaluzney** on a path to write from an early age, but a series of coincidences and mishaps changed her life's path. She ended up enjoying and sometimes cursing a long career in animal welfare. Thirty years later she is now writing about the compelling stories that shaped the course of her life.

Meet Amy Newmark

Amy Newmark is the bestselling author, editor-in-chief, and publisher of the *Chicken Soup for the Soul* book series. Since 2008, she has published 196 new books, most of them national bestsellers in the U.S. and Canada, more than doubling the number of Chicken Soup for the Soul titles in print today. She is also the author of *Simply Happy*, a crash course in Chicken Soup for the Soul advice and wisdom that is filled with easy-to-implement, practical tips for enjoying a better life.

Amy is credited with revitalizing the Chicken Soup for the Soul brand, which has been a publishing industry phenomenon since the first book came out in 1993. By compiling inspirational and aspirational true stories curated from ordinary people who have had extraordinary experiences, Amy has kept the thirty-year-old Chicken Soup for the Soul brand fresh and relevant.

Amy graduated *magna cum laude* from Harvard University where she majored in Portuguese and minored in French. She then embarked on a three-decade career as a Wall Street analyst, a hedge fund manager, and a corporate executive in the technology field. She is a Chartered Financial Analyst.

Her return to literary pursuits was inevitable, as her honors thesis in college involved traveling throughout Brazil's impoverished northeast region, collecting stories from regular people. She is delighted to have come full circle in her writing career — from collecting stories "from the people" in Brazil as a twenty-year-old to, three decades later, collecting stories "from the people" for Chicken Soup for the Soul.

When Amy and her husband Bill, the CEO of Chicken Soup for the Soul, are not working, they are visiting their four grown children and their spouses, and their five grandchildren.

Follow Amy on Twitter @amynewmark. Listen to her free podcast — Chicken Soup for the Soul with Amy Newmark — on Apple, Google, or by using your favorite podcast app on your phone.

Thank You

We owe huge thanks to all our contributors and fans. Here at Chicken Soup for the Soul we want to thank our Associate Publisher D'ette Corona for reviewing our story library and presenting us with hundreds of dog stories to choose from for this new collection. Publisher and Editor-in-Chief Amy Newmark made the final selection of the 101 that are included here, all personal favorites, and D'ette created the manuscript. None of these stories appeared in previous Chicken Soup for the Soul books about dogs. They were compiled from our books on other topics.

The whole publishing team deserves a hand, including Senior Editor Barbara LoMonaco, Vice President of Marketing Maureen Peltier, Vice President of Production Victor Cataldo, and our graphic designer Daniel Zaccari, who turned our manuscript into this beautiful, entertaining book.

About American Humane

American Humane is the country's first national humane organization, founded in 1877 and committed to ensuring the safety, welfare, and wellbeing of all animals. For more than 140 years, American Humane has been first to serve in promoting the welfare and safety of animals and strengthening the bond between animals and people. American Humane's initiatives are designed to help whenever and wherever animals are in need of rescue, shelter, protection or care.

American Humane is the only national humane organization with top ratings and endorsements from the key charity watchdog groups. The organization has earned Charity Navigator's highest "Four-Star Rating," the Platinum Seal of Transparency from GuideStar USA, and is one of the few charities that meets all of the Better Business Bureau's Wise Giving Alliance's 20 Standards for Charity Accountability.

American Humane's certification programs that help verify humane treatment of animals are wide ranging, covering animals in film, on farms, in zoos and aquariums and even those in pet retailers. The iconic "No Animals Were Harmed®" certification, which appears during the end credits of films and TV shows, today monitors some 1,000 productions yearly.

Through rigorous, science-based criteria that are independently audited, American Humane's farm animal welfare program, Conservation program and Pet Provider programs help to ensure the humane treatment of more than one billion animals living on certified farms and ranches, in zoos and aquariums, and at pet provider locations. Simply put, American Humane is the largest certifier of animal welfare in the world.

Continuing its longstanding efforts to strengthen the healing power of the human-animal bond, American Humane also pairs veterans struggling to cope with the invisible wounds of war with highly trained service dogs, and also helps reunite discharged military working dogs with their former handlers.

To learn more about American Humane, visit AmericanHumane. org and follow them on Facebook, Instagram, Twitter and YouTube.

AMERICAN★HUMANE
FIRST TO SERVE

Editor's Note: Chicken Soup for the Soul and American Humane have created *Humane Heroes*, a FREE new series of e-books and companion curricula for elementary, middle and high schoolers. Through thirty-six inspirational stories of animal rescue, rehabilitation, and humane conservation being performed at the world's leading zoological institutions, and eighteen easy-to-follow lesson plans, *Humane Heroes* provides highly engaging free reading materials that also encourage young people to appreciate and protect Earth's disappearing species. To download the free e-books and learn about the program, please visit www.chickensoup.com/ah.

Sharing Happiness, Inspiration, and Hope

Real people sharing real stories, every day, all over the world. In 2007, *USA Today* named *Chicken Soup for the Soul* one of the five most memorable books in the last quarter-century. With over 110 million books sold to date in the U.S. and Canada alone, more than 300 titles in print, and translations into nearly fifty languages, "chicken soup for the soul®" is one of the world's best-known phrases.

Today, thirty years after we first began sharing happiness, inspiration and hope through our books, we continue to delight our readers with ten to twelve new titles each year, but have also evolved beyond the bookshelves with super premium pet food, a podcast, adult coloring books, and licensed products that include word-search puzzle books and books for babies and preschoolers. We are busy "changing your life one story at a time®." Thanks for reading!

Share with Us

We have all had Chicken Soup for the Soul moments in our lives. If you would like to share your story, go to chickensoup.com and click on Books and then Submit Your Story. You will find our writing guidelines there, along with a list of topics we're working on.

You may be able to help another reader and become a published author at the same time! Some of our past contributors have even launched writing and speaking careers from the publication of their stories in our books.

We only accept story submissions via our website. They are no longer accepted via postal mail or fax. And they are not accepted via e-mail.

To contact us regarding other matters, please send an e-mail to the webmaster@chickensoupforthesoul.com, or write us at:

Chicken Soup for the Soul
P.O. Box 700
Cos Cob, CT 06807-0700

One more note from your friends at Chicken Soup for the Soul: Occasionally, we receive an unsolicited book manuscript from one of our readers, and we would like to respectfully inform you that we do not accept unsolicited manuscripts, and we must discard the ones that are sent to us.

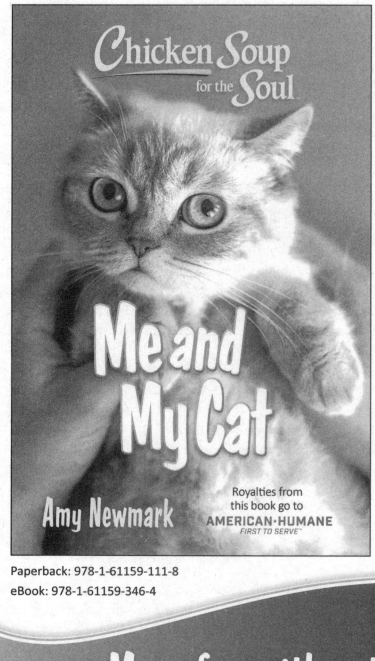

Paperback: 978-1-61159-111-8
eBook: 978-1-61159-346-4

More fun with pets,

Chicken Soup for the Soul

Lessons Learned from My Dog

Royalties from this book go to
AMERICAN·HUMANE
FIRST TO SERVE

Amy Newmark

Paperback: 978-1-61159-098-2
eBook: 978-1-61159-335-8

our furry family members